PROVINCETOWN AS A STAGE

PROVINCETOWN AS A STAGE

Provincetown, The Provincetown Players, and the Discovery of Eugene O'Neill

LEONA RUST EGAN

PARNASSUS IMPRINTS
ORLEANS, MASSACHUSETTS

To the memory of Marguerite L. Young

Contents

Acknowledgments

I AM DEEPLY GRATEFUL to friends and scholars who gave their time and encouragement.

If not for the inspiration of Reginald "Reggie" Cabral and his enthusiasm for the history and culture of Provincetown, I doubt that this book would have been started or finished. Reggie embodies the complex nature of Provincetown, that is, the interweaving of art, commerce, and the maritime tradition. He comes from a family of Portuguese whalers and Grand Bankers, whose descendants, changed—as did the economic base of Provincetown—to enterprising services for tourists. As a child, Reggie developed an intense interest in the theater and the arts, which has lasted over his lifetime, as evidenced in his unique collection of Provincetown memorabilia.

I am truly indebted to my dear friend, Jean Hanson Johnson. Over the years, Jean has always been generously available to look at early drafts, to give advice, and to talk about Provincetown, especially her childhood summers there. What I treasure is the memory of those long winter afternoons at her home in Brookmont, Maryland, overlooking the Potomac River. While we envisioned shifting dunes and white sails, I watched the dogwood tree in her garden slowly shed its casings and turn pink—my signal to return to Provincetown.

To others who read all or part of my manuscript and gave advice and encouragement, I am thankful: Molly Malone Cook, Mary Evans Collins, Lily Harmon and, in particular, Claire Sprague.

Acknowledgments

I am particularly grateful to Professor John Tamplin, Penn State University, as well as to Shirley Snyder, Librarian, who over the years generously provided me with books, documents, and literature searches.

Also I thank Travis Bogard, Professor Emeritus, University of California, and Professor Dee Garrison, Rutgers University, for their encouragement. My appreciation also extends to Roseanne Adams, Clive Driver, and Margaret Mayo, Provincetown Pilgrim Museum; to Hope Merrill, Curator, Cape Cod National Seashore; and to John Skoyles, Director, Provincetown Fine Arts Work Center.

I appreciate the graciousness of Alice N. Nash, New York City, in providing the Nash family letters; John Raposo, Providence, R.I., for his guidance on Portuguese-Americans; and Diana Linkous, Catherine Small, and Andrea Vojtko, Washington, D.C., for their computer advice.

I am especially grateful to my niece, Patricia Fetty Schmidt, for being there when all else failed.

To the many in Provincetown who gave me information and advice, I give my thanks. I am indebted in particular to Francis Alves, Mary Avellar, Sheila Costa, Miriam Hapgood DeWitt, Ruth Dwyer, Emily Farnham, Lee Feroba, John and Edith Gaspa, Jane Gildersleeve, Grace Collinson Goveia, Phyllis Higgins, Frank and Halcyon Hurst, Alice Joseph, Madeline L'Engle, Mary Lewis, Anna Enos and Manny Lewis, Joseph C. Patrick, Barbara and Joseph Perry, Richard Prowell, Mark R. Silva, Joyce Tager, Heaton Vorse, and Hazel Hawthorne Werner.

Introduction

And thus it comes about that the spot where the Pilgrims first landed is the spot where one may look for the "last word" in literature and art.

—*Boston Post*, September 1916[1]

THE FRIDAY EVENING PERFORMANCE, July 28, 1916, of Eugene O'Neill's sea play, *Bound East for Cardiff*, on a derelict wharf in Provincetown Harbor, marked a turning point for the novice playwright and for the American theater. That night was O'Neill's successful premiere as a playwright. Moreover, the poetic realism of his first performed play inspired an amateur troupe of bohemians to organize as the Provincetown Players and look for a New York stage. The Provincetown Players were also successful in creating a pioneering, experimental art theater that fostered the careers of native playwrights, notably O'Neill.

In a relatively short period, O'Neill gained an international reputation, culminating in his being awarded the Nobel Prize in 1936, the only American dramatist ever so recognized. And through his innovative and artistic efforts, American drama came of age. George Jean Nathan, in his introduction to O'Neill's 1923 collection of sea plays, said that O'Neill raised American theater out of its "stereotyped dullness . . . Many plays have heart. It has remained for O'Neill . . . to add the blood."

O'Neill's theatrical debut changed his personal life. He stopped drifting and made Provincetown his home, where he stayed until 1924. For O'Neill the summer of 1916 was an emotional resurrection from a period of depression and dissolution. The year before, he had not written anything of consequence; his plays had been rejected by the Washington Square Players in New York; and once again he had succumbed to drinking and despondency. In Provincetown, the sea spiritually and physically restored him.

Summer 1916 was O'Neill's introduction to Provincetown. He explored the oceanside dunes on the outskirts of Provincetown, and in particular, the site of the old Peaked Hill Life-Saving Station that had been elegantly renovated by the socialite Mabel Dodge. Three years later, following a second marriage in Provincetown to Agnes Boulton, the former Station became his first home. In 1930, when O'Neill turned it over to his son, Eugene, Jr., he said: "That place meant a lot to me . . . as a solitude where I lived with myself it had infinite meaning." At Peaked Hill, surrounded by sand dunes and the sea, O'Neill wrote himself out of his apprenticeship and gained world-wide attention. His time there, at the edge of the Atlantic Ocean, was one of his most productive periods. Over half of his dramas—nineteen short and seven long plays—were written before 1920, and twelve of them dealt with the sea.

THE PROVINCETOWN PLAYERS' PRIVATE LIVES became their public art. What they talked about in their bedrooms and private salons was grist for their scenarios. As part of a generation that demanded new social, political, and artistic liberties, they experimented widely—with free love, open marriage, psychoanalysis, peyote, Buddhism, and political demonstrations. There were few perceptible boundaries between what they did and what they wrote. Neith and Hutch Hapgood, for instance, in *Enemies*, dramatized on Lewis Wharf in Provincetown, their persistent arguments about their own open marriage. In the largest role of his short acting career, as a mulatto castaway in *Thirst*, O'Neill displayed his passion for Louise Bryant, who was the lover of his friend, John Reed. Reed, the nonpareil bohemian, met the gossip head-on, and wrote—as well as acted in—*Eternal Quadrangle* as a way of telling his friends that he knew and did not care.

Susan Glaspell, in *Road to the Temple*, talked about the "great summer" of 1916: "We would lie on the beach and talk about plays—every one writing, or acting, or producing. Life was all of a piece, work not separated from play." In recounting the activities of the Players, particularly during the creative summer of 1916, I relied heavily on their writings, with emphasis on the plays because, in most cases, they mirrored their active lives and magnified their thoughts. John Reed, for example, signalled his shift from poetry to communism in *Freedom*, a self-parody of himself as a poet-poseur. Reed's former lover, Mabel Dodge, was derisively portrayed by her friends in *Constancy* and *Change Your Style;* these plays also disclosed the sophisticates' attitude toward modern love and modern art.

It was especially important to scan the writings of the reclusive O'Neill, for he rarely revealed his interior world except through his art. In his poem, "Submarine," written the summer of 1916, O'Neill declares his detachment: "I will hide unseen beneath the surface of life." In addition to his two plays staged on Lewis Wharf (*Bound East for Cardiff* and *Thirst*), O'Neill wrote a full-length play during the 1916 summer, *Now I Ask You*. It was his satirical commentary on the antics of the bohemian crowd. I also cite the torrid love poems O'Neill wrote to Louise Bryant, as well as the cool letters that he was simultaneously sending to Beatrice Ashe, his New London sweetheart.

IN TELLING THE STORY of the Provincetown Players I have concentrated on their time in Provincetown, especially the two years, 1915 and 1916, when they staged their plays on Lewis Wharf in Provincetown Harbor. I found that previous accounts had given only minimal attention to the Provincetown years. I began by looking for the fortunate accidents, the literary and social antecedents as well as the accident of Provincetown's geography, that led to O'Neill's debut. I soon realized that to understand the complexity of Provincetown, I needed to talk about its history. Finding no ready reference, I developed in Chapter 3, "City of Sand, City of Canvas," a retrospective look at Provincetown, focussing on writers and artists who preceded the Players. In exploring Provincetown's past, I was searching for clues that would explain the town's attraction for the avant-garde Greenwich Villagers who aethestically mined the vulnerable, yet enduring, peninsula town.

Following the arrival of the railroad in 1873, Provincetown became a motherlode for palette and pen. Writers were led to Provincetown by the artists, who earlier had discovered the special light of a town that hunches low in the sea. All the Players wrote about Provincetown in various ways: in memoirs, plays, poems, short stories, novels, and magazine articles. Some Players, as did O'Neill, made their home in Provincetown; some stayed on a lifetime and died there.

That July night on Lewis Wharf in 1916 was likewise a defining moment for Provincetown, which, in the 19th century, had been a thriving, international fishing port. Provincetown acquired a new reputation—as a mecca for the artistic avant-garde. When World War I sent America's bohemians back home from Europe, Greenwich Village bohemians en masse discovered Provincetown. Most located in the East End of Provincetown where they drank and smoked in public, went bathing in the nude, and couples, who were not married, lived together. On an abandoned fishing wharf in Provincetown Harbor, in 1915 and 1916, the Provincetown Players performed plays that, on the whole, re-created their new social freedom.

Provincetown is a tolerant and fatalistic town, that over the years has been pummeled by all the furies—storms, foreign invasions, and sandy avalanches. Time and again it has been discovered anew, mainly because it is geographically remote. It reaches twenty-five miles into the Atlantic Ocean, situated on the land's end of Cape Cod—as well as Massachusetts. "Hard to get to and get out of," wrote O'Neill in 1919 from his Provincetown home. Early explorers and mariners chanced upon its harbor, and found it a safe haven from the shoals and storms of the North Atlantic.

In the winter of 1620 the Pilgrims moored in Provincetown, diverted from their assigned destination, the Virginia Colony. They explored the surrounding area, and, like previous explorers, found it inhospitable because it lacked arable land and sweet water. After five weeks, they left Provincetown, their first landing place in America, and headed west to Plymouth. For the next two hundred years, Provincetown was virtually ignored by the pious theocracy of mainland Massachusetts. It thrived as a waystation, a free port for renegade colonists, smugglers, and roving Indians, a legendary helltown of vices.

Provincetown stretches out for three miles along a circling waterfront, at the end of a low-lying sandy peninsula. The town is built on a bed of sand sculpted from the sea by wind and waves. Henry David Thoreau, in 1849, saw it as "a filmy sliver of land lying flat on the ocean . . . a mere reflection of a sand-bar on the haze above." There are few hiding places, no outside tracts of land or large buildings to mask an industry. Nathaniel P. Willis, a highly popular journalist of his day, observed in 1848 that Provincetown's one main, narrow street—its "one accountable path"—permits no secrets. Today, Commercial Street, a narrow twenty-two-foot-wide passageway that runs the full length of Provincetown, is in summer an impromptu stage on which all are free to parade in outlandish costume and to behave in a manner that elsewhere might be considered bizarre.

Provincetown is a quick study. A glance at the activity across its wide, natural harbor tells immediately what it is about. This has been true since its beginning. Today there are two long wharves filled in the summer with pleasure craft, charter boats, whale-watching boats, Plymouth and Boston ferries, and launches for visiting ocean liners. Its once predominant fishing fleet is now berthed in one small section of a single wharf. How different the view is today from the one Henry David Thoreau had on an October afternoon when he watched a fleet of two hundred mackerel schooners tacking about the harbor. It was a spectacular sight for the Concord native as he imagined the white sails to be a "city of canvas."

Provincetown then was an international port. There were wharves for drying cod and pickling mackerel; piers for coopers, chandlers, and sailmakers; and longer wharves for berthing the Grand Banks schooners and whaling vessels that flocked to Provincetown, the only deep harbor on Cape Cod. As the fishing and whaling industries declined, so did Provincetown's more than fifty wharves. At the turn of the 20th century, *plein-air* artists dominated the waterfront, replacing fish flakes and windmills. With their easels and smocks and outdoor display of talent, they were an attraction for the increasing number of tourists arriving by train.

Early 19th-century travelers journeyed to Provincetown to see its peculiar geography, in particular, the towering sand dunes that border the town. For over two centuries, trees and vegetation had been wantonly destroyed, leaving the dunes unanchored, a sahara of moving sand which nearly buried the town. There are three sand ridges that separate the town from the Atlantic Ocean. On the far outer ridge fronting the ocean is Peaked Hills, the site of O'Neill's former home. A few miles to the south of Peaked Hills, Thoreau was inspired to write his classic line, "A Man may stand there and put all America behind him."

Peaked Hills is a significant part of Provincetown's history. If footprints leading to Peaked Hills could be unearthed, they would be artifacts as historically telling as sunken ships. There would be the prints of moccasins and the bare feet of unnamed Nauset Indians, and the bootprints of European mariners, fishermen, and shipwreck survivors. There would be the tracks of brigades of Surfmen and Coast Guardsmen who patrolled the beach and pulled the drowning from the sea; and of the families, friends, and tourists who visited the Life-Saving Stations. There also would be the footprints of the lovers who sculpted a sandy bed; the artists who reinvented the dunes; the novelists, the playwrights, and the journalists who recorded their journeys across the sands.

Among those who can be named are the writers Henry David Thoreau, Eugene O'Neill, John S. Reed, Mabel Dodge, Edmund Wilson, and John Dos Passos; the painters Maurice Sterne, Charles Demuth, Marsden Hartley, and even the actor, Henry Fonda. They are names from America's literary and artistic past. Each made the pilgrimage for many of the same reasons: curiosity, inspiration, health, and solitude. Many went to see what others had already described. And so, too, this retracing of footsteps is a walk across time, to see again what centuries of travellers saw as they crossed the mile of sand from Cape Cod Bay to the Atlantic Ocean.

CHAPTER ONE

Eugene O'Neill's First Stage: Provincetown

The seamen's forecastle of the British tramp steamer Glencairn *on a foggy night midway on the voyage between New York and Cardiff.*

—Eugene O'Neill, *Bound East for Cardiff*

EUGENE O'NEILL, a twenty-seven-year-old untried playwright, came to Provincetown the summer of 1916 looking for a stage. He found it perched on the waterfront, scruffy and salty, awaiting his debut. The histrionic O'Neill may have swaggered a bit as he walked down a ramshackle wharf into a salt-encrusted, sea-washed fishing shack that housed a narrow stage. He knew from his theatrical experience with his father, the popular actor James O'Neill, that this setting was a natural one for his sea play. *Bound East for Cardiff* takes place mid-ocean in a cramped, noisome forecastle on a foggy night. O'Neill helped to direct the play, insisting on a minimum of props. And with a beginner's luck, on premiere night the sea provided a bonus of special effects: a thick fog, a wailing foghorn, and a high tide rushing in and splashing beneath the floorboards. O'Neill, the former sailor and now poet-of-the-sea, had found a new home. He stayed on in Provincetown for nine years, one of the most productive periods of his career.

The stage itself nearly floated on water. It was on the first floor of a two-story converted fishhouse at the far end of rickety Lewis Wharf, which reached about 100 feet into Provincetown harbor. Throughout the performance incoming waves, swelled by a new moon, flooded the tidal flats and battered the spindly pilings under the fishhouse. For days the weather had been muggy and damp, not at all unusual in the summer when a tropical front stalls off the coast of Cape Cod. Just before 8:00 P.M. on Thursday, July 28, 1916, the wind changed to the north and the freshening breeze locked the town in a moist, cool fog.

The fishhouse theater was layered with smells of the sea and of sailors: oilskins and rubber boots, pipe tobacco, and sweat reeking from the actors crammed into makeshift bunks. There was also the fetid scent of burned wood as well as of fresh paint. Three weeks earlier, the west wall of the fishhouse had been badly scorched by an accidental fire and the adjoining walls had been painted black to mask the damage. There was the lingering smell of old wharves—a mixture of fish oil, turpentine, and tar. As if all these stage effects weren't enough, the fortunate young playwright also had the mournful sound of an intermittent foghorn echoing from Long Point Lighthouse, two miles across the harbor. So with a lapping tide, an enveloping fog punctuated by a warning horn, the stuffiness of nearly one hundred people jammed into a rough-hewn, odoriferous fishhouse measuring only 25 feet by 35 feet, it took no scenic magic for the audience to believe that they were indeed in the cramped forecastle of a tramp steamer stalled mid-ocean.

2

On the outside walls of the fishhouse were two large sliding doors a story high, one facing south, the other west. These doors had been conveniently rolled back when fish, freight, and dories were unloaded from fishing vessels. The sliding door at the south end of the wharf was cleverly incorporated as a stage backdrop. It measured about 10 feet by 12 feet. When the weather allowed, the door was rolled back for scenic effect—revealing a seamless horizon of sea and sky.

The new owner of the wharf, Mary Vorse O'Brien, a popular fiction writer, had rented the top floor of the fishhouse to the New York-based Modern Art School. It was run by Bror Nordfeldt, artist and inventor of the white-line block print. She had also managed to rent out her small cottage at the foot of the wharf. The summer before, the cottage had been a fish market, but the rent was long overdue. John A. Francis, the realtor and long-time friend and ombudsman to Provincetown's writers and artists, wrote Mary O'Brien on March 3, 1916, about the delinquent rent: "I told him [Manuel Morris, the fish dealer] that he already owed you for three months rent . . . It strikes me that the only way you can get this money is to take fish for it in the summer."[1] The fish dealer, however, took to the street and peddled his fish from a cart.

Summer 1916 was actually the second season of theatricals for the group of amateurs who became the Provincetown Players. Their first season had also been in Provincetown, during the summer of 1915. It was a spontaneous beginning. On July 15, at 10:00 in the evening, after the children had gone to bed, the writers Neith Boyce and her husband Hutchins Hapgood amused their friends with some theatricals staged on their summer veranda facing the harbor. Neith Boyce's one-act play, *Constancy,* was the first performed. It is a spoof about the romance between Mabel Dodge, a wealthy socialite, and John [Jack] Reed, poet, journalist, and future revolutionist. All knew the plot beforehand, for the love affair was the talk of Greenwich Village.

The vacationing scenic designer Robert [Bobby] Edmond Jones arranged the impromptu set. He simply moved about some pillows and lamps to create a set on the veranda; then he turned the audience about to face the living room for the second play, *Suppressed Desires*. This too was a spoof—of Freudianism—by the newlyweds, novelist Susan Glaspell and her writer husband, George [Jig] Cram Cook. The group was delighted. Jig thereupon arranged a second bill of two new one-act plays on Lewis Wharf. Jig staged his own play, a satire about the feud between current artistic schools in *Change Your Style*; and he staged *Contemporaries*, a parable about the homeless in New York City, the work of the young writer Wilbur Daniel Steele.

After the 1915 summer productions in Provincetown, the winter talk in Greenwich Village switched from Marxism, free love, and Freudianism to theater. It was Jig Cook who spearheaded the efforts to create new drama, modelled after the theater of ancient Greece. Jig wanted the theater to be an artistic community: "True drama is born only of one feeling animating all the members of a clan."[2] Jack Reed was at first co-leader, and characteristically enthusiastic; however, he was professionally overcommitted and relinquished control to Jig Cook.

Those who had taken part in the plays in Provincetown in 1915 formed a loose vanguard directed toward a new American theater that would break free from the hackneyed melodramas and frothy comedies on Broadway controlled by commercial syndicates. Except for Jack Reed and his play *Moondown,* their attempts to get their own plays staged in New York by the Washington Square Players had failed. They envisioned a change toward psychological real-

4

ism, as found in the Abbey Players of the Irish theater. Their dream materialized in Provincetown the following summer of 1916 with O'Neill and his *Bound East for Cardiff*.

O'Neill's premiere was on the second bill of the 1916 season. The first bill began two weeks earlier on July 14, 1916, and consisted of three traditional one-act plays. There was *Winter's Night* by Neith Boyce Hapgood, a journalist and fiction writer, in which she parodied her own marital conflicts. *Not Smart*, a spoof of both the Provincetown Portuguese and the bohemian attitude toward sex, was by the otherwise serious, short-story journeyman Wilbur Daniel Steele. ("Not smart" was a localism for getting pregnant.) *Freedom*, a political farce by John Reed, completed the bill. Little is known of these premieres, so overshadowed were they by *Bound East*. On the second bill with *Bound East* were two other plays: a reprise of Steele's *Not Smart* and a debut of *The Game*, an allegorical drama by the journalist Louise Bryant.

Bound East is a one-act play that reflects the seafaring experience of its youthful, obsessively autobiographical author. Its mood recaptured O'Neill's dreary, homeward voyage to New York from Buenos Aires on the *Ikala*, a British tramp steamer. Eight months earlier O'Neill had been ecstatic when he sailed from Boston on the *Charles Racine*, a fetching Norwegian windjammer. Eugene's father, James O'Neill, a successful actor and theatrical entrepreneur, had paid the $75 fare, hoping that his dissolute younger son would profit from a sea adventure. Once in Buenos Aires Eugene reverted to his old habits of excessive drinking and cavorting with derelicts and pariahs, as he had in Manhattan. He slept in flophouses and with the readily-available Brazilian prostitutes. When his money ran out and his health failed, he signed on with the freighter as a "scenery bum," one who works his passage from port to port.

O'Neill's original title for *Bound East*, written in 1914, was "Children of the Sea." It is a story about the fatalism and the helplessness of seamen. The plot centers on Yank, who is dying from a shipboard accident that crushed his chest. The action is restricted to the cramped seamen's quarters of the steamer *Glencairn*, a "rusty lime-juicer," as it lumbers eastward across the Atlantic in fog and darkness. Shipmate Driscoll mercifully stays with Yank, who is afraid to die alone. "For God's sake don' leave me alone!" The play begins with humorous, fantasized memories as Cocky, a "weazened runt," boasts to his shipmates about his love affair with the "queen of the cannibal isles." Through his characters O'Neill relates his own waterfront days in Buenos Aries. "D'yuh remember the times we've had in Buenos Aires? I do that; and so does the piany player. He'll not be forgettin' the black eye I gave him in a hurry." The mood shifts to grim reality as Driscoll and Yank talk of their bittersweet memories, centering on their disillusionment with the sea. "It must be great to stay on dry land all your life and have a farm with a house of your own." The play ends when death comes as a "pretty lady dressed in black."

O'Neill directed *Bound East* with the help of the professional actor Edward [Teddy] Ballantine, who took the part of Cocky. Despite the protests of the artists, who had constructed abstract, art deco sets for other productions, O'Neill insisted on realistic scenery and props. William Zorach, sculptor and painter, who with his wife Marguerite designed memorable, cubistic scenery for the group, complained that O'Neill resisted his designs. "Gene insisted everything had to be factual. If the play called for a stove, it couldn't be a painted box."[3] Jig Cook, philosopher-turned-farmer, turned-writer, turned-carpenter, supervised the props for this and most other sets. For the wharf productions he designed a stage

6

"in four sections which could be picked up by hand and set at various levels and angles."[4] Three bunks were built along the far wall of the fishhouse adjacent to the sea; wooden benches were placed in front of the bunks; portholes were painted on the canvas behind the bunks; and a wooden pail and a hanging kerosene lantern completed the arrangements. Costumes were simple: the all-male cast wore oilskins and walked around in their heavy woolen socks.

The premiere casting cannot be fully reconstructed. Of the eleven characters, it is known that the part of Yank was played by Jig Cook and that of Cocky by Teddy Ballantine. There is some evidence that the actor Frederick Burt played Driscoll. Journalist Jack Reed, soon to be acclaimed for his first-hand coverage of the 1917 Russian Revolution, *Ten Days That Shook The World*, and Wilbur Steele, soon to be recognized as one of America's leading short-story writers, most likely took minor acting parts. True to the group's democratic spirit, writers, actors, and artists exchanged roles and duties.

It is well-established that O'Neill himself played The Second Mate, the least demanding role. He had one line, "Isn't this your watch on deck, Driscoll?" Although O'Neill was reportedly terrified about his role, he nevertheless later bragged about his acting debut. He chided the director of a later production that it might not have been as good as the original "because I didn't play the Mate, what?" Furthermore, from out-of-the-wings could be heard the drone of O'Neill's measured, baritone voice, for he prompted the poorly rehearsed players throughout the performance.

IN THE SUMMER OF 1916 Provincetown was a crucible of creative activity, seething with bohemians from Greenwich Village. The summer colonization of Provincetown, which had begun slowly in 1914—when World War I restricted travel to the artistic haunts of Europe—peaked in 1916. Artists were everywhere, painting on the streets, wharves, shacks, or exhibiting in Town Hall and in the new Provincetown Art Museum. Writers congregated on the beach and on the narrow sidewalks and streets and talked about their assignments for popular magazines like *Scribner's* or revolutionary magazines like *The Masses,* and in the usually quiet East End of town there was concentrated activity as this energetic group of writers and artists banded together to produce some experimental, amateur theatricals on Lewis Wharf.

The waiting audience that lingered on the wharf that foggy Thursday evening to gossip and preen was excited about seeing O'Neill's play. News of the play's tryout had spread quickly through the close-knit summer colony. Almost everyone had some personal involvement in these non-commercial play productions, either as creative artists, theatrical aides, or subscribers. No one got paid. The money was raised only to cover production costs—scenery, lighting, seats, curtain, and costumes. The most expensive production was less than $13. Jig found the summer group to be ready subscribers. For the 1916 summer, the first bill of three plays was priced at fifty cents and sold out immediately. For the next three bills, or nine plays, subscriptions were sold for one dollar. No licenses were required because admission was by prior subscription. This was a way of avoiding licensing fees both in Provincetown and in New York.

One can imagine the fascination of Provincetown residents and the summering Bostonians as they watched the chattering bohemians gather on Lewis Wharf before the performances. In her signature outfit, a red cape over white linens, Louise Bryant doubtlessly was ringed by male admirers. Among her summer entourage were the avant-garde artists

Charles Demuth, with his black shirt and purple cummerbund, and Marsden Hartley, wrapped in a flowing navy-blue coat accented with a gardenia boutonniere. Also in attendance was Max Eastman, editor of the controversial magazine, *The Masses*, sporting his proletarian uniform of brown corduroy shirt and trousers. Bryant was the season's much-talked about beauty, with her striking red hair, green eyes, and flawless complexion. The prevailing rumor, later substantiated, was that Bryant was romantically involved with O'Neill, even though she was virtually engaged to Reed.

The waiting bohemians were well-travelled cosmopolites. Jack Reed, tie-less and tousled, was an internationally known war correspondent. Demuth and Hartley were habitués of Gertrude Stein's famed Paris salon, as were the writers Neith Boyce and Hutchins Hapgood. Also among Stein's coterie were the smock-clad artists Ethel Mars and Maud Squire, who had left America's staid Midwest to enroll in life classes in Parisian ateliers. Artists Marguerite and William Zorach had travelled to Europe as well as to the South Pacific to search out the haunts of the French painter Paul Gauguin. In 1913 both Zorachs had exhibited at the landmark New York Armory Show, as had Marsden Hartley.

One way these Greenwich Village bohemians protested was in their manner of dress. Women bobbed their hair, removed their corsets, and wore loose garments; men wore open-neck working-class shirts of flannel or corduroy and, if artists, wore smocks and berets in the Continental fashion. Purple was the season's rage—in all its shades: mauve, plum, lavender, and magenta. It accented women's make-up and dress and even men's clothes. There were the more conventionally attired, such as Mary O'Brien and Susan Glaspell, who had bought Provincetown homes, just a little "up-along" Commercial Street from Lewis Wharf. They were talked about in town, not for their clothes necessarily, but for their wild parties, where women were seen to drink liquor and smoke cigarettes.

While theater history was being made on Lewis Wharf, what might have been the random thoughts of those first-nighters? Surely Mary O'Brien was reliving a deathwatch as she heard Driscoll say his long goodbye to the dying Yank. The previous Fall she had comforted her husband Joe as he lay dying in a New York hospital. Although of a different sort, Max Eastman was rehearsing a goodbye scene. That summer he was planning to tell his wife, Ida Rauh, that he was leaving her for another woman. Jig Cook and Sue Glaspell recently had had their share of goodbyes. When they decided to marry, they were virtually exiled from their native, conventional Iowa because of the notoriety attached to Jig's divorce. The seriously ill Jack Reed was preoccupied with death; in a few weeks he was to undergo major surgery to remove a diseased kidney. There were others with less tragic thoughts, such as Louise Bryant, who that night was awaiting her debut as a playwright. She was thinking of that dark-haired, dark-eyed, handsome and mysterious O'Neill, her new love interest.

Neith Boyce was no doubt concerned about her husband Hutchins and his worrisome affair with Lucy Collier. That summer Lucy had taken a nearby cottage. While waiting for his own play to be staged that night, Wilbur Steele was annoyed with the valuable time these summer theatrics had taken away from his professional writing. He was especially worried about his minister father's reaction to the summer's frivolity. For many of the others, professional writers and artists, their thoughts turned to their careers, to whether or not their future lay in the theater. It is safe to say that O'Neill alone was thinking of little else but his play. He had decided even before that night that the theater would be his whole life.

BOUND EAST WAS A SIGNAL SUCCESS. Susan Glaspell vividly recalled the premiere in her memoir, *The Road to the Temple*: "It is not merely figurative language to say the old wharf shook with applause."[5] Only days before, *Bound East* had been enthusiastically selected by the democratic caucus of bohemians. The play was read by the actor Frederick Burt in Glaspell's Provincetown parlor while the taciturn, brooding O'Neill listened from the adjoining dining room. Approval was unanimous. Spontaneously the assemblage rushed to congratulate their new playwright. They knew immediately that O'Neill's play was different; it was the breakthrough they had hoped for.

Why this instantaneous approval of O'Neill? Most of the artists and writers were familiar with the leading playwrights of Europe, such as Strindberg and Ibsen, whose work had inspired O'Neill. O'Neill had adopted the Europeans' melancholy and introspective themes to become America's own apostle of woe. Until O'Neill, no American dramatist had brought the new genre to home shores. He was the first to challenge the century's materialism; the first to stage the lower-class idiom and life on an American stage; and the first American playwright to work solely as an artist. Many of the innovative techniques that he later employed in his major dramas—poetic use of light and sound, dialect, dramatic narrative—had their beginnings in this germinal play, the one he selected for his premiere. In 1922, after he had won a Pulitzer Prize for *Beyond The Horizon*, O'Neill recounted that in the winter of 1913 and 1914, he had written: "eight one-act plays, two long plays. Of these *Bound East for Cardiff* [was the] only one worth remembering."[6]

The audience filed out more slowly and more somberly than they had entered, for they had witnessed a magic moment, a turning point in theater history. All the memoirists in the audience, and there were many, talked and wrote about O'Neill's premiere and that "remarkable summer" of 1916 in Provincetown. Some turned to playwriting, others to directing or scenic design. None but O'Neill lasted as a playwright. In September, before they left Provincetown for subsequent successful seasons in New York City, they became a formal group, the Provincetown Players. In one way or another the Players organization lasted over a decade. Their failure was due to their success—they eventually were absorbed by the commercial theater they had revolted against.

CHAPTER TWO

Mrs. O'Brien's Fishing Wharf

We dragged out the boats and nets which still stood there.
We made the seats of planks put on sawhorses and kegs.
We ransacked our houses for costumes and painted our
*   own scenery.*
Out of these odds and ends we made a theater.

—Mary Heaton Vorse O'Brien, *Time and the Town*[1]

WHY A GROUP OF WRITERS AND ARTISTS from Greenwich Village were on a wharf in Provincetown Harbor during the summers of 1915 and 1916 staging amateur plays may be traced directly to the efforts of Mary Heaton Vorse O'Brien. Over the years she had actively encouraged her friends to come to Provincetown and when they needed space for a theater, she made room on her fishing wharf. From the moment in 1907 when she bought a whaling captain's house, Mary Vorse had never stopped talking about the delights of living in Provincetown. She had talked about Provincetown to her radical associates on the magazine, the *Masses,* to the artists and writers at the Liberal Club, and to friends who frequented the basement restaurant in the Hotel Brevoort.

When in 1914 Lewis Wharf was put up for sale, Mary Vorse and her second husband Joseph O'Brien immediately placed a bid. It was a stage in disrepair, a former Grand Banks wharf, a souvenir of Provincetown's past, as was Vorse's whaling captain's home. It was through her properties that Mary Heaton Vorse relived Provincetown's past. She was both a romanticist and an activist. She was an ardent defender of immigrant laborers and, early in her career, a popular writer of sentimental, drawing-room fiction. Vorse had ancestral ties to New England and an affinity to the sea. On her first visit to Provincetown she experienced an epiphany, a coming-together of the disparate elements of her life: the sea, the Pilgrims, and romanticism. She knew as she first "drove around the town in a horse-drawn accommodation . . . that here was home."[2]

The sale of Lewis Wharf to Mary Heaton O'Brien by the heirs of Isaac Lewis was announced July 15, 1915, in the *Provincetown Advocate*. The sale price of $2,200 included the wharf and three buildings thereon, and the land and Arequipa Cottage at the foot of the wharf. The *1880 Atlas of Barnstable County* shows Lewis Wharf extending over 300 feet, probably its maximum length. By 1915 its length had been reduced by two-thirds, a casualty of storms and ice; only about 100 feet remained, on which were two small shacks and one larger, two-story building, a fishhouse.

Because of financial and legal difficulties, final settlement was delayed another year. Mary O'Brien had recently refinanced her house to pay for a new wing designed by a friend, Donald Corley, architect and writer. Seamen's Bank was reluctant to refinance the mortgage a second time. Also, there was a question of back taxes as well as problems related to obtaining clearances from the Lewis heirs. After two years of negotiations, the deed for the property "situated in Provincetown and bounded as follows, on the north by Commercial Street, on the east by the land of Joseph Mayo, on the south by the sea, and on the west by the land of Joseph Weeks" was finally recorded June 6, 1916. This was just weeks before the opening of the second season of the Provincetown Players on Mary O'Brien's Wharf.

Lewis Wharf, like other Grand Banks codfishing wharves, had become obsolete when consumer tastes changed from salted cod to fresh and frozen fish. "Today, the once humble flounder is ardently courted."[3] Along with the popular mackerel and whiting, the newly palatable bottom fish, flounder and halibut, were caught in local waters and shipped by rail to off-Cape markets. The canvas-rigged Grand Banker had been replaced by gasoline-driven trawlers. For a Grand Banker to sail into Provincetown Harbor was newsworthy. For "the first time in quite a number of years a vessel flying a Grand Banks flag entered the harbor... The schooner, *Governor Russell* had a full cargo of cod."[4] In the late 19th century, Provincetown had been an international fishing and whaling port, with approximately fifty-five wharves for servicing vessels. When the Grand Banks and whaling industries declined, the wharves fell into disrepair and eventually crumbled under winter storms and ice. The ferocious Portland Gale of 1898 exacted a large toll. There was no economic incentive to rebuild.

Consolidated Wharf, immediately to the west of Lewis Wharf, operated one of the six cold-storage plants in Provincetown. In addition to its freezing operations, Consolidated was experimenting with the canning of tuna, which was locally plentiful, hoping to compete with the canned-salmon market. Trawlers or draggers, with their large nets, landed most of the fish caught in local waters. The small-scale weir or trap fishing, once prominent in the harbor, had become outmoded. The few remaining traps were strung littorally within the long, sloping, protected curve of the Cape tip, beginning in Provincetown Harbor and extending south along the Truro coast and around Long Point to Herring Cove on the outside of the harbor. The weir-fishing crews who worked for the storage plants earned 50 percent of the market price of the catch; generally the traps were pulled once or twice daily, from April through December. Trapboats—large dories with live fish wells—were about 30 feet long with a 10-foot beam, powered either by oars or two-cycle engines. Fish caught locally were frozen into fifteen-pound blocks, shipped to market in railroad cars, dripping water all along the way from Provincetown to Boston, New York, and cities westward.

It was a favorite pastime for summer visitors to go out with the trapboat fishermen as they tended their weirs. The literary critic, Edmund Wilson, who also wrote plays for the Provincetown Players, described one of these early morning trips in his memoirs. Wilson's breakfast was "shredded wheat biscuit and condensed milk and coffee, with orange-peel alky [liquor] in it."

> Everything was dark on the gray long pier, with its wooden apparatus overhead and its stink of fish . . . They got down into a dory, five of them . . . and rowed out toward the traps with regular and funereal rhythm of oars, not saying a word. We visited a series of four traps—the laborious pulling up of the nets: the butterfish, great flapping silver flakes . . . The squid would usually be the first to appear . . . the mackerel, with their clean-clipped tails . . . a big goosefish . . . dogfish with their mean smug shark's mouths . . . a few whiting and cod-headed hake—rather prettily mottled sand dabs.[5]

Most of the trapped fish described by Wilson were jettisoned, because only the mackerel and whiting were marketable. The discarded fish littered the waterfront beaches, emitting a constant stench.

In the crowded summer of 1915, Lewis Wharf, now Mrs. O'Brien's Wharf, was one of the few available spaces large enough to accommodate a stage. "Our wharf, with the fishhouse on the end was conveniently at hand to serve as a theater."[6] It was also in the center of the bohemian East End and almost directly across the street from the home of Jig Cook, who was organizing the productions. Its three buildings were filled with dead storage, for Consolidated Wharf had neglected to dispose of its outmoded weir rigs. Therefore, it fell to Mary O'Brien and her friends to dispose of the nets, tackle, and dories to make room for the theater. Despite the uncertainty of ownership, Mary O'Brien rented the second floor of the largest building on Lewis Wharf to the Modern Art School of New York City and permitted Margaret Steele to set up an easel on the first floor. In July the plays, which had been first performed in the Hapgood's East End summer cottage, were moved to Mrs. O'Brien's Wharf farther "up-along" Commercial Street. To make way for the new theater, Margaret Steele packed up her easel and relinquished the first floor of the fishhouse.

By August 1915 the theater on the wharf was ready for the first night's performances, as Mary O'Brien recounted in *Time and the Town.*

> Four people stood in the wings with lamps in their hands to light the stage. Lanterns with tin reflectors were placed before the stage like old footlights. Four people stood beside the lamp bearers with shovels and sand in case of fire, and with these lights the fishhouse took on depth and mystery . . . In spite of its raining in torrents, everyone had come down the dark wharf lighted here and there by a lan-

tern. People had leaned their umbrellas against one of the big timbers which supported the roof. I noticed an umbrella stirred, then slowly slid down an enormous knothole to the sand thirty feet below. With the stealth of eels, other umbrellas went down the knothole to join their fellows under the wharf.[7]

The 1915 theater-on-the-wharf performances were so successful that the players decided to stay the winter in Provincetown to plan for the 1916 season. Suddenly all changed when Joe O'Brien became seriously ill and was hospitalized in New York City. Mary at first remained with the children in Provincetown and took the time to reassess her life. She read and burned old letters—"Old letters hold the past very closely." She wrote Joe about their debts. "The everlasting pressing clutch of bills." "What we need is $1,050 [her agent had offered only $350 for her fiction.] . . . so we can even get your jewels out of pawn [and] live anywhere in ease . . . in spite of wharfs [sic] and buildings." Mary spoke of her anguish in staying behind in Provincetown. "For it was very hard to let you go away without me and there were tears in my heart. I wanted to run after the train just to see you once more. I shall never get used to going away from you."[8] Joseph O'Brien died of stomach cancer on October 27, 1915. Mary Vorse O'Brien was a widow, for the second time in five years.

Joe's death was a shock, for no one had realized that he was seriously ill. Wilbur Steele went to New York to assist Mary O'Brien, while Mary's half-brother, Fred Marvin, an artist, took care of the three children in Provincetown. Hutch Hapgood, who had visited Joe daily in the hospital, also provided emotional support. Susan Glaspell wrote an elegiac poem, "Joe": "I only know my throat's all tight with the longing to have you open the door of my house and brightly call 'Hello!'"

Mrs. O'Brien's Fishing Wharf

* * *

ON JULY 13, 1916, the Provincetown Players opened their second season on Mary O'Brien's wharf.[9] Jig Cook, with a crew of volunteers from the troupe, had worked rapidly to build a stage, a movable set, and seating. Electricity was also installed. The *Provincetown Advocate* reported on the activity: "The studio on Lewis wharf (so called) now owned by Mrs. Mary Heaton O'Brien is in the hands of carpenters, who are making sundry interior changes."[10] Also, Arequipa cottage, which had housed a fish market, was made into a summer residence for Jig Cook's mother. Mary Heaton O'Brien lamented the alterations to her wharf. It was no longer the romantic setting of maritime adventure and bravery she and Joe had fallen in love with. The conversion to a theater symbolized the passing of an era, for her and for Provincetown.

As a forty-one-year-old widow, with three children to support, large debts, and a diminishing career as a fiction writer, she was understandably depressed. Donald Corley, her thirty-year-old friend, became her confidante and, for the summer, her lover. Don empathized with her about the wharf. "[I love] your personification of piles and girders and plankin', and the 'guilty leisure of lofts and fish market.' . . . Wharfage is a fascinating employment . . . I am lonely for you. I'd like to be walking homeward with you along the flat."[11]

The 1916 summer theater season was nearly aborted when, one week before the scheduled opening, an artist's oil stove ignited in the fishhouse, severely charring the western wall and roof. One of the two shacks on the wharf was destroyed. The *Provincetown Advocate* reported the incident.

The building was occupied by Mrs. Myra Mussleman Carr, of New York, and the Modern Art School . . . which building by-the-way, occupies a wharf site only a few feet re-

19

moved from the burned structure . . . The fire had gained good headway when discovered, and, although streams were directed upon it without undue delay, by hose one, hose two and the chemical engine, the building and contents were destroyed, while the outside western wall and the roof of the Modern Art School building were quite badly damaged.[12]

Don consoled Mary: "The poor wharf must look tragic with half of itself gone—what a shame you should have had that now, too, when it has just paid for its new clothes."[13]

"IT IS JUST A MONTH SINCE WE CAME UP ON THIS TRAIN," Don wrote to Mary in June while enroute from New York to Provincetown. "An appalling wait at Yarmouth—quite useless—with only two golden days—how can a heartless railroad rob one of half-an-hour? When my heart runs out to meet you beyond the dunes." On the return trip, he wrote, "The little grey town has slipped out of sight with you, and my heart aches."[14] In early Fall Don abruptly ended the affair and secretly married Harriet Works in New York City. Heaton Vorse remembered Don Corley as a "special friend" of his mother, though he had not known Corley's wife. Hutch Hapgood's characterization of Corley may well have applied to Hapgood himself: Corley later in life was "under the influence of unlimited booze and the unstemmed flattery of women."[15] Corley also became a member of the Provincetown Players, and devoted more time to the theater than to his career. He wrote plays, helped construct sets, and acted, taking the part of "a Norwegian" in the first New York production of *Bound East for Cardiff*.[16]

Mary O'Brien in 1916 had only minimal interest in the Wharf productions. She took small acting parts and tried her hand, unsuccessfully, at playwriting. She turned increasingly to the career that would continue the rest of her life, that of labor journalist and crusader. Mary nearly lost her wharf entirely in October 1916 when two dredging scows moored off Consolidated Wharf broke loose during a storm and narrowly missed the wharf. The incident was reported in the *Advocate*. "How they escaped striking and wrecking the Mary Heaton O'Brien wharf and building thereon passeth all understanding . . . Had the heavy scows hit the wharf, one or two bumps would have been sufficient to level that ramshackle affair, theater building and all."[17]

MARY HEATON VORSE O'BRIEN called her first five years in Provincetown "The Age of Innocence." That was about how long her imaginative affair lasted. Paradoxically, in creating her Shangri-La, she destroyed it. She campaigned for Provincetown, persuading her friends in Greenwich Village to share it with her. The first wave came slowly—with her intimates: Hutchins and Neith Hapgood, Wilbur and Margaret Steele, and George Cram Cook and Susan Glaspell. Then came the groundswell: colleagues and acquaintances, artists and writers who in 1914 left the unsafe bohemia of Europe and flooded Provincetown. Decades later a third wave came, which she called the "summer froth," unknown and ill-mannered tourists, jammed into automobiles, who trashed the town and left. Mary Heaton Vorse stayed on in Provincetown for sixty years, until her death in 1966. Through the years she watched her intimate, fictive town disappear as each wave took it farther and farther away.

In 1914, when tourism hit its first peak, the exploits of whalers, privateers, and renegade squatters were but town legends. Also gone were some of the specters of the past— isolation, long sea voyages, and unshackled sand. With the opening of the Cape Cod Canal there were fewer shipwrecks on the treacherous outside sandbars. Fishermen had mastered the currents of the nearby fishing grounds of Georges Bank, thus obviating the longer, more hazardous trips to the Grand Banks. Whalers roamed the well-charted Atlantic Ocean, seldom rounding Cape Horn or venturing into Arctic regions. With the coming of the railroad, a sea voyage was not the only expedient way to Boston. With the successful planting of beach grass, cascading dunes had been slowed down. The town had slowly drifted into the Twentieth Century.

BORN IN NEW YORK CITY and raised in Amherst, Massachusetts, Mary Heaton came from a financially secure, conservative Republican family. Her formal schooling was limited, but she learned German and French and studied art during European travels with her parents. At the time of her marriage to Albert Vorse in 1898 she had no career. Albert White Vorse, a descendant of Peregrine White, who was born aboard the *Mayflower* in Provincetown Harbor, readily agreed to the purchase of a Provincetown house. Bert was an avid boatman, a member of the New York City Explorers' Club, and a friend of Donald B. MacMillan, an Arctic explorer and Provincetown native. As a journalist Bert had gone to the Arctic on a Peary Relief Expedition.

Mary began to write for publication so that Bert would be able to quit his job and write full-time. After two years Bert had published little. Mary's earnings from her writing supported the family. Bert then devoted himself full-time to yachting and to philandering. According to Dee Garrison, Mary Heaton Vorse's biographer, "Bert believed himself a lover, a maverick, and a writer. He would enjoy real success at the first two endeavors."[18] At the time of Mary's first pregnancy Bert began to have affairs. There was a separation, then a reconciliation followed by the birth of a second child. Finally, after another of Bert's affairs, the couple permanently separated in 1910. That same year forty-five-year-old Bert unexpectedly died while in a Staten Island hotel. In an interview, his son Heaton described his father as a wastrel: "He may have died of syphilis."

AT THE TIME OF HIS DEATH Bert Vorse was in the vicinity of Viola Roseboro, one of his paramours. Known as the Duchess of New Dorp (in Staten Island), she was an archetypical, independently successful New Woman, a striking, dark-eyed "female bachelor" who publicly smoked cigarettes at a time when it was quite scandalous for women to do so.[19] Roseboro was a novelist, but she was better known as a *McClure's* editor, and for her professional advice that helped to launch the careers of Booth Tarkington and O. Henry. Roseboro often read manuscripts outside of *McClure's* office: on a park bench in New York, in her Staten Island home, or in Provincetown. In this way she was able to avoid the frequent and sometimes violent staff quarrels.

The staff was restive because the owner, Sam McClure, was spending vast sums of money taking young women on grand tours of Europe. While McClure gallivanted, his long-suffering wife stayed home and worked in the office. McClure's behavior particularly angered Ida Tarbell, the social reformer and renown muckraker, who instigated a staff rebellion that ended in a massive walk-out. Sam McClure quickly hired Willa Cather, a young writer teaching in Pittsburgh, to fill an editorial position in his depleted staff. Roseboro stayed on. Her notes at the time re-affirmed her loyalty to Sam; she greeted him with "Hail to the Chief" and signed herself as "your loyal Clubwoman."[20]

Viola Roseboro preceded the Vorses to Provincetown.

As the editor for both Mary and Bert at *McClure's*, she was an inducement for their going to Provincetown. According to Heaton Vorse, "Painters Charles Hawthorne, Ambrose Webster and Oliver Chaffee and novelist Viola Roseboro were already paying property taxes to the town treasurer before my progenitors arrived."[21] Roseboro bought her cottage in 1906. "I've just returned from a three months stay at Provincetown, Cape Cod. My balcony overhung the beach and I had all kinds of joy from the water . . . I've bought a house in Provincetown, on the beach. It is a long way, but Mr. McClure approves, they send MSS down there." Viola wrote enthusiastic letters from Provincetown—about the old wharves, the church steeples, even the standpipe, and the odor of fish. She walked the sand dunes and rowed a dory in the harbor. "The particular attraction is going barefoot."[22]

During the summer of 1908, Mary caught Bert cavorting with Viola. The two had wandered over Snail Road to the dunes at Peaked Hill, a favorite trysting place. Mary hired a horse and carriage and caught up with them. In his dapper white ducks, Bert emerged from the dunes, and coolly confronted Mary with "Ah, such is the way of the world."[23] After that summer Mary's associations with Viola were strictly professional. Viola gave up her summers in Provincetown and relocated to Staten Island. She rented out her cottage, at one time to the honeymooners Susan Glaspell and Jig Cook and later to the newlyweds Wilbur and Margaret Steele. In 1915 she sold it.

WILBUR DANIEL STEELE'S FIRST VISIT to Provincetown was in 1908. He roomed with Mary Heaton Vorse, who claimed he was Bert's distant cousin. Wilbur had met Mary in Paris where he was continuing the art training he had started at the Boston Museum of Fine Arts under the renowned artist

Philip Hale. Mary at the time was travelling with Bert, Bror
Nordfeldt, and Bror's fiancée. Mary and Bror were collabo-
rating on a series of travel articles for *Harper's* and *Outlook*.
Over a six-week period Nordfeldt taught etching to Steele.
When the foursome left for Italy, Steele followed along, leaving his mother and sister behind in Paris. It was in Florence,
with Mary's encouragement, that Steele began to write. He
sequestered himself in a room for three days and came out
with a short story.[24]

Despite a twelve-year age difference, Mary and
Wilbur became lovers. She nicknamed him "the kid." Mary
actively encouraged Wilbur's apprenticeship; she sent his stories to Viola, who also saw promise in Wilbur's early efforts.
Viola sponsored him for reporting assignments and commis-
sions for illustrations. His first *McClure's* piece—an adventure article, "Moving-Picture Machine in the Jungle"—was
published in January 1913. Even after the infatuation cooled,
Mary continued to promote Wilbur's career; he returned frequently to Provincetown for her support.

> The story I'm working on now is about Helltown . . . I hate
> to leave Provincetown, now that the leaving becomes immi-
> nent. It is actually home to me, Mary—I know I couldn't
> call any other place home, with anything like an equal de-
> gree of truth. Thank you very much, dear Mary, for Prov-
> incetown.[25]

Wilbur married in 1913, about the time of Mary's second marriage. Much to Wilbur's dismay, Mary did not ap-
prove of his fiancée, the painter Margaret Thurston. Wilbur
wrote Mary about his dilemma:

> Your letter—the part about Margaret troubled me a good
> deal. I can't make out just the ground under me. For Mar-

garet has said the same thing about trying to make you like her—almost *exactly* the same words. I believe you both. God—I don't know what to do.[26]

In 1913 Mary Vorse married a red-haired Irishman, Joe O'Brien, who was a free-lance reporter from Berryville, Virginia. In contrast to Bert, Joe was a feminist who willingly lent support to Mary's career and shared family responsibilities. Unfortunately, Joe's weakness was drinking, which diminished his earnings. Nevertheless, he was profligate with both money and his time. He freely volunteered his support for labor causes and prison reform, especially the I.W.W. "Wobblies" programs. Together Mary and Joe covered major strikes, such as those of the garment workers in Lawrence, Massachusetts, in 1912, and the silk workers in Paterson, New Jersey, in 1913. As she had with her first husband, Mary found herself the sole support of the household.

Mary was a charter member of the Liberal Club, of the feminist Heterodoxy Club, and both she and Joe were editors of the radical magazine *Masses*. Max Eastman, managing editor, described Mary as a "popular story writer . . . pale and fragile, and although abounding in energy had a permanently weary look."[27] Mary was constantly travelling between New York and Provincetown on the Fall River Line. Lawrence Langner, a founder of the Theatre Guild, described her as one of the most popular members of the Liberal Club and someone "who was always in a dither over a new husband or a new child, and kept the railroad tracks busy between the Village and Provincetown, running from one to the other."[28]

MARY VORSE'S CIRCLE of Provincetown intimates increased in 1911 when Hutchins and Neith Hapgood began summering there, and again in 1913 when George and Susan Cook came to settle. Having heard about Provincetown from Mary Vorse, Hutch arranged a meeting in Boston with Bert Vorse. "We both got drunk on red wine, and he gave me a vivid picture of Provincetown . . . He left on me an impression of a dark vivid man with a lively temperament, more sensuous than mental, with a passion for boats and the sea."[29] Neith then went to Provincetown to look for a rental cottage for her family of four children. She wrote Hutch about available housing:

> I am quite in love with this place and think it would be an ideal place for the children . . . I looked yesterday at cottages—There are a lot of them along the beach—fisherman's houses—with the sea coming right up in the back-yard! I found one, quite comfortable, furnished, good bathroom, large yard, good bathing beach for $100 for the 2 months—Aug & Sept Boyce would have Heaton Vorse to play with . . . The journey down, mostly by boat, is not expensive . . . food is not expensive . . . food very good and cheap, also vegetables.[30]

In 1913 Jig Cook arrived in Greenwich Village several weeks ahead of his fiancée, Susan Glaspell, "Davenport's leading novelist." He had left Chicago immediately after his divorce from his second wife. He and Sue had kept secret their marriage plans, even from friends in the Village. He wrote to Sue in Chicago: "I haven't told anybody about us yet.[31] Finally, he did write to his mother. "[I] wish I had been telling her about our marriage five years ago."[32] After their marriage on April 14, 1913, in Weehawken, New Jersey, at "ten minutes of eleven" and lunch at the Brevoort, Jig and Sue boarded the 5:00 P.M. Fall River steamer for the first leg of their journey to Provincetown.

The *Provincetown Advocate* took note of the two new

summer residents. "Mr. and Mrs. Cook are now in Provincetown at the Roseboro Cottage, where they will spend the summer."[33] The *Advocate* also reprinted a *Boston Post* announcement of the wedding entitled "Novelists are Secretly Wed." While there was no mention of Jig's prior marriages, the article discretely stated that it was a "marriage of more than ordinary interest in literary circles" and that "they spent many happy childhood days together." Jig was new to Provincetown, but in 1912 Susan had rented the Roseboro cottage with her long-time friend and Des Moines newspaper associate Lucy Huffacker. Huffacker later married Edward Goodman of the Washington Square Players.

THE FEW YEARS BEFORE THE OUTBREAK of World War I were halcyon times for the Provincetown writers: the Cooks, the Hapgoods, the O'Brien's, and the Steeles. They had nicknames for each other. Steele was called the "Kid"; the Cooks, "Jiggedy-and-Sue"; the O'Briens were "Joseph-Mary." "Has your wedding certificate got a picture of Jesus on it? and the Holy Ghost," quipped Sue in a letter to the honeymooning O'Briens.[34] The *Provincetown Advocate* was delighted with its new "colony of literary folks" and made frequent note of their comings and goings in its Personals column, and the town library accessed copies of the short stories and novels of its famous resident writers, Glaspell, Vorse, and Steele.

In his memoirs Hutch recalled these years as relaxed and pleasant times. "We were living simply and happily, as writers, mothers and fathers, husbands and wives, and friends, in a little community . . . things so . . . ordinary that they were almost indescribable."[35] There were family picnics, walks across the dunes, sailing parties, and almost nightly get-togethers after the children had been put to bed. They worked hard and played hard. Frequently their drinking parties got out of hand. Provincetown had been dry since the 1880s. There were no bars or liquor stores, but little was done to curb the sale of bootleg whiskey. Moreover, physicians could freely prescribe whiskey for medicinal purposes. Sue tells of a drinking episode centered around a birthday party for Jig:

> Last week Jiggedy Cook had one stunning birthday party . . . The party threatened to go on the blink because of . . . the lack of faith of Pierces of Boston. I sent to them for claret, saying send it collect. Seems it's against the law and day before the party comes a letter saying they are holding the wine for the money. Damn all such merchants. We beat it to the Express office, always a faithful friend in time of direst need, but even they said booze couldn't arrive before eight thirty the night of the party. All was gloom . . . Floyd Dell wanted to get Jig a birthday present. Said I, get it from Dr. Curley; he has lovely birthday presents. So we had sherry to tide us through dinner . . . I shall never forget the picture of Jiggedy as he threw open the door [of town hall] for that eight thirty booze. He was wearing his white suit and we had made him a wonderful turban and sash of orange calico from the New York store. Neith, who had made the birthday cake, robbed the noble structure of its red carnations and decorated everything about Jig that was decoratable [*sic*]. Looking like a float in a flower parade he threw wide the door to Adams Express, crying in a grand manner: "Well, well—what is this?"—and I think they felt like returning: "What is *this*?"[36]

PROVINCETOWN WAS KNOWN as an art colony before Mary Heaton Vorse and her writer friends arrived. Charles Webster Hawthorne in 1899 began his Cape Cod School of Art. Hawthorne, the son of a Maine sea captain, had served as assistant in the Southhampton art school of the popular and successful William Merritt Chase and had studied in Holland.

He selected Provincetown for some of the same romantic reasons as did Mary Vorse—its Old-World appearance and its maritime past. Subscribing to the *en plein air* theory of painting popular at the time in European art colonies, Hawthorne conducted his classes out-of-doors. He emphasized the beauty of colors and tones best distinguished in bright sunlight. His school advertisements told of the special light in Provincetown, "a jumble of color in the intense sunlight accentuated by the brilliant blue of the harbor." In the School's 1901 folder, Hawthorne promised students that "Provincetown had kept its refreshingly primitive character, not having been rendered colorless by the inroads of summer excursionists." Hawthorne, in white flannels, held weekly demonstration classes on a wharf or on the beach and often one hundred or more students and spectators gathered to watch him apply spots of color on the canvas until forms magically appeared.[37]

Further "up-along" (then meaning eastward) from Lewis Wharf were several wharves that housed artists' studios. On P. A. Whorf's Wharf, once 800 feet long, vessels designed for Grand Banks fishing and for the West Indies trade had been built and outfitted. Whorf's Wharf was now as dilapidated as Lewis Wharf. "The big building formerly used as a sail-loft and storage house at the head of P. A. Whorf's Wharf . . . has been furnished with large windows at the north end to provide artists painting quarters."[38] Artists had been taking over fishermen's shacks and sailing lofts for a decade or more. In 1915, with the formation of a theater on Lewis Wharf, playwrights and actors were not only taking over a wharf, but also moving into artists' space.

The transition from fishhouse to artists' studio to theater chronicled a changing Provincetown. In the 19th century the entire waterfront of wharves and windmills was devoted to the fishing industry. Beginning in 1899 with Charles

Hawthorne's school of art, the waterfront blossomed with artists' studios on the wharves and artists' classes on the beach. In 1915 theater found its small niche on the waterfront. Not only were trawl lines and half-barrels, sweep nets and dories displaced but also, on Lewis Wharf, an artist's easel. To Henry David Thoreau's "city of canvas" was now added the canvas of theatrical scenery to take its place alongside the painter's stretched canvas. Provincetown had added a new signature.

In selecting Provincetown as the location for an art colony, Hawthorne was following in the 19th century European tradition. As part of a back-to-nature movement, *plein-air* artists gravitated to rural areas, where subjects were painted out-of-doors rather than in the confines of studios. One of the earliest and most renown sites chosen by the artists was Barbizon in the forest of Fontainebleau, forty miles south of Paris.[39] Its popularity increased after 1849 when the railway was extended from Paris to Fontainebleau. Provincetown likewise met all the requirements for a turn-of-the-century art colony. It was rural, remote from the classical restrictions of urban centers, and yet it was accessible by train and by boat. For the Greenwich Village writers, a compelling reason for settling in Provincetown was the convenience of travel on the Fall River steamship railroad line. It was a pleasant, sometimes inspirational, journey, essentially portal-to-portal transportation from the docks near Greenwich Village to the wharves of Provincetown. Many love letters and poems were composed as the Players shuttled back and forth between villages on the old Fall River Line.

Hawthorne was fascinated by Provincetown's colorful Portuguese community, whose population by 1875 had outnumbered the residents with Yankee backgrounds. Throughout his career, he produced scores of canvases of the

Portuguese fishermen and their families. Mary Heaton Vorse in 1911 published her first article about Provincetown; it was about "The Portuguese of Provincetown."

> The fishing business has passed, during the last twenty years, the time of the great change in the fishing business from salt to fresh fish, almost entirely into the hands of the Portuguese. They own boats; Portuguese capital owns the handsome one-hundred foot schooners, as beautiful as any yacht; Portuguese captains command them, and Portuguese men sail them.[40]

For the Provincetown writers the Portuguese were a source for their "local color" fiction. In this genre was Steele's play, *Not Smart*, staged by the Players in 1916 on Mary Heaton Vorse's wharf. The Portuguese offered another significant and attractive element, a European ambience valued by the Village bohemians. These radicals had gravitated en masse to Europe to escape the creative and sexual restrictions of their conventional small hometowns. In America their center was Greenwich Village, essentially a non-interfering, Italian neighborhood. Because of the Portuguese, Provincetown seemed like the Village, European. This element was one of the persuasive reasons the unconventional Provincetown Players settled in Provincetown rather than in more orthodox colonies like Woodstock or Southampton.

Another reason for choosing Provincetown was its affordable housing. Cheap accommodations became available as the fishing industry declined. "None of us had much money, these were small houses we lived in: they had been fishermen's homes before they were ours," recalled Susan Glaspell in *Road to the Temple*. Inexpensive whaling captains' homes in disrepair were up-for-sale. Mary Heaton Vorse and Wilbur Daniel Steele each bought one. Also available for sale and rent were scores of vacated wharves. The summer crowd of painters and writers found these wharves especially to their liking, as they did the wide array of other housing lining the waterfront—deserted fishermen's shacks, boathouses, and sailing lofts. O'Neill's first summer lodging was T. A. Snow's deserted boathouse in the East End. His first home was also an abandoned structure, the Peaked Hill Life-Saving Station, situated between the Atlantic Ocean and the edge of the dunes.

Provincetown also had nostalgic appeal. In some ways it was like coming home, for many of the Players had New England ties. There were those who had been born elsewhere but had ancestral roots in New England: Hutchins and Neith Hapgood, Susan Glaspell, Jig Cook, and John Reed. For O'Neill it was like his seaside boyhood home in New London, Connecticut, the only permanent home his peripatetic theatrical family had known. There was also the Harvard connection; many had attended school and/or taught there, most notably, Jig Cook, Hutch Hapgood, Jack Reed, and Eugene O'Neill.

After Mary Heaton Vorse had lived in Provincetown for thirty-five years, she wrote *Time and the Town*, her Provincetown chronicle, in which she complained about the tourists:

> There are times that the summer froth becomes so dense it seems like some monstrous growth climbing up over the little white houses, and one wishes that an equally monstrous hose could be taken to it, making the place clean again.[41]

How different had been her feelings in 1907 when she first approached Provincetown aboard the Boston steamer *Longfellow*. She saw Provincetown rise in magic fashion from the sea; she fell in love with the "seafaring place that lived from the sea." Her love affair with Provincetown lasted a lifetime, her initial passion in time giving way to harsh yet tender accommodation. What Mary Heaton Vorse fell in love with was an imaginary world of "adventure, improbable escapes, heroism, and sudden death . . . of hairbreadth rescues." In time these images died and with them the romance of the sea, the heroics and opulence associated with whaling and the golden era of Provincetown.

In 1922 when Mrs. O'Brien's Wharf collapsed, so also collapsed Mary Heaton Vorse's romantic fantasies and, symbolically, the rich maritime history of Provincetown. Mary grieved its passing:

> Now that fishermen no longer tramped down the wharf in their rubber boots and loads of fish no longer came over the side, the old fish wharf could not go on living. In the winter of 1921 the ice crushed the wharf, leaving only Lucy L'Engle's studio tottering precariously on a few piles.[42]

THE STORY OF LEWIS WHARF, a.k.a. Mrs. O'Brien's Wharf, is central to the story of the Provincetown Players. Likewise, a study of the metamorphosis of Lewis Wharf—as it changed from a housing for commercial fisheries, to studios for artists, to a theater for the avant-garde, and even its collapse—is integral to the history of Provincetown. For wharves tell the history of Provincetown.

Provincetown began with the building of a small fishing stage in the 17th century, then accelerated in the 19th century with the rapid erection of fifty-five or more wharves to accommodate its new status as an international seaport. In the early 20th century, when its glory years as a maritime port were over and its neglected wharves were tumbling into the harbor, Provincetown welcomed a new identity: that of an art colony and the place where the Provincetown Players began.

CHAPTER THREE

City of Sand, City of Canvas

a filmy sliver of land lying flat on the ocean . . .
a mere reflection of a sand-bar on the haze above.

—Henry David Thoreau, *Cape Cod*[1]

THE ESSENTIAL PROVINCETOWN is today what it was in the 16th century, a fishing station on a broad, protective harbor. The rest is sand and insularity. Provincetown sits on the narrow end of a sandspit that extends into the Atlantic Ocean at the far eastern reach of New England. These geographic realities write its history.

Provincetown began with the building of a make-shift wharf, a fishing stage. Most likely it was fashioned by a 16th-century Basque, Norman, or Portuguese fisherman who sought the safety of Provincetown Harbor after a northeasterly gale had blown his ketch from the codfishing banks of Newfoundland. He stayed on through the fishing season because there were marketable codfish in nearby waters, and mackerel and alewives for bait alongshore. At that unrecorded time, the sandy peninsula that protects the harbor from the Atlantic Ocean was covered with trees to the water's edge. To construct a stage, the fisherman needed to walk only a few steps back from the shoreline to fell pine, red oak, or cedar. There was also an abundance of small boughs and bramble to build drying platforms, called flakes. He gutted and split the codfish, soaked it in salt water, and spread the fish on the flakes to dry. When his fishing vessel was filled with sun-dried, cured cod, destined for the lucrative European market, he left.

BEFORE THE 18TH CENTURY, no one stayed on—neither fisherman nor explorer nor Pilgrim. However, many vessels sought out Provincetown's harbor. Time and again European explorers took soundings, and re-mapped and renamed the harbor and the surrounding peninsula. In 1606 Samuel de Champlain called the peninsula Cape Blanc because of its towering white dunes; John Smith in 1614 renamed it Cape James after his royal patron; but Cape Cod, the name Bartholomew Gosnold had given it in 1602, prevailed because of the abundance of codfish nearby. Gosnold's crew loaded their small bark, *Concord,* to the gunwales and reported "we had pestered our ship so with codfish, that we threw numbers of them overboard again."[2]

Provincetown missed its chance for wider historical fame when, in 1620, the Pilgrims decided against remaining there, their first landfall in America. Thanks to early fishermen and explorers, Captain Jones, the pilot of the *Mayflower,* had charts and soundings of Provincetown [then known as Cape Cod] Harbor. So when he was thwarted by the rip tides of Chatham presumably on his way to Virginia, Jones tacked around and sailed into what he knew was a protected harbor. (Current opinion is that, for religious reasons, the Pilgrims never intended to settle in Virginia, as originally authorized.)

For five weeks the *Mayflower* lay at anchor in the "harbor wherein a thousand sail of ship may safely ride."[3] Here the Pilgrims drafted the *Mayflower Compact,* witnessed the birth of Peregrine White, the first English child born in New England, and suffered the death of four members, including the depressed young Dorothy Bradford, who threw herself into the icy waters. They ate shellfish, either sea clams or large mussels, and became quite ill; they contracted pneumonia from wading ashore in the frigid winter waters; and they watched helplessly as whales circled and bumped into their vessel. Had they had the "right instruments" for whaling they might well have stayed on. But it is doubtful that the artisans, merchants, and farmers aboard the *Mayflower* would have survived as fishermen.

Although the surrounding waters of Cape Cod were well charted, not much was known about the land. What accounts had reached Europeans led them to believe that it was a "hideous and desolate wilderness, full of wild beasts and wild men." Actually, the "wild men" of Cape Cod, the Nauset Indians, were game hunters, foragers, and cultivators of tobacco (pokeweed) and maize. Nevertheless, the Pilgrims' fears were not altogether unfounded. Prior to 1620, about fifty unaccountable deaths of Europeans had occurred in New England. Encounters between Indians and Europeans turned violent in the 16th century when Edward Harlow kidnapped four Cape Indians and took them back to Europe as slaves.[4] The Pilgrims' fears were confirmed when they explored the peninsula and unearthed the remains of a blond-haired European, apparently a sailor, with Old-World objects, "a knife, a pack-needle . . . and old iron things."

In 1636, sixteen years after the *Mayflower* had left for Plymouth, Harvard College was founded, but Provincetown, the Pilgrims' landfall across the bay, was still a fringe society.

Well into the following century, Provincetown had neither families, nor schools, nor a hint of civilization. It belonged to roving Indians, fishermen, and sea dogs. Plymouth Colony's faint attempt to collect revenues from bass fishermen to help support its emerging schools was skillfully thwarted. These renegade fishermen also traded in contraband with European smugglers. "There was no place so well suited to these lawless fellows to carry on unlawful traffic as the head of the Cape; called by the settlers, 'Cape Cod'."[5]

This community of rogue fishermen banded together not only with the European smugglers but also with the Indian braves who, during hunting and fishing season, set up a nearby camp of circular bent-sapling-and-straw houses. The fishermen traded glass buttons and rum for Indian venison, tobacco, and corn. The Indians taught them "hubbub," a form of dice made with painted plumb stones. The Indians took this game seriously. There was much shouting of "hub, hub, hub, accompanied by the slapping of breasts and thighs. They cast the stones in a Tray with a mighty noyse and sweating."[6]

It was indeed an outlaw society. All flotsam and jetsam that washed upon the shore was fair game, be it drift whale, wrecked cargo, or bejeweled corpse. This rapinous activity lasted well into colonial times. In 1722, the six-weeks-old corpse of Hannah Robinson was washed up on Herring Cove, a little within Race Point. It was discovered by Indians. "The corpse was identified by papers found in her stays and by a gold necklace which had been concealed from the natives by the swelling of the neck. A finger had been cut off, probably by other natives to obtain the gold ring which had disappeared."[7]

Life was much freer for these Colonial bachelors in their bacchanalian fishing station than in the theocratic confines of the Pilgrim community. There unmarried men were unfairly taxed for what was considered the selfish luxury of the solitary life. Trivial misbehavior—such as using tobacco, playing cards, and uncleanliness—was unduly punished. All conduct was closely monitored and severely punished in accordance with the laws of the Old Testament. Eavesdropping, neglecting work, "profane dancing," sleeping in a meeting, and picking peas on the Sabbath were punishable crimes, often with corresponding physical abuse such as cropping ears, slitting noses, branding hands, and putting sticks through tongues. Excessive drinking was a common offense. In addition to physical punishment, the guilty person had to wear a letter "D" on his garment. Incest offenders wore an "I." The letter "A," as worn by Hester Pryne in *The Scarlet Letter,* stood for adultery. One can surely sympathize with the New World's first streaker, the frustrated man who was convicted of running "naked into the meetinghouse."[8]

Punishments were often gruesome. A teenage lad in Plymouth was convicted of buggery with "a cow, two goats, five sheep, two calves, and a turkey." A large pit was dug and the condemned boy was made to stand at the edge, where—before his eyes—each animal implicated was slaughtered and thrown into the pit. As the boy watched, first a mare was marched to the edge, then a large cow, then smaller cattle, each animal killed in order of size. Finally the condemned teenager was executed and thrown into the carnage on top of the bleeding and mutilated animals.[9]

The prying theocrats had their hands full, for—contrary to popular belief—Plymouth Plantation erupted after its first decade into a "brothel house of sin." Drunkenness was endemic, robbery common, and sexual offenses grew to the point where tribunes were called "bawdy courts." William Bradford, in his history of Plymouth Plantation, writes about the sexual offenses, claiming that there was "incontinency between persons unmarried . . . but some married persons also. But that which is worse, even sodomy and buggery (things fearful to name) have broke forth in this land oftener than once."

Race Run was the site of Provincetown's bachelor fishing station. It is an inlet outside Provincetown Harbor, at the roiling junction of Cape Cod Bay and the Atlantic Ocean. To this day it is a rich fishing ground because of the abundant nutrients in the sea. This locale is no doubt the source of the modern-day legend of "Helltown," a rendezvous for those with unlicensed appetites. Provincetown has never shed the notoriety of this fishing camp. Historians invariably equated all of Provincetown with this legendary station. The 19th-century historian Shebnah Rich referred to Race Run as the "poker flats of Cape Cod" and to Provincetown as a "town of many anomalies." In the 20th century, the historian Henry Kittredge characterized the town as a "lawless gang of polyglots." The contemporary writer, Norman Mailer, a seasonal resident of Provincetown, continues the nefarious legend of Helltown in *Tough Guys Don't Dance,* suggesting that there were brothels there. It is doubtful there were bawdy houses in these primitive surroundings. Prostitutes were located closer to the center of town in places accessible to seamen and mariners. What licentiousness the Puritans suspected long ago has now become a modern-day legend.

Until the 19th century, Provincetown was virtually uninhabited. It developed slowly because of its remoteness and its lack of natural resources. It is at the end of a sandspit, a geological afterthought, a pace or two behind the mainland. By land Provincetown is situated full circle from Boston. Enroute one will box the compass—that is, first head south, then east, then north, then west to reach the outer edge of Cape Cod and of Massachusetts. As one makes his way down the Cape, he will run out of rocks, topsoil, and fresh water. When the first United States Census was taken in 1790, no census taker came to Provincetown. The journey was long and the residents were few. It has been estimated that 424 residents lived there in 1790, a small number considering that Provincetown had been given township status in 1727. Householders left when the pelagic fish moved on and when foreign navies raided the town. During the Revolutionary War in 1776, there were 205 inhabitants; by the end of the War the vulnerable port had been abandoned. Some returned after the Revolutionary War, but the town did not gain population until after the War of 1812. The federal census of 1820 counted 1,252 residents.

During the Revolutionary War fishermen were exempt from military service and colonial taxes. On the other hand, they were given no protection. Fishing schooners were captured, cargo confiscated, mariners impressed into foreign service or imprisoned, some in leaky, crowded prison-ships where, at every rising tide, they had to pump for their lives. Some fishermen armed their boats and, as legalized pirates, preyed on enemy commerce. These successful adventurers provided the Continental Congress and themselves with scarce munitions, stores, and clothing. England closed off the Grand Banks to fishing. Colonial ports were crowded with disintegrating and grounded vessels. In Gloucester, grass grew on the wharves; in Boston, the port was closed; and Provincetown was under siege by the English frigate *Somerset*.

Once again Provincetown inhabitants practiced expediency, as they had earlier with sea rovers and Indians. Arrangements with the British were amicable, for the town had little in common with the rebels in Boston. For example, on Sundays the captain of the *Somerset* preached in the meetinghouse and, in return, the town supplied the crew with fish, butter, and eggs. The ship's surgeon ingratiated himself by providing medical services and eventually married a Truro woman. However, when the *Somerset* was wrecked on the backside shore on November 8, 1778, the residents of Provincetown took advantage of the situation. They complied with the authorities by capturing the British sailors, who were then marched from Truro to Boston, but they looted the ship. The Boston official who investigated the incident found no trace of the booty: "From all I can learn, there is wicked work at the wreck, riotous things. The Truro and Provincetown men made a division of the clothing, etc. . . There is a plundering gang that way."[10]

To become a town, Colonial residents were required to have both a proper meetinghouse and an appropriate name. Provincetown resisted both. A meetinghouse was expensive; for example, it cost at least £500 to build one in 1680 in Hingham, Massachusetts. This was ten times the cost of an average house and seven times the yearly cost of running a town.[11] To encourage its residents, the General Court in 1717 gave £150 to "Provincetown, alias Cape Cod" to build a meetinghouse for itinerant ministers. In 1727 Provincetown was eventually incorporated, but for the next fifty years it did not keep adequate town records:

> Unwarrantable liberties appear to have been taken with the records . . . Very many pages have evidently been cut out from . . . a Book of Records; [later] a wholesale sacrilege has doubtless been committed. Our indignation burns toward the vile perpetrators.[12]

Decorum was hard to come by. As late as 1775, the Court ordered that "for every dog that comes into the meeting-house on the Sabbath-day in the time of meeting the owner shall pay one-half dollar or kill his dog."[13]

Then there was the question of the town's name. This was tied in with the matter of land sovereignty. In its official documents the General Court had assumed the practice of addressing the settlement as "Provincetown" and "Provincetown, alias Cape Cod." This was before it had official status as a town with a corresponding name. It was commonly identified on maps as "Cape Cod" or "Cape Cod Harbor." By calling it Provincetown, the General Court was reasserting its supremacy over the land. It did so on the grounds that the settlement was part of the "Provincelands" of the Massachusetts Bay Colony, which included the Harbor and extended around Long Point, the far tip of Cape Cod, to the strategic backside fronting the shipping lanes of the Atlantic Ocean. When the General Court incorporated Provincetown in 1727, it kept the land; the residents continued to be squatters. This arrangement lasted almost until the Twentieth Century. And as for the name? The General Court had its way: Provincetown. It was not what the residents asked for; they wanted to call it Herringtown.[14]

> They are the sea made land
> To come at the fisher town
> And bury in solid sand
> The men she could not drown.
>
> —Robert Frost, "Sand Dunes"

PROVINCETOWN BEGAN AS A FISHING SETTLEMENT with the felling of trees for a stage. And it almost ended in the same way. Wood was scarce and was not replenished; with each season the early itinerant fisherman had to walk farther into the slim tip of the peninsula to find timber and brush. He tapped pine trees for tar and turpentine; cut pine, cedar or oak to replace a spar; and gathered bayberry bush to insulate a cobhut and to start a fire. When householders settled in, the destruction accelerated. Woods were decimated to build wharves, houses, salt vats, and windmills. It was estimated that a householder with two fireplaces needed over thirty cords to carry him through the year. Distilling seawater to produce salt robbed the land even more. It took a cord to convert seawater into eleven bushels of salt. After only one generation of settlement, dunes and hollows were stripped of tree and bush; the unanchored sand nearly buried the town.

THIS WAS INDEED A BIZARRE PERIOD in Provincetown's history; it was a one hundred-year incurious struggle against avalanching sand. Provincetown faced up to this threat as it had to others, with prolonged indifference. The Colonial government was likewise indifferent. It finally took action, not because houses and roadways were threatened, but because the sand was clogging the harbor. After all, Provincetown was a strategic harbor. The government encouraged its settlers to be informers about the movement of foreign navies, as well as shipwrecks, poaching, and any other illegal trafficking. It commended one four-year resident who in 1705 complained about foreigners taking "her majesty's" beached whales. (These so-called "drift whales" were by law the property of the clergy and a chief means of support.)

One of the first conservation acts designed to save Provincetown Harbor and the Provincelands was written in 1714; it restricted the felling of trees "to keep the sand from being driven into the Harbour by the wind." This was followed by a series of laws from 1740 to 1786 attempting to limit the unrestricted pasturage of "neat" cattle and "horsekind" on dunes and salt meadows. All went unheeded.

> The court might as well have forbidden the winds to blow or the sun to shine. Provincetowners cared nothing for

laws, and continued to cut wood and turn cattle loose for the next hundred years.[15]

ALL OF PROVINCETOWN IS BUILT ON SAND. The glacial moraines that created Cape Cod stopped a mile or so to the east of town at High Head. Provincetown is at the narrow end of a geologically recent sandspit, formed by sand transported by wind and waves from southerly Atlantic cliffs, shoals, and beaches. There are three parallel ridges of dunes bordering Provincetown. Before the 20th century all three ridges were loosely cascading onto town streets and roadways and into harbors and inlets. Today the first ring of sand hills circling the northern rim of Provincetown has stabilized. The more distant two dune ranges still walk—that is, they are blown southward by strong northerly winter winds. Repeated plantings of beach grass and restricted use slow down the migration.

The Peaked Hills range, the outer ridge, borders the Atlantic Ocean and reaches from Race Point to the glacial deposits at High Head. This outer range is older and more stable than the middle range. In 1790, however, Peaked Hills range was barren and mobile; an anonymous observer described the area as a "desert of white sand, five miles in length parallel to the sea. The tops of the trees appear above the sand, but they are all dead."[16] A far cry from the lofty forests of "oaks, pines, sassafras, juniper, birch, holly" touted by the Pilgrims. The middle range of dunes, running west of Pilgrim Lake to within a mile of Hatches Harbor at Race Point, unless checked by plantings of beach grass, will walk into the lake and onto the highway at an annual rate of 15–20 feet. Trucks cart away tons of sand from Route 6 and, during high winds, windshields are pitted by the swirling sand.

* * *

EARLY IN THE 19TH CENTURY, excursionists made their way into Provincetown, attracted by its peculiar geography, particularly its dunes. With the publication of the 1784 text, *Geography Made Easy,* literary America became intrigued with the new science of geography and, with notebook in hand, launched forth into America's unexplored countryside. What they saw in Provincetown was a wasteland of sand: denuded dunes swirling about; roadways that led through rutted sand troughs and across the bottom of the sea on an outgoing tide; houses and schools filled with sand; and shifting beaches that periodically made Provincetown an island. Strangers were amazed by the indifference of the townspeople to the blowing, shifting sands. To the foreign eye, Provincetown was a vast desert, a miniature Sahara, a "city of sand."

Edward Augustus Kendall, a British free-lance writer, in 1808 reported that in Provincetown "there is nothing under the foot but a deep white sand, which is driven by the wind into banks, like snow . . . Heaps are sometimes driven against the houses; and it appears that they would be buried under them, but for the contrivance of raising them on piles, and thus allowing a passage for the drift, beneath their floors."[17]

In 1810 Timothy Dwight, President of Yale University, rode his private chaise into Provincetown over sandy ruts and flooded roadways "where a horse wades with excessive fatigue." It was an uncertain and hazardous trip as stages often got stuck in the sand and sometimes capsized into the ocean. Dwight prophesied that the "whole township of Province Town, will one day, and that at no distant period of time, be swept away by the ocean," for the sand that had been "a barrier against the ambition and fretfulness of the ocean" had become "the sport of every wind."[18]

The 1839 woodcut by John Warner Barber, the first

46

known illustration of Provincetown, depicts residents ankle-deep in sand. Engravings for a long time thereafter pictured Provincetowners without feet. Barber noted that the town was "on the margin of a beach of loose sand . . . [the sand] is so light that it drifts about the houses . . . similar to snow in a driving storm. There were no hard surfaces; upon stepping from the houses the foot sinks in the sand."[19]

Timothy Dwight, dubbed "the old Pope" for his excessive piety, was saddened by the "russet and melancholy" short grass on the barren dunes and hillsides, the result of unrestrained foraging and too many animals on too little land. He reported that in 1810 Provincetown had, in addition to its 936 residents, two horses, ten yoke of oxen, and 140 cows. There was one large common pasturage situated between Provincetown and its neighbor Truro, an extensive salt meadow bordering East Harbor (what is now Pilgrim Lake). "Each inhabitant being entitled to pasture a certain number of animals, and take away a certain quantity of hay." This arrangement was disregarded.

Provincetown blamed its neighbor Truro for the wanton use of pasture lands and Truro blamed Provincetown. Truro had more at stake, because the unanchored sand was filling in Truro's main anchorage, East Harbor. Truro called for outside help, and in 1826 the federal government appropriated $3,500 for the planting of beach grass. Once again restrictions were placed on foraging. But the struggle was not over.

In 1833 the Federal Government took further action by assigning Major James Graham to conduct a three-year survey of Provincetown Harbor because of its strategic military location. It is "an important rendezvous for any naval force. During the greater part of our late war with Great Britain, it was occupied by the enemy, who kept a strong squadron almost constantly stationed here."[20] Of concern was silting at both the east and west ends of the harbor, caused by breaks in the outer beaches: one north of East Harbor, the other at the west end near Hatches Harbor. The survey resulted in the erection of earthen dikes and the planting of beach grass.

Despite these measures, valuable salt marsh acreage was lost to erosion. Shebnah Rich in 1883 observed: "Stout's Creek, once several hundred yards wide, and where a number of tons of hay were annually cut, now scarcely exists, being almost entirely choked up with sand."[21] Adjoining the salt marsh in the west end, an earthen dike was erected extending from Long Point to what was then called Stevens Point. Beach grass was planted on the dike, but in short order the grass was killed; townspeople piled salt hay on top the dike and suffocated the grass. In 1911, a rock dike was built.

A continuing problem at the East End of town, which is the only approach to town by land, was sand erosion. Maps as early as *Carey's American Pocket Atlas* (1808) show Provincetown as an island, separated at East Harbor from the adjoining peninsula. When the road was washed out—a common occurrence—the only way into Provincetown was along the Atlantic Ocean beach, preferably at low tide. The first road to reach Provincetown was the King's Highway in 1719. This route led from Truro across the ocean cliffs, then along the beach, then around the salt meadow skirting the northern rim of East Harbor.

At first the beach was the only roadway, then it became a preferred one because the sand flats were firmer than the sandy roads. At times during major storms, however, the entire beach was washed out and the Atlantic Ocean cut through to East Harbor. For example, during the ferocious winter gale of 1851, when the Minot's Ledge stone lighthouse in Boston harbor was destroyed, a breach was cut and a stack

of timber lying on the Atlantic Ocean beach on the backside
was propelled through the breach into East Harbor on the
Cape Cod Bay side. Beach grass was periodically planted to
shore up the narrow sandy roadway around East Harbor.

HENRY DAVID THOREAU VISITED PROVINCETOWN four times
(1849, 1850, 1855, and 1857). His first approach from the
Truro cliffs was around East Harbor by way of the Ocean
beach. He observed that the roadway had been rebuilt with
sod, the sides lined with six feet of brush, and beach grass
planted on the adjoining banks to prevent further erosion,
"thus Cape Cod is anchored to the heavens, as it were, by a
myriad of little cables of beach grass."[22] The less frequently
used approach was on the Cape Cod Bay side; this was pass-
able only at extreme low tide because East Harbor flowed
into the Provincetown Harbor at this juncture. Not until 1854
was a bridge built over the inlet to East Harbor, but it was
periodically washed out. Not until 1873 when the railroad
arrived was the bridge replaced by a permanent roadway.

During each of Thoreau's four visits, Provincetown was
plagued by sand avalanches. "The sand is the great enemy
here . . . There was a schoolhouse . . . filled with sand up to the
tops of the desks."[23] Thoreau walked the length of Provincetown, using wherever possible the four-plank wooden sidewalk along Front Street (Commercial Street). Supposedly the
townspeople had objected when the Federal Government had
constructed this sidewalk in 1839. To show their resentment
many avoided the sidewalk and continued to wade ankle-deep
in the sandy road or to walk along the beachfront.

While the Federal Government was fighting erosion
on the dunes, silting in the harbor, and impassable roadways,
Provincetowners were acting in characteristic ways, thwarting the remedies or capitalizing on the crisis. "I could hardly

believe my eyes," said Thoreau, for there amid the teeming mountains of sand, one entrepreneur had posted a sign, "Fine Sand for Sale Here." Then there were those opportunists who shoveled the sand out of their houses, streets, and hillsides into wheelbarrows and carts, and dumped the sand into the harbor. Thereby they created new land and extended property lines into the sea.

> From the high hill in the rear of the town, also at the east part of the harbor, cars have been for years employed in bringing down sand by railways to the wharves, for the purpose both of making land and especially to furnish ballast for vessels. Many thousand tons are thus annually supplied ... A mountain of earth has already been removed, and additional house-lots have been furnished thereby.[24]

Thoreau reported on his first visit that the dooryards were all sand and that he "did not see enough black earth in Provincetown to fill a flower pot."[25] All the topsoil or large rocks now in Provincetown have been brought in by man, in many instances carried as ship's ballast. On the other hand, vessels were not allowed to take stones from the beach for ballast "therefore their crews used to land at night and steal them."[26] In his 1874 *Gazetteer,* Elias Nason reported that "the man now lives ... who made the first artificial garden here."[27] To the astonishment of the town this pioneer spread ballast loam upon the beach sand and planted a garden. When landowners talked of their dooryards being part of China, Peru, or Madeira, they meant that their topsoil came by ship from ports in those foreign lands.

"People in Provincetown do not regard houses as stationary objects. A man will buy a piece of dune land above the town and a cottage on the front shore, and presently up the hill toils the little house."[28] This observation of the 20th-century

Provincetown resident, Mary Heaton Vorse, is much like that of the 19th-century visitor Thoreau, who was amazed at the unanchored houses riding on stilts above the moving sand. And yet even today older Provincetown houses rest on sand and are easily moved. Many have been floated from Long Point to the center of town, from Truro to Provincetown, and from one end of town to another. The preferred way to add on a story is not to build a second floor but to jack up the whole structure and build from the bottom. Cellars are circular because that is the best geometric form for withstanding shifting sand.

Provincetown was indeed slow to raise itself out of the sand. As late as 1874, Nason echoed a familiar observation: "[the town] consists of loose, white sand, into which the foot sinks somewhat as into snow . . . The land is destitute of vegetation, and hence there is not a single farm in the whole township." By the time of the completion of the Pilgrim Monument in 1910, the town had become sufficiently concerned about the fragile environment that a guard was assigned to keep visitors from stepping on the newly planted fragile grass. Tourism had become a thriving business by then.

SAND SCULPTS PROVINCETOWN HARBOR in equalized sweeps, for it is a natural harbor, one of the world's largest. When dredging is required, it is mainly to correct man-made modifications, such as groins, breakwaters, or wharves, or to increase the depth of the harbor to accommodate deeper-draft boats.

Fresh water is critically scarce in Provincetown. There is no bedrock; sand acts as a sieve. What little fresh water there is, is trapped, in the shape of a lens, atop the heavier salt water. Today water is piped in from neighboring Truro. When there is heavy usage of water one tastes the salty underbelly of Provincetown.

Provincetown's harbor shapes its industry and the

sand shapes its appearance. Its geography makes it noticeably different from the rest of Cape Cod—a compact and somewhat scruffy town at the end of a well-manicured peninsula. Provincetown is a vulnerable yet dynamic outpost resting on a sliding man-made stage, forever a city of sand. The town crouches low, between rings of dunes and a sloping beach. It rests on a thin skin of transplanted soil and pockets of sweet water. Its houses are low-scaled, easily moved around on malleable sand. There are the narrow streets and narrow houses squeezed and jumbled together in all directions; there is the spacious, iridescent harbor, attracting fishing vessels and strange ships and strangers with novel palettes and ideas and there are the towering dunes and long stretches of beach.

PROVINCETOWN HARBOR in the 19th century was one gigantic wooden stage on which the town dramatized its new-found prosperity. These were the glory years, between the end of the War of 1812 and the start of the Civil War, when Provincetown was the fishing and whaling capital of Cape Cod. In its wide harbor, fishing vessels multiplied and grew larger: gunwales higher, beams wider, and keels deeper. Thereupon wharves multiplied and grew wider and longer. Once again this low-lying, malleable town dramatically and visually displayed its metamorphosis, this time from a "city of sand" to a "city of canvas."

Wharves and piers and stages rose out of the sandy harbor, long and short, narrow and wide, wooden tentacles that crawled out to meet the scores of canvas-rigged vessels tacking about. At the end of each street leading downward to the sea was a stage, a pier, or a wharf. There were small cobwork platforms, stages for drying fish, and piers for stowing fishing gear. And there were the long wharves, which reached out into depths of two fathoms, beyond the tidal limits, where Grand Banks schooners and whaling brigs and packet steamers tied up. No longer necessary were hand-carts and horse-drawn jiggers for ploughing across the sand flats to pick up and unload cargo and passengers.

> When the demand came for larger vessels and longer voyages, the creek harbors of the Upper Cape became worthless, while a fleet of schooners swung easily at anchor inside Long Point, and fishermen flocked to Provincetown as deer to a salt-lick.[29]

There was a host of other visual changes. An entire satellite settlement—houses, school, wharves, salt works—which for a generation had populated Long Point at the entrance to the Harbor, was picked up, set on log rafts, and floated over to the town proper. Long Point settlement disbanded when the marketable mackerel and herring alongshore moved away, probably chased out to sea by ravenous bluefish. A new federally owned lighthouse was erected on Long Point, guiding ships from thirteen miles out around the shoals and into the priceless harbor.

Dismantled were most of the pervasive salt works, victims of abolished protective salt tariffs and the recently found, cheaper salt deposits. Acres of wooden salt works—vats, troughs and windmills—were cannibalized to erect houses and other structures. In 1812 there had been over a million and a half square feet of vats and troughs.

Also gone was the town's landmark, a sailor's beacon—a windmill that sat high on the horizon, on the highest dune, High Pole Hill (now Monument Hill). It was replaced in 1854 with a new landmark, a Town House, which contained both town offices and the high school. Climbing High Pole Hill was arduous; during high winds it was dangerous, for roof tiles flew off and, on one occasion, gale-force winds picked up a student, impaling her on the iron picket fence and running a picket through her cheek.[30] In 1879 the Town House was torched by unknown hands. In 1886 a new Town Hall was situated conveniently in the center of town.

Townspeople finally took to the despised plank sidewalk along Front Street (Commercial Street), for traditional pathways on the beach were blocked by wharf footings. In addition, Front Street—laid out in 1835, then and now only 22 feet wide—was jammed with streams of carriages and jiggers heading in both directions on the hardened roadway, newly paved with seashells and with blue-clay taken from Truro's Highland Pounds. Scattered along the heavily trafficked street were a few shade trees, lawns, bushes, and artificial gardens. As legend goes, the first three trees were willows, propagated from slips brought to town by a whaling captain from Napoleon Bonaparte's grave at St. Helena.

But Provincetown's main focus was neither Front Street nor the dunes; it was the harbor where there were new walkways, the wharves. There a new town had been created, a newly staged town riding on water.

Provincetown Harbor rests high on the continental shelf and is subject to extreme tides; twelve-foot drops are not uncommon, and the tidal flow is even more extreme at times of the syzygy of moon, sun, and earth. Every six hours, at low tide, it appears as though someone has pulled the plug as the water drains out of the harbor. Without wharves, mariners must wait for diurnal high tides to launch and moor their vessels.

Around 1830 when Thomas Lathrop built the first wharf, he did so against the advice of the townspeople, "who believed that the sea would soon cut away the sand from the piles and destroy the wharf."[31] Despite the risks, Lathrop's critics followed his lead. By 1835 there were twelve wharves. Thereafter, an average of one was built each year until the start of the Civil War.

Enterprising Provincetowners had once extended their land by dumping tons of sand into the harbor; now they expanded the town by building wharves and erecting sheds on the wharves to house sail-makers, blacksmiths, chandlers, coopers, and lumber and coal purveyors. The new satellite town was created not from local trees, for they had been destroyed, but from lumber shipped from Maine, Nova Scotia, and the Southern states. Lumber schooners unloaded at Hilliard's wharf, built in 1846 especially to accommodate these ships.

There was scarcely enough space for all the fishing activities. What did not fit on the wharves, such as fish flakes, barrels of pickled mackerel, and half-barrels for trawl lines, was crowded into the sandy dooryards and side streets. In *Cape Cod*, Thoreau observed that "A great many of the houses were surrounded by fish-flakes . . . so that instead of looking out into a flower or grass plot, you looked onto so many square rods of cod turned wrong side outwards."[32] The work of tending the flakes most often fell to women who spread and turned the fish for drying. There were a few remaining windmills to make salt for local use; Thoreau described them as "huge wounded birds, trailing a wing or leg."[33] They were wedged between the wharves and connected to umbilical cords of wooden troughs that wound through the streets and terminated in turtle-shaped evaporation vats among the dunes.

The *Provincetown Banner* reported that in 1856 Provincetown had 100 vessels fitted out for codfishing, many of them locally owned. Fish landings were at an all-time high.[34] In 1860 Provincetown handled over one-half of the codfish landed on the Cape: 62,181 quintals of the total 107,548. (A quintal was 100 weight, or about 30 salted codfish.) Mackerel landings were second only to those made in Wellfleet (27,350 versus 19,350 barrels). By 1885 Provincetown accounted for over 16 million of the 18 million pounds of cod landed by Cape vessels.[35]

There were marine railway wharves that were used for building and repairing fishing vessels and whalers. After the war of 1812, according to the historian Henry Kittredge, more small vessels were built in Provincetown than in any other town on the Cape. He further claimed that after the Civil War, John Whitcomb built a number of whaling schooners there. As a home port and as an outfitting and repair station, mid-century Provincetown was not only the hub of fishing but also of whaling activity.

The 1850 census reported that 25 visiting whalers lay in Provincetown Harbor; later estimates of visiting whaling ships ran as high as 175. As in Colonial times, Provincetown was thwarting custom officials by destroying records. In his 19th-century statistical report of American whalers, Alexander Starbuck noted that whaling records in Provincetown "are extremely hard to get at; vessels are reported arriving, with no date of sailing, and sailing, with no date of arriving; and the product is often wholly ignored in the reports."[36]

To accommodate its increasing popularity, Provincetown each year rolled out another wharf to greet each new class of vessel: Grand Banks schooner, mackerel clipper, whaling brig, and packet steamer. Packet trips to and from Boston became more frequent, and steamships were added to the scheduled run of sailing vessels. In 1863 Bowley's Steamship Wharf was extended into deep water to berth the large Boston-bound steamship, the *George Shattuck*. Thoreau, who had died in 1862, one year before, was denied the convenience of Steamship Wharf. To board the packet steamer, *Naushon*, he had to trundle over thirty rods of tidal flats on a wide-track, slewing horse carriage. With the availability of Bowley's Steamship Wharf and other long wharves, it was an easier transit from the narrow streets downward to the sea.

ON A BRIGHT OCTOBER AFTERNOON, as Thoreau walked the beach and ocean bluffs toward Provincetown, he followed the mackerel fleet's jagged course. In the Fall, the fatter and higher-priced mackerel return to Cape Cod waters on a slow seasonal migration from southern waters. Mackerel vessels flocked together to stalk the mackerel in its swift and erratic flight. At sunset high atop the highest dune overlooking the Harbor, Thoreau saw the canvas-rigged schooners tack about on the outer rim of Provincetown Harbor. Thoreau had a panoramic 360-degree view of the broad harbor that reaches southward into the horizon, of Cape Cod Bay to the west, and of the Atlantic Ocean to the north and east. An inspiring scene. That October day there were about 200 mackerel schooners skirting the Harbor. For Thoreau these white-winged schooners sailing across the horizon and into port were a migrating city of canvas.

THOREAU, A MAN OF THE INTERIOR, was not interested in what life was like aboard a fishing vessel. For a description of this, one needs to turn to Charles Nordhoff, writer and editor for Harper & Brothers and a contemporary of Thoreau. (His grandson and namesake co-authored *Mutiny on the Bounty*.) As an enterprising journalist, Nordhoff rendered an eyewitness account of mackerel fishing. In the mid 1850s, he shipped out as part of a twelve-man crew from Harwich aboard a two-masted clipper schooner. He was outfitted with oiled clothes and an apron, and was issued jig hooks and lines, a bait knife, mittens, and a barrel. His total pay for two voyages, comprising nine weeks of grueling, boring work, was $40. He complained of an overcrowded forecastle that smelled "villainously of decayed fish" and of the monotonous wait for mackerel.

"Mackerel go in large schools" but are like a "needle in a haystack," demanding "unwearying patience." Mackerel vessels traveled in groups, 600 to 1,000 cruising as one vast body over miles of water. Within five minutes, every vessel within ten miles knew when a vessel had spotted mackerel. All rushed to the spot, tangling booms and smashing masts as they tacked in and out. As Nordhoff described the scene,

> ... every heart beats loud with excitement, and every hand hauls in fish and throws out hooks with a methodical precision, a kind of slow haste. The mackerel ... a moment ago fairly rushing on board ... in that moment disappeared so completely ... The sea if tolerably rough, the vessels lie so closely together that one could almost jump from one to the other.[37]

When feeding slacked, mackerel were dressed and salted. Salt burned into cuts in the hands and muscles ached from hours of fishing. At night "groans and growls resound[ed] from every corner" of the forecastle.

Mackerel became an important market fish in the 1850s. Its price overtook that of cod, a long-time leader. In 1830 mackerel went for $5 a barrel; in 1856 the price jumped to $19. A quintal of cod in the same period rose only from $2.12 to $3.75. In 1851, the Massachusetts mackerel fleet numbered 1,000. About that time the clipper ship was introduced into mackerel fishing; its use lasted a generation. The mackerel clipper weighed 100 tons or more, had a large sail or two, which made it swift and, unfortunately, a shallow draft that made it unstable. It was designed for speed, to equip it for the race to the fresh fish markets in Boston or Gloucester. The highest daily market price went to the first cargoes into port. In the race to an early market, clipper captains took extreme risks. Every storm brought disaster.[38]

Boston and the so-called codfish aristocracy had turned its back to the sea about the time Provincetown was outfitting scores of vessels for Grand Banks fishing. Early in the 19th century, Boston began its development as the railroad hub of New England, with an eye to broader Western markets. It was immersed in manufacturing and industry as well as in cultivating the arts, and in trying to fashion a new Athens. Fishing activities were relegated to less-developed ports like Provincetown. Crews were no longer native-born but were recruited from the new immigrants who were fleeing from various misfortunes: the Irish from the potato famine, Canadians from political differences, and the Portuguese from poverty.

To bolster a diminishing codfish market, Massachusetts gave codfishermen a bonus of $8 to $12 a year, provided they shipped out for at least four months a year. For a while some mackerel fishermen illegally collected the cod bonus, a scandal that was exposed in 1840. Before things could be sorted out, mackerel prices so overtook cod prices that the bonus question faded. Codfishing techniques, beginning in the ghostly past of fishing history, did not change until after the Civil War. Codfishermen were called "high-liners" because they fished with handlines from the deck of high-gunwaled vessels. At times they would fish around the clock, half-asleep and lashed to the rigging to keep from falling overboard. Setting trawl lines from dories began in the 1860s. In the dense and protracted Newfoundland fog, dories became separated from the mother ship and untold numbers of crews were lost.

* * *

IN CONTRAST TO ITS ACCESSIBILITY BY SEA, Provincetown was difficult to reach overland. For 19th-century journalists it became a challenge to visit and report on the anachronistic town, described as an *Ultima Thule* (Land's End) and *terra incognita.* Provincetown furnished ideal material to titillate arm-chair travellers, who included a growing number of magazine and newspaper readers, particularly women who had shunned rigorous travel. Travel writers of that era were, in some ways, similar to today's foreign correspondents, ready to endure uncomfortable journeys and unusual risks to report on exotic, remote landscapes. To heighten interest they frequently over-dramatized the dangers. Nathaniel Parker Willis, writing for the *Home Journal,* claimed he had made out a new will before setting foot on Cape Cod. For *Harper Magazine,* Samuel A. Drake described the Cape as a passage onto "a gangplank pushed out over the side of the Continent." And in a lecture to the Concord Lyceum, Thoreau described the six-hour sea voyage from Boston to Provincetown as quite long, "indeed . . . twice as far as from England to France."[39]

Travel by common carrier was uncertain, uncomfortable, and hazardous. Stagecoaches were crowded, the high-back seats were covered with prickly horsehair and the dusty floors were covered with straw. They pitched and yawed and at times rolled over. If all went well, the overland trip by stage from Boston to Provincetown took a minimum of 14 hours. Thoreau, wedged into a crowded stagecoach, saw little of the landscape from Sandwich to Orleans. He observed that they were forced to time their "inspirations and expirations" to assist the driver in closing the coach door.

Train travel was equally uncomfortable and, in most cases, as slow and unpredictable as the stage. Locomotives spewed blinding steam and pulled unstable, rocking cars whose lofty ceilings made them look like small churches on wheels. For Cape Codders, commented Shebnah Rich, "Going to Boston by land was less common than a voyage to China."[40] The fastest passage was by boat if the weather was fair and the vessel sea-worthy. Sailing packet owners, however, were more interested in hauling freight than passengers; travelers were squeezed in between barrels, hogsheads, sides of beef, jugs of vinegar, and crocks of molasses.

Men of wealth like Nathaniel Willis and Timothy Dwight hired well-appointed private chaises when they travelled overland to Provincetown. Thoreau, on the other hand, used the public railroad and the stagecoach, and then walked. Upon leaving Provincetown, all these correspondents took the preferred routing, the packet, back to Boston.

"THE PLACES WHICH I HAVE DESCRIBED may seem strange and remote to my townsmen."[41] Thus Thoreau began his report to the Lyceum audiences in Concord on January 23 and 30, 1850, about his first visit to Cape Cod. In his day, the ingredients for a successful travel lecture or essay were that the locale be strange and that the account be humorous and anecdotal. So Thoreau played to his audience; he stressed the peculiar and the strange and, uncharacteristically, he was amusing and witty. The audience "laughed until they cried," according to his friend and sponsor, Ralph Waldo Emerson. In February Thoreau repeated his lecture in Danvers and received $10.00 toward his expenses.

Bolstered by these appearances, Thoreau turned to preparing his materials for publication. To collect more information, he returned to Cape Cod the following summer (1850) and again in 1855 and 1857. Only one small series of his Cape Cod essays was published during his lifetime in the 1855 summer issues of *Putnam's Magazine*. Editors objected, among other things, to his patronizing treatment of Cape Codders. *Cape Cod,* a book that integrated three of his four trips into one account, was published posthumously in 1865. Readers bought it then not for its author but for its title.[42]

The *Cape Cod* essays were for Thoreau a departure in style: informal, witty, and almost debonair, the "most human" of his travel accounts.[43] In the fall of 1849, when Thoreau first set out for the Cape, he was virtually unpublished, except for a few minor essays in the new magazine *Dial.* He was thirty-two years old, dark-haired, with a long nose, saved from ugliness only by his fine blue eyes and sensitive mouth. He was a Harvard graduate and had had a checkered career as teacher, surveyor, live-in tutor, handyman, and—only when absolutely necessary—as an artisan, albeit quite productive, in his father's pencil factory. Thoreau had completed his two-year stay on Walden Pond on land borrowed from Emerson and was looking for funds to publish privately his account of his Walden Pond experiment in "living deliberately."

NATHANIEL PARKER WILLIS, a popular 19th-century journalist, sent travel sketches from Cape Cod and Provincetown to fill the columns of his own New York City weekly, the society magazine, *Home Journal.* These travel letters, as well as essays from the magazine, were collected in *Hurry-Graphs,* published in 1851 in New York and London. Willis achieved early fame. While still an undergraduate at Yale, he became nationally known for his verses that paraphrased biblical themes. When only twenty-three he quite successfully established the *American Monthly Magazine* in Boston.

At that time he assumed an affected personal and stylistic pose—in the manner of Oscar Wilde—that offended sober-minded critics, who referred to him as Namby-Pamby Willis. James Russell Lowell, on the other hand, found Willis's dandyism humorous and, in *A Fable for Critics,* called him "the topmost bright bubble on the wave of the Town." Oliver Wendell Holmes described the twenty-five-year-old Willis as "already famous . . . He was tall, his hair, of light brown color, waved in luxuriant abundance."[44]

When Willis traveled in Europe, his wit and flamboyance charmed European society, who esteemed him almost as much as they had Washington Irving and James Fenimore Cooper. Willis socialized with Prime Minister Disraeli, Charles Lamb, and the poet Walter Savage Landor. Present-day scholars have re-evaluated the importance of Willis; he is now receiving recognition for his early support of Edgar Allan Poe.[45] On his part, Poe praised Willis's successful romantic play, *Tortesa the Usurer,* as "by far the best play from the pen of an American author." Willis's pallbearers were among the New England literary greats: Oliver Wendell Holmes, Richard Dana, Henry W. Longfellow, and James Russell Lowell.

In an 1885 study of Willis, Henry A. Beers noted that both Willis and Thoreau wrote about "the same piece of geography," Cape Cod.

> Both men had quick eyes, and had taught themselves the art of observation. But Willis's letters were the notes of an "amateur casual," or "here-and-therein," on a flying trip over a sand-spit inhabited by queer people, who was always on the lookout for points which would interest the lady readers of a metropolitan journal. Thoreau, on the contrary, was like a palmer on a solemn pilgrimage to one of nature's peculiar shrines, with loins girt up and staff in hand, tramping along the heavy sands.[46]

Despite their philosophical differences, Thoreau and Willis mirrored one another in describing certain aspects of their trips. Since Willis preceded Thoreau, there is the possibility that Thoreau read and was influenced by Willis's light-hearted account. For example, both saw the configuration of Cape Cod in anatomical terms. For Thoreau, it was "the bare and bended arm of Massachusetts"; to Willis, it was "the raised leg of New England." Willis described the mackerel boats as "flocks of snow-white birds painted upon the blue table of the sea." Thoreau calls them "fowls coming home to roost." Both had similar impressions of the stagecoach driver. Willis calls him, "Agent, parcel-carrier, commission-broker, apologist, and bearer of special intelligence for the whole population." Thoreau found the driver to be "free and easy," stopping often for "Uncle Sam's bag" and collecting pieces of gossip along the way.

They shared some of the same prejudices about Cape Cod folks. Older men are described as rugged and handsome and young boys cute and bright, while older women looked "pinched up" or "flat-chested and round backed." At Race Point overlooking the Atlantic, Willis stepped to the water's edge and had the "realizing sense . . . that I was outside man of you all, for the space of a minute. One likes a nibble at distinction, now and then." There is the echo of Willis in one of Thoreau's most quoted observations: "A man may stand there and put all America behind him."

Thoreau, the naturalist, and Willis, the hedonist, had their marked differences. Willis came to the Cape in balmy summer weather. For the sensuous Willis,[47] the Cape Cod journey was marked by "a full moon rising before us . . . a delicious southern breeze laden with the breath of sweet-briar and new hay." Thoreau's first trip was in autumn, when he encountered a torrential storm. Willis relished the Gifford Hotel's breakfast of fried fish, a type of "turbot," of "great delicacy and sweetness." Thoreau, on the other hand, complained: "I did not taste fresh fish of any kind on the Cape . . .

That is where they are cured, and where, sometimes, travelers are cured of eating them."

Willis's style was deliberately geared to the ladies. For instance, he compares the sowing of beach grass to "love, which binds the spider's webs that grow into cables, the slender filament of . . . Nature's productions." He comments on ladies' fashions: women were wearing a "visite" or "polka," a brown over-jacket, in Yarmouth and Provincetown, a rage imported from the mainland. Whether this jacket covered the flat "proportions of the female bust," Willis did not know, but he did know about the cause of the flat chests. He believed that the arid climate had denied women the juices of nature as it did the rose and lily in the deserts of Asia. Further he conjectured that women had worked their bodies into muscle by assuming the labors of their seafaring husbands. For he did see them at work: picking cranberries, wheeling fish to the flakes, herding cattle, and raking hay.

As for Provincetown, Willis's social observations were most insightful: he characterized it as a place with "no secrets, where there is but one accountable path in the whole neighborhood. Everybody at Provincetown knows every time everybody goes out, and every time anybody comes in." Willis further observed: "The close quarters of the town only bind them into a family with their neighbors." After all, "men who are two-thirds of the time seeing the world elsewhere, are kept liberal and unprovincial."

Willis took the steamer *Naushon* back to Boston, as did Thoreau on a later visit. Both had to trundle across the broad sand flats to board the packet. Willis observed: "There is no wharf running to deep water at this place, and, chancing upon low tide for our time of departure, we were obliged to drive over the muddy bottom of the harbor in a wagon, and, at horse-belly depth, take a row boat for the steamer." Willis's six-hour passage was pleasant enough; "we bobbed up and down." He summed up Provincetown as a "delightful thing—a peculiar place," the inhabitants "hearty and honest," and the "girls looked merry."

Writers like Willis were different in style and purpose from the ponderous didactic writers such as Timothy Dwight and Edward Kendall who travelled in search of virtue and truth. Their accounts might have bored Thoreau's Lyceum audiences, who were knowledgeable in the tradition of the English familiar essay and wanted to be entertained with puns and amusing anecdotes. In his *Cape Cod* accounts, Thoreau entertained and did much more. He produced a classic that lured wave after wave of landscape writers, artists, and photographers to Cape Cod. He inspired several of the Provincetown Players. Jig Cook, the motivating force of the group, wanted to be a "Greek Thoreau living with Homer ... the sailors and the sea." O'Neill attempted to make his dune-encircled Peaked Hill home into another Walden. In fact, he re-created the Walden shack for the setting of *Touch of the Poet*.

Thoreau disdained commercial enterprises, preferring naturalistic, transcendental experiences. "I love a broad margin in my life ... It is not necessary that a man should earn his living by the sweat of his brow, unless he sweats easier than I do." In Provincetown, he was particularly inspired when he transcended the bustling waterfront and took a seat "upon the highest sand-hill overlooking the town, in mid-air, on a long plank stretched across between two hillocks of sand, where some boys were endeavoring in vain to fly their kite ... looking out over the placid harbor."[48]

Like the explorers before him, Thoreau wanted to give Cape Cod a new name, in his imagination, a "more poetic" one. This inspiration came as his packet was leaving Provincetown Harbor. Thoreau said that Provincetown was "the most maritime of towns we were ever in." Despite this, and despite the sight of scores of Grand Banks schooners in the harbor unloading tons of cod, of acres of dried cod turned outward on the flakes, of rotting racks of codfish on the crowded beach, what Thoreau saw as he left Provincetown harbor was a "filmy sliver of land lying flat on the ocean . . . a mere reflection of a sand-bar on the haze above." For him this sight deserved a name "more poetic" than Cape Cod.

EVERY TIME THE YOUNG MISSIONARY, Lorenzo Warriner, had to leave his home in Worcester and travel to Provincetown he got sick. He arrived with either a "terrible headache" or a "shocking cold" or "bilious diarrhea." Travelling in 1831 "from the forest trees of my native land" to that "sterile place" was arduous and frightening for the young man. As a Methodist circuit rider he was assigned for a month at a time to teach in Provincetown's seminary school. He packed in his portmanteau a Bible, a medical book or two, and turn-keys for extracting teeth. He knew beforehand that he would be teaching young men and women about salvation. If fortunate, he might be asked to assist the local minister in his ancillary profession of physician; and if really fortunate he would earn much-needed money by extracting teeth. Competition for clients was fierce, because all types of tradesmen—auctioneers, hardware and furniture dealers, and barbers—practiced dentistry as a sideline. The treatment for dental problems was extraction and the main tool for that a turn-key.

In an 1831 letter[49] to his mentor Samuel Nash, Lorenzo brashly and humorously described his trip to Provincetown, beginning with his first train ride aboard the newly inaugurated Boston–Worcester railroad.

I paid $1 for the fare, the first bell rung, and we were soon on our way to the Metropolis . . . The steam, which terrible monster ahead called engine would spew out, obscured our vision for a moment. I gazed a few moments at fields . . . then the cars would slacken and stop. The agent would stick his head into the car, and bawl out "any passengers for Newtown?" . . . We went five minutes longer, till we came to another village when the same ceremonies would be repeated. At the end of 2 hours we were dragged into Boston. Friend Sam, if you wish to travel and see the country, I advise you to keep off the railroad.

The next leg of the journey was the 50-mile trip from Boston to Provincetown aboard the packet schooner *Avenal*. Among other mishaps, the wind laid down and the trip took thirty-six hours, for a crossing that ordinarily took six hours in fair weather.

Friday P.M. I engaged a passage on board the schooner *Avenal,* as she was to start out that night. I engaged a hand-cartman to lug my trunk down to the vessel, for which I gave another ½ dollar; so you see how they catch our coppers in great cities. We got outside as the seamen say in the evening, but, as there was no wind we came to anchor, and lay there till 2 o'clock in the morning, when there being a gentle breeze we went ahead about 18 miles, and not being able to go on for want of wind, we 'bout ship and went back to Georges Island and came to an anchor . . . We stayed in that place till 1 o'clock Sunday morning, when, as there was a good wind, almost a gale, we put to sea.

I turned in to a berth a part of the time and part of the time on deck. It was my delight to see the little bark heave, pitch and plough through the billows, though I was much troubled to keep the center of gravity and was once or twice prostrated to the deck, yet I was not seasick in the least, and now I think I should like to make a voyage to Liverpool. At length I turned in, and after a while hearing an unusual noise on deck, such as running, and the commands given in a louder and quicker tone, I immediately "turned out" and went on deck. I found they had carried too much sail for the wind, and their main sheet had split in two, and the main boom had gone overboard, and was ploughing along at a great speed. Being not far from Long Point Light, they run her ashore and mended matters. About 9 o'clock we made the upper part of the town.

Lorenzo arrived in Provincetown with a "shocking cold," which was treated by "Mother," the nickname for Mrs. Benjamin Gifford of the Gifford House. She gave him some "quack medicine . . . together with hot brick and a half cord of bed-blankets got me into a profuse perspiration." Mother's cure worked; the very next day Lorenzo was able to meet his class of "40 scholars . . . who are anxious to make more noise than I am in the habit of allowing." With Mother's care and cooking, he was also well enough in a few days to notice one of the young girls who helped out, Sally B. Snow, "a lively girl, and a real go ahead," but one who did not make him "languish and caterpillar." [*sic*] He recovered sufficiently to cross the dunes to the ocean, where at each summit "new hills presented themselves." He wrote to Nash, "Do send me a Dromedary, a llama, or a pair of snowshoes."

Methodist missionaries brought with them the temperance movement, which produced much divisiveness and hostility. In 1795 the Methodists, then a new denomination, tried to build a church in Provincetown. Fervid Congregationalists tore down the framework, dragged the dismantled lumber to the highest dune, High Pole Hill, set it afire, and on top of the blazing pile threw the effigy of the Methodist minister. Thereupon the Methodists relocated to Truro and stayed there until tempers cooled. When they returned, they brought back the temperance movement with regained force.

Traditionally, Puritans and Congregationalists exercised a flexible conscience toward drinking; they publicly denounced it, while privately they promoted the highly profitable rum trade. Fiery, unrelenting Methodist circuit riders, on the other hand, preached total abstinence. By 1810 the Methodists had taken over Provincetown; they were using the Town Hall for their meetings and on one occasion refused to allow a town meeting to assemble. They stationed themselves behind closed doors, triumphantly singing Methodist hymns to the locked-out, angry crowd. As time went on, those who drank "like the hunted . . . sought the covert of the forest."[50]

Methodists objected to public bars, so local drinkers were relegated to fields, backrooms, and key-clubs in hotels. Liquor was distilled on the outskirts of Provincetown and in nearby Truro, and was also smuggled into town aboard packets and fishing vessels. Visiting sailors and fishermen drank openly along the streets. "Hundreds of fishermen . . . drawn onshore by the odor of rum, mingled with our citizens, crowding the streets, rife for mischief, their passions aroused by the contact of alcohol."[51] Rich merchants and ship owners drank in private clubs. For these "educated gentlemen" of the town, there was a key club. Each member was given a special key to open a club room, where there was a "stock of a superior quality of liquors" and where members might meet "away from wives and home, [to] pursue unmolested their round of dissipation."[52]

The teetotaler Thoreau did not indulge in spirits. "The barroom may be defined as a place to spit" he wrote in 1857 when he stayed in a small attic room over the noisy bar in the Pilgrim House. His was a sleepless night. Added to the noise of the carousers was the caterwauling of cats that "swarmed on the roofs of Provincetown like the mosquitoes on the summits of its hills." However, there was another type of traveller, such as a group of foreign correspondents, who sailed in during the summer of 1858 intent on finding a drink.

ROBERT CARTER, A JOURNALIST for the *New York Tribune* assigned to Washington, D.C., sailed into Provincetown Harbor on the *Helen*, a chartered sloop. He found the fishing excellent, the dentists suspect, and the town dry of spirits. Similar to Willis and other traveloguists of the day, Carter wrote lightheartedly for a ready audience. Carter's stated reasons for cruising the coast of New England was pleasure, to escape the Washington summer, "a long succession of hot nights and days," to fish, and to report back to his editor. Dr. William Stimpson, a naturalist, wanted "one specimen of every creature that swims the sea or dwells on the bottom." Francis Henry Underwood, a novelist, was interested neither in fishing nor collecting specimens but in drinking. He found to his dismay that Provincetown, like most of the Northeastern ports, was dry, the result of the crusades of temperance zealots.[53]

In *A Summer Cruise on the Coast of New England,* 1858, Carter recounts a moveable feast of seafood caught and eaten. In detail he describes each species, its appearance and habitat, as well as the tackle and bait needed to catch it. The cruise was a fisherman's and epicurean's dream-come-true. Fish were abundant and varied: bluefish, cod, cunners, flounder, halibut, and lobsters. Upon entering Provincetown Harbor, the sports fishermen bought twelve lobsters at three cents apiece from a Long Point lobsterman "lying-to just outside the harbor." Some lobsters were eaten and others cut for flounder bait. "The lines hardly reached bottom before the flounders began to bite so rapidly that they kept us actively employed . . . in the course of an hour we had caught twenty or thirty, all large ones, weighing several pounds each."

Underwood said he despised flounder fishing and went into Provincetown for cocktails. He found that no one knew what a cocktail was and that the apothecary was "the only man in town who kept for sale anything to drink" and that was "an almost forgotten bottle of sherry bitters." Back aboard the ship Underwood, with his concocted cocktail in hand, smoked a cigar, another vice frowned upon. (Smoking in public was a crime in Boston until 1824.)

Carter, who had a toothache, went into town looking for a dentist. As in Warriner's day two decades before, Carter found that most dentists were engaged part-time in other occupations. For instance, the *Provincetown Banner* of June 1856 lists Dr. A. S. Dudley in the Business Directory under "Dentists, Watchmakers and Jewelers." Carter judiciously chose the practitioner whose only business was dentistry, and happily reported that he "relieved me of my offending molar in a dexterous manner."

Carter and his friends took the *de rigueur* jaunt across the dunes to see the Ocean. They "hired a wagon, a span of horses, and a queer little urchin of a driver, to conduct us thither over the sand-hills." The horses had "rumps unusually developed from working always fetlock deep in sand." Provincetowners at that time were being paid by the government to plant beach grass. The "urchin busied himself with separating the clumps of beach grass and transplanting it." This twinged the conscience of the debonair Carter, who was "languishing with the ocean's roar"; he first attempted to help the urchin, but after sinking in the grass, gave the boy a dime to continue planting alone, and then another dime to continue the planting out of sight.

Carter's was one of those seaside vacations, devoted to

exploring, hunting and fishing, and sailing, that only men took. When trains improved and made it easier to travel with luggage, household paraphernalia, and servants, families—and sometimes unescorted women—were able to travel to the seashore. Vacationers, however, most likely stayed the season, renting or buying summer "cottages." Not until the days of the automobile and good roads were short trips to the seashore possible.

PROVINCETOWN WAS AN INTERNATIONAL PORT. Thoreau observed that "men from all parts of the globe touch there in the course of the year." The 1850 census gives some idea of the global mix because it reports for the first time personal data such as nationality, occupation, age, and schooling. Isaiah Gifford, the enumerator, counted 200 residents who were born outside the country, mostly in Canada and Portugal; some few others were from England, Spain, Sweden, and France. One wonders about these new immigrants and about those sojourners from foreign ports aboard the brigs, barks, and schooners in the harbor. To the 1850 enumerator the crews of the twenty-five whaling ships lying in the harbor were only names: "Their names is [sic] all that can be learned of them." Gifford gives us only a count of the transient fishermen and mariners from Portugal and domestic servants from Ireland who stayed in boarding houses. Their personal histories are untold stories. One wonders about the life of Elisa Hamilton, a nineteen-year-old Massachusetts resident staying at the Gifford House, who gave her occupation as "mariner." And one may only speculate about the life of the one lone black, an eighteen-year-old lad from Virginia, living in the William Cook household.

"Whaling ships were floating hells," remarked historian Samuel Eliot Morison. Whaling crews died from brutality, starvation, and drowning. Life aboard other ships, while less brutal, was equally dangerous. Untold numbers of fishermen were lost in the foggy and icy waters of the Grand Banks and from unstable clipper ships racing dangerously to market.

Travel writers glossed over these grim truths, for the style of the day was to entertain and amuse. It was through fiction writers, not travel journalists, that one learns of the actual hell of life at sea. Those writers who did it best, like Herman Melville and Eugene O'Neill, actually sailed out. Thoreau, for his part, found shipboard life distasteful. His only reported fishing excursion was a day-trip aboard a mackerel schooner from Duxbury to Clark's Island, a mere three miles into the Gulf of Maine. Thoreau cared more for the poetry of fishing than the "whole of it." Repulsed by the "foul juice of mackerel," he, with fellow passengers, spent the short trip gathered "about the helmsman and told stories."

We learn about the agonies and intricacies of whaling from fictionalized accounts of real voyages, in Melville's *Moby Dick* and O'Neill's *Ile*. We learn about Grand Banks fishing from the Englishman Rudyard Kipling in *Captains Courageous*. Mackerel fishing had no fictive counterpart. Wilbur Daniel Steele began in 1915 to write short stories and novels about the Portuguese fishermen. These were serio-comic, sentimental accounts. Some were about mackerel fishing. Steele's "The 'Killers' of Provincetown" humorously related the ruthless race to the fresh fish market by two "killer" mackerel schooner captains.

Herman Melville, Thoreau's coeval, sailed out of Fairhaven, Massachusetts, in 1841 aboard the *Acushnet*, a 350-ton whaling ship, bound for the Pacific. Nearby New Bedford was the whaling center of the world, the port where the sperm oil kings were "as tight-fisted, cruel and ruthless a set of exploiters as you can find in American history."[54] Melville jumped ship in the Marquesas. Most greenhands were encouraged to do just that so the owners would not have to pay them at the end of the voyage. It was easy enough to pick up new crews in isolated and primitive ports around the world. Even those who stayed on and withstood the cruelty and depriva- tion of a two-to-four-year voyage seldom received money, for the owners contrived to have the crew's wages eaten up by their debts. In the mid-nineteenth century an estimated 3,000 to 4,000 whaling men deserted annually.

One of the first Provincetown tales Eugene O'Neill heard was about the crazy Viola Cook, who would race down Commercial Street shouting obscenities at strangers. Viola had learned these vulgarities aboard her husband's whaling vessel when she accompanied him on prolonged Arctic voy- ages in search of right whales. John Cook was a proud, ag- gressive, obsessive "high-liner," who would not return to port without the largest booty or at least a full cargo of oil.

During his first winter in Provincetown in 1917, O'Neill wrote *Ile,* a one-act play about Viola and the tragic voyage that precipitated her madness. The setting and action of *Ile* follows closely the actual voyage of Captain John A. Cook into Arctic waters. *Ile* takes place aboard a whaler locked in the Arctic ice. Against the wishes of his wife and the crew, Cook stayed on when the ice moved in because he had not reached his self-prescribed quota. The crew mutinied and Viola went insane. John Cook, tall and muscular, with "hands like iron mauls," punished the mutineers, isolated his wife, and still did not leave. Cook's cruelty was so extraordinary that the muti- neers were not imprisoned, as was the custom, but were awarded restitution for being held beyond their contractual time. Viola never recovered from the effects of the agonizing isolation and her husband's cruelty to the crew.

Agnes Boulton, O'Neill's wife, wrote to him about Viola in a 1920 letter:

This will amuse you. Today I was walking up to the village when a refined, well-dressed woman of sixty or there-abouts, very sweet looking, crossed the street in front of me, and I got the impression that she was making some remarks to kids playing in the snow; but when I caught up behind her I discovered that she was talking, (in a loud, vigorous tone) to herself. Imagine my surprise when she suddenly came out with: "The goddamned f—ing (your pet word) son of a bitch. I show him. To hell with him!" . . . No one seemed to pay any attention to her. I went into the ice-cream place and said "Miss Livingston, *who* is that woman . . .?" "Why that's poor Miss Cook . . . She ain't crazy but she has these spells . . . She used to come in here last summer when she got that way and set at one of my tables and talk so terrible and so nasty that women would get up and leave . . . She got that way up in the Arctic when they was froze in."[55]

In 1916, the year O'Neill first came to Provincetown, John Cook undertook his last voyage. Whaling as a profitable enterprise had been over for a generation, but Cook continued to sail his brig *Viola* despite what economics dictated. For his last voyage Cook had arranged for John Waite of Boston, a motion picture photographer, to accompany him and docu-ment the trip. (This film is now in Provincetown's Pilgrim Monument Museum.) The *Viola* left New Bedford in April 1916 and returned four months later with 5,000 feet of pic-tures and 500 barrels of sperm oil. In November, Cook showed his film, "Sperm Whaling," in Tremont Temple in Boston. At the same time that the Provincetown Players were mounting their productions on a dilapidated wharf in Provincetown Har-bor, John A. Cook of Provincetown was closing out the whal-ing era. He lectured, wrote *Pursuing the Whale,* and then lost his whaling fortune in unwise petroleum investments.

CHAPTER FOUR

Railroad Wharf:
No Longer an Island

Strangers rumble down from Boston by hundreds at a time.
—Nathaniel Hawthorne[1]

PROVINCETOWN'S WHARVES came to an undignified end. It was a slow death, mirroring Provincetown's decline after the Civil War, the end of its glory years as a major fishing and whaling port. Wharves slowly collapsed as supporting knees and footings gave way, dragging twisted, decomposed planking into the water. Mackerel and cod resources dwindled, as did the whale population; this, coupled with the reduced demand for salted fish and whale oil—the latter because of the discovery of petroleum—brought about economic decline. Provincetown's large fleet of mackerel and cod schooners had shrunk from more than two hundred vessels in 1850 to a mere fifty or sixty by 1875. Whaling brigs and barks outfitted for extended round-the-world voyages were retired. Only a few whaling schooners survived to chase the dwindling number of whales in waters closer to home—the Caribbean Sea, Gulf of Mexico, and North Atlantic.

Standing erect and well-groomed among the shriveled wharves was Steamship Wharf. Here the *George Shattuck* tied up daily, depositing freight and passengers from Boston. Until the railroad arrived in 1873, steamship companies monopolized service to Provincetown and Cape Cod. Overcoming the opposition, the Old Colony Railroad in 1849 started a slow, tenacious crawl down the peninsula. The railroad courted and won each town along the way. Within a year after the railroad arrived, the *George Shattuck* discontinued its Provincetown run. Steamship Wharf was then renamed Railroad Wharf.

Provincetown was virtually an island dependent on the sea until the railroad nailed down a permanent iron connection. Its only access to the rest of the peninsula had been either a precarious wooden bridge leading to sandy roadways or beach routings. During major storms these approaches washed out. The Old Colony Railroad built a high embankment that sealed off East Harbor and formed a permanent access impervious to weather. Later, in 1877, a parallel, companion road was built. Triumphantly, the railroad laid its tracks on the embankment, then proceeded into the center of town, not stopping at the terminal but continuing on into the harbor, running 1,650 feet of glistening new rails right down the middle of Steamship Wharf. The long wooden wharf was practically covered with iron. Thus the railroad stamped its claim both on the town and on the harbor.

At one o'clock on a sparkling summer afternoon, Tuesday, July 22, 1873, the special excursion train from Boston pulled into Provincetown. From that moment on, Provincetown lost its insularity; it was now attached to the rest of Cape Cod, to Boston, and all points West. Winter and summer, in gale or fair breeze, "citizens and strangers" could depart or arrive twice daily. "We have long felt our isolation," reported the *Provincetown Advocate* on that joyful day when the train finally "brought low" the "hills of sand."

It was a new day for tourism. The railroad had already brought industry and some vacationers to the Upper Cape; for Provincetown it brought primarily excursionists. Although it was a six-hour trip between Boston and Provincetown whether by rail or by steamer, the train—because it was less subject to weather—became the preferred mode of travel. It was possible to leave Kneeland Street Station in Boston in the morning, arrive in Provincetown for lunch, stroll along Commercial Street, make a quick trip across the dunes, and leave at sunset for the trip back to Boston. For the first time, "day-trippers" to Provincetown were reasonably assured of returning home the same day.

The inaugural excursion train was nearly filled to capacity with dignitaries and tourists even before it left Boston. A few Cape Codders squeezed in along the way, but no one could board after Orleans. A red-funneled engine, the "fiery steed," with *Mount Hope* painted on the sides, pulled thirteen bright yellow coaches "packed and jammed with its living freight." Conductor Osborne sparkled with gold accessories: he wore a double-breasted frock coat with gold buttons and gold monograms on the collar, and a straight visor cap with gold cord and a gold badge. Framed by the yellow coaches, Osborne leaned out and saluted the crowd that was decked out in holiday attire and was good-natured despite being stranded on hilltop and roadside. The *Provincetown Advocate* reported that "At Truro quite a large crowd was assembled displaying the stars and stripes, waving handkerchiefs and giving cheers as the train swept along."[2]

Detraining passengers formed a procession at the terminal on Back Street (now Bradford Street) and marched up

High Pole Hill to a tented pavilion with seats for a thousand. The tent was festooned with flags and flowers and a huge illustration of a locomotive boldly lettered *Provincetown*. After a sumptuous banquet of hot turkey and chicken, lobster salad, fruits and vegetables, the crowd listened to speeches by—among others—Massachusetts Governor William B. Washburn and the governor of New Hampshire. Later many worshiped "at the shrine of Terpsichore," for Porter's six-piece Quadrille Band played after dark in the dimly lit tent for the two hundred couples who danced to the "All Aboard" polka and "Down Brakes" waltz.

Charles Nordhoff returned to Cape Cod in 1873, not to ship out on a mackerel schooner as he had in 1853, but to report to *Harper's Monthly* about recreational travel. As a journeyman writer he had endured the hardship of commercial fishing, the chilling, damp, monotonous routine of searching for, gutting, and pickling mackerel. Now as an older, recognized member of the fourth estate, he strongly objected to the smell of fish:

> Besides the sand, the most striking thing in Provincetown . . . is an all-pervading odor of fish . . . [There is] every imaginable offense which a fish can commit against the sense of smell from the time he is first split open and washed in a bucket of water, through all the stages of frying, boiling, broiling, salting, pickling, washing out, drying in the sun, packing away in a storehouse . . . trodden under foot, rotting on the beach, or hanging up in a shop door.[3]

Nordhoff was but one of the legion of travel writers scurrying about America's countryside exhilarated by the liberating ease of rail travel. Thoreau's *Cape Cod*, posthumously published in 1865, served as a regional Baedeker. Thoreau, to the railroad generation, was a daring pioneer. As Nordhoff

remarked: "Thoreau was thought to have accomplished a notable feat" in his exploration of Cape Cod, for it "lay so far
outside of the regularly traveled routes." With the arrival of
the railroad, Cape Cod has been transformed from a "peculiar and strange" place of "ancient habits and customs" to a
popular seaside resort. The new wave of travel writers looked
first through Thoreau's lenses, then copied, magnified, and
re-focused his mid-century views for a later generation.

Train passengers' first glimpse of Provincetown, seen
from the heights of Truro, was as "a filmy sliver of land"
circling the crescent harbor. Then, after a descent to East Harbor and a short run across the embankment, they sighted the
eighty- to ninety-foot-high dunes—undulating waves of wilderness—rising from the east. This sight impelled most tourists to cross the dunes, a bold adventure, notwithstanding that
a wide-wheeled horse carriage was often hired for the trek.
Sand, to Nordhoff, was not the threat of Thoreau's day: "[it
was] flying about . . . as it is supposed to do in the great
desert." Beach grass had nearly tamed the shifting sand; the
dunes were but a "toy sahara."

Mainland gentility had filtered into Provincetown.
Reverend Elias Nason reported in his 1874 Gazetteer that the
town had a lyceum and five churches. The Methodist church,
the most recent denomination in Provincetown, sported the
highest steeple. There was a new library that had been
founded with seed money from the Sons of Temperance. Telephone service reached the town in 1883, and the next year
Commercial Street, in the center of town, was lighted.
Helltown had disappeared. In 1875, at Race Point, the travel
writer Samuel Adams Drake inspected a cluster of abandoned
fishing shacks and observed that "the doors were open . . .
The sand had drifted to a considerable depth within."[4] Squatters on the outer harbor had been crowded out by Life-Saving

Stations newly manned in 1873: Wood End, Race Point, and Peaked Hill. These stations were a popular tourist attraction, as were the oil works.

Sprawling about at Herring Cove, the approximate site of Helltown, was the Nickerson Whale and Menhaden Oil Works. At the peak of operation in 1890, the oil works had twenty-five to thirty employees, with try-works for reducing whale blubber and a bone mill for making fertilizer from menhaden. There were seine boats, a steamer, and a wharf that extended 400 feet into the Bay. Gales and ice and a scarcity of whales and menhaden destroyed the operation. By 1911 the oil works was gone, but free whale souvenirs were still available, as William Nolen pointed out:

> At the old, abandoned blubber works . . . there was a shipload of [finbacks] waiting to be carried away by curiosity hunters. A little upholstering will convert a big vertebra into a comfortable stool.[5]

In the east end of town, David Stull, the so-called "ambergris king" of Provincetown, was finding little ambergris but enough blackfish (small whales) to run a try-works. Here he refined the melons, a hemispherical mass of blubber in the head of the blackfish. He shipped his refined oil worldwide to makers of watches and precision instruments. By 1915 the *Provincetown Advocate* reported that Stull was sending whale artifacts, for use in window displays, to Filene's Department Store in Boston. Fishing armamentaria had been retired; the glorious maritime past was now garnishment.

In 1898 Katherine Lee Bates—on a train ride to Provincetown from Falmouth, her birthplace—noted with distaste the extensive ornamental array of whale vertebrae, scallop shells, lobster pots, and codfish weathervanes scattered along

82

the way. Bates, a Wellesley College professor of English, on a trip to Pike's Peak in 1893, had been inspired to write the patriotic hymn, "America the Beautiful." Bates did admire some pockets of scenic beauty, such as the tapestry of Provincetown's dunes, quoting Thoreau's sensitive description: "It was like the richest rug imaginable . . . no damask nor velvet . . . nor the work of any loom, could ever match it." And she astutely captured the architectural signature of Provincetown, its crooked streets and jumbled houses:

> Back Street copies the curve of Front, and the two are joined by queer, irregular crossways, that take the abashed wayfarer close under people's windows and along the very borders of their gardens and poultry-yards . . . There are bunches and knots of houses in sheltered places, looking as if the blast had blown them into accidental nooks . . . built close and low, tucked in under one another's elbows.[6]

Professor Bates was one of the so-called New Women, the economically independent career women who emerged at the end of the 19th century. Among their newly won freedoms was that of traveling about without a male escort. As early as 1842 Charles Dickens commented on the ladies' car on a train bound for Lowell from Boston:

> In the ladies' car, there are a great many gentlemen who have ladies with them. There are also a great many ladies who have nobody with them; for any lady may travel alone, from one end of the United States to the other, and be certain of the most courteous and considerate treatment everywhere.[7]

Among the throng of train riders, Hawthorne's "strangers . . . hundreds at a time," were now women travelling alone. Trussed with whalebone stays, with whalebone hoops ballooning their skirts, and adorned with whalebone combs, female tourists gathered from the beaches and shops of Provincetown other whale by-products, such as vertebrae for footstools. Among these excursionists was a new breed— women artists and women travel writers who rendered pictorial descriptions of a day at the seashore.

One of the early artists to arrive with the new train service was Marcus Waterman, who came specifically to paint the dunes, as he had in Algiers. Waterman coaxed Ross Moffett and other Boston painters to travel to Provincetown to see the blinding white, shifting dunes. Moffett, in *Art in Narrow Streets,* said that Waterman painted Provincetown dunes as he had Sahara scenes, "with his pretty Italian model in desert costumes."

Initially, Americans were thrilled with the railroad and registered few complaints. Thoreau in 1849 saw nothing peculiar and strange about his train ride from Bridgewater to Sandwich, except the irony of calling Sandwich the "terminus of the Cape Cod Railroad," for Sandwich lies not at the end but at the beginning of Cape Cod. Liberated armchair travellers rode the train just for the joy of the trip. President Grant in 1874 and President Cleveland in 1889 took the train into Provincetown for a day's excursion. Ulysses S. Grant was a train aficionado, riding free, disdaining even a pass, counting on his mere presence as passport. This was challenged one day by a lone gatekeeper who insisted that Grant pay his own fare as well as the fares of his eighteen tag-along friends.[8]

Charles Dickens, however, complained about American trains:

> There is a great deal of jolting, a great deal of noise, a great deal of wall, not much window, a locomotive engine, a shriek, and a bell. The cars are like shabby omnibuses . . .

holding thirty, forty, fifty people. The seats, instead of
stretching from end to end, are placed crosswise. Each seat
holds two persons . . . In the centre of the carriage there is
usually a stove, fed with charcoal or anthracite coal . . . It is
insufferably close.[9]

By modern standards, early train rides were uncomfortable, tiresome, and seemingly interminable. As highways
appeared, complaints increased. In 1916 Hildegarde Hawthorne fretted about the trip to Provincetown:

> There is nothing wild and dashing about the train that takes
> you to Provincetown. It stops at every station and looks
> about, while passengers get slowly on and off, chat with
> brakemen, and swap news among themselves.[10]

Helen Henderson, whose art critiques in the *Philadelphia Inquirer* were noted for their wit and sarcasm, was one
of Provincetown's pioneer art colonists. John Sloan especially
was offended by her critical reviews of his paintings and said
of her, "the cidevant art student and now 'critic' of the Philadelphia Inquirer staff, was as usual amusing in her ignorance
coated with sarcasm."[11] Henderson, a summer resident of
Provincetown, in 1916 described the train trip down Cape:
"Things on the Cape have changed very little since Thoreau's
day, and the lumbering . . . train is but an amplified stage
coach." Along the Cape there was not much to see, only a few
glimpses of the sea, scrub-pines, bayberry bushes, and station
after station. Passengers slept and ate cold lunches. When the
conductor roared "Brewster," "a sleepy voice inquired 'How
many Brewsters have we yet to go through?' 'I don't know,' a
woman answered, 'but I dread the Truros.'"[12]

Truro had three train stations and many random flag-
stops. Warren Chamberlin, a long-time Truro summer resi-

dent, recalled his train rides from Quincy, especially during the summers that he travelled with his grandparents and their two cats. The cats were packed in a valise, then enroute were tethered on long cords and released to scamper about in the overhead baggage rack. When the train labored up the slope at Great Hollow Road, where the Chamberlin summer cottage is still located, it slowed down just enough to allow an unauthorized stop—his grandparents jumped off, dragging with them large trunks, bags of groceries, and two re-parcelled cats.

The spectacular approach to Provincetown over the seaward cliffs of Truro was frequently described by train riders. There, spreading out to the left was the end of the Cape, Long Point spiraling back into Provincetown harbor, and to the right was Highland Light. This lit the sky at night with an intermittent, intense white beam synchronous with the softer green beacon from Long Point lighthouse. Mary Heaton Vorse, in *Footnote to Folly*, recalled the happy, involuntary tears she shed when, in 1915, she returned from the war in Europe and saw Provincetown unchanged and tranquil from the Truro heights.

Nearly everyone in Provincetown came out to meet the evening train, for it brought—along with visitors—the mail and out-of-town newspapers. Horse-drawn carriages, jiggers, and handcarts scurried among the crowds. Some tourists were carriaged to the newly refurbished Central Hotel, where "delectable seafood, chowders and broiled fish" were served, and rooms "big and full of sea wind" looked down on the harbor. The view was especially pleasant from the "upper veranda with great rocking chairs." Helen Henderson provides a witty account of the townspeople's rush for newspapers and mail.[13] Mail was transferred to jiggers and carted to the post office located across from Adam's Pharmacy. Boys with pushcarts took the evening newspapers to the village shop nearby. Crowds followed behind; there was "an undignified scuffle," but the papers were "doled out by a rigorously impartial hand." Even more frantic was the crush for mail. "Hopeful letter seekers . . . peering critically through the pigeon holes at the harried clerks, like expert card sharks, watching the clumsy efforts of an inexperience dealer, and itching to get a hand at it themselves." The crowd disappeared as quickly as it had materialized, like "a scene from grand opera," where the "chorus at a given signal streams upon the bare stage . . . only to fade away again . . . at the voice of the prompter . . . The night seems to soak up the villagers like a sponge."

TO SURVIVE, STEAMSHIP COMPANIES frequently merged with the railroad. Such was the case with the New York, New Haven & Hartford Railroad, which had replaced the Old Colony Railroad and then took over the Fall River Steamship Line. This monopoly provided a convenient connection, an easy way for New Yorkers to escape to New England for the summer. At the turn of the century, it brought a new summer resident to Provincetown—the Greenwich Village bohemian.

Nothing delighted the captains of industry—such as "Commodore" Cornelius Vanderbilt and Jay Gould—as well as the bourgeoisie more than cruising on the Fall River steamers. For ninety years, beginning in 1847, a fleet of elegant, massive, side-paddled steamships travelled daily year-round on Long Island Sound between New York City and Fall River, with a stop at Newport. Robber barons, railroad magnates, peripatetic presidents—all the eastern elite—sailed on these vessels, which were furnished as regally as any of the Newport "cottages" they served.

America developed its inland and coastal waterway shipping because England—with its Cunard Line, started in

1840—had monopolized transatlantic steamer traffic. Many American side-wheeled steamers were as large as ocean vessels. Some, such as the *Priscilla* of the Fall River Line, were indeed larger and more elegant. Some were showy and flamboyant; for instance, Jim Fisk, a self-made millionaire, flaunted his wealth on his grand Long Island steamer. He lined the salons and corridors with 200 canary birds in gilded cages, and dubbed himself "Admiral," meeting passengers in a gold-braided uniform. "If Vanderbilt's a Commodore, I can be an admiral."[14]

The *Priscilla* began service in 1894. It was 359 feet long with a 93-foot beam; it had 359 staterooms with 1,022 passenger berths and carried up to 1,500 passengers. Its two enclosed side-paddles were each 35 feet in diameter. There was usually a waiting list for staterooms; those without staterooms were given mattresses or cots and slept in the carpeted salons. By departure time at 5:00 P.M., the largest dock on the lower North River in New York City was jammed with trunks, barrels, crates, and noisy horse carts and cabs and carriages, as passengers and tons of freight were loaded. White-gloved black porters escorted passengers up the rubber-covered, rail-protected aisle into the quiet elegance of the mahogany-paneled, gold-leafed, many-mirrored, illuminated interior of the *Priscilla*. As the *Priscilla* left Pier 14 at night, New York City became

> a majestic cluster of sparkling lights. The lofty towers of commerce, the Woolworth Building, the Hudson Terminal, the Singer Building, . . . tiers of man-made stars against the dark sky. The *Priscilla* rounded the Battery, . . . the East River . . . the illuminated "el" trains and trolleys . . . under the Brooklyn Bridge . . . through the tortuous channel at Hells Gate.[15]

The Fall River Line was the favorite passage for the Provincetown Players, and leading the way was Mary Heaton Vorse. Season after season, twice-widowed Mary marshalled her three children, a French governess, Italian cooks, a secretary, and endless baggage aboard the steamer. After twelve hours overnight on Long Island Sound, passengers were escorted, again by white-gloved porters, down the gangplank at the Fall River wharf and onto the waiting railroad coaches for the hour ride to Middleboro, where connecting trains awaited for the final leg to Provincetown. Not once along the way did passengers have to touch their luggage. Each year more and more New Yorkers took summer cottages on the New England seashore, lured by the convenient extravagance of the Fall River boat-train.

After thirty years of commuting, Mary Heaton Vorse lamented the end of the Line, particularly the dining service:

> For years two of the most perfect headwaiters in the world set the tone of elegance and recalled the urbanities of the past on the Fall River Line. Thompson and Wilson on one or another of the vessels made one as welcome as though one were the lord of the manor returning to his ancestral halls. White carnation in button hole they ushered one to a seat attentively. They bent over you as you ordered, with a sense of having, after horrid exile, come home at last.[16]

Decades later the offspring of the Provincetown Players—Heaton Vorse, and Miriam and Trixie Hapgood—remembered fondly their passage on the Fall River Line. These former Provincetown travellers could even render the chorus of Harry von Tilzer's 1913 song:

On the old Fall River Line
I fell for Susie's line of talk
And Susie fell for mine
Then we fell in with a parson
And he tied us tight as twine
But I wish "oh Lord" I fell overboard
On the old Fall River Line

IN ADDITION TO THE SEA, the sand, and the strange geography, a new element in Provincetown arrested the visitor's eye—the Portuguese. After the Civil War the number of these exotically dressed Europeans dramatically increased. This European ambiance appealed to the well-travelled artists and writers who began to frequent Provincetown. In 1875 Samuel Drake delighted in the colorfully costumed Portuguese women with "handkerchiefs tied about their heads, and shawls worn sashwise and knotted at the hip—bright bits of warm color contrasting kindly with the dead white of the sand."[17]

Portuguese fishermen took over the fresh fish business, both the weir fishing inshore and the Grand Banks fishing offshore. By the last decade of the 19th century, nearly 50 percent of the population of Provincetown was Portuguese, in contrast to the rest of Barnstable County, where 90 percent was of English descent. Provincetown, always an international port, became more so with the Portuguese immigration.

The Portuguese were by no means new to Provincetown nor to America. They were Grand Banks fishermen long before the English thought of settling in the New World. By 1527 the Portuguese had fishing colonies on Newfoundland, that is, trading stations for drying codfish.[18] It was from the Grand Banks that many worked their way to Provincetown. Portuguese were recruited by American whaling captains in the Azores, an important way-station for whalers roaming the Atlantic. Azorean sailors, once in America, abandoned whaling for other fishing, or for farming or other occupations. By the 1850 census, there were more than fifty respondents in Provincetown who designated Portugal as their native land. The first birth from Portuguese parentage recorded in Provincetown church records was in 1853. By 1880 the *Provincetown Advocate* reported that "One third of the town's population" was Portuguese. The others were of English, Scottish, and Irish descent.

Portuguese migration peaked after 1880 and declined as the result of immigration restrictions in 1920. Military conscription and poverty precipitated Portuguese and other European immigration to America during these decades. Portuguese immigrants settled in southeastern Massachusetts, principally in the city of New Bedford. Of all the Cape towns, Provincetown witnessed the greatest influx of Portuguese.[19] Provincetown's overall population zenith coincided with the decades of highest Portuguese immigration (1880–1920). Provincetown's peak population was reported as 4,642 in the 1890 census. Since the census of 1920 (4,246), the population of Provincetown has never exceeded 4,000.

Provincetown in time grew accustomed to "strangers," but it was overwhelmed on two summer days in 1907 and 1910, when President Theodore Roosevelt and President William Howard Taft, respectively, came to dedicate a Provincetown monument to the Pilgrims. There was marvelous pageantry: flotillas of yachts, Navy destroyers, marching sailors, bands, buntings, flags, and presidential yachts that docked at Railroad Wharf. Provincetown now had national recognition and a monument that on a clear day can be seen across Cape Cod Bay by an observer in Plymouth, a reminder to the guardians of the Plimouth Plantation that Provincetown was the first landing place of the Pilgrims. Private citizens sponsored the monument, and the Federal Government subsidized its erection, to provide a lookout in case some foreign navy decided to invade Provincetown. It was stipulated that the monument should have ramps for Army caissons.

The military specifications for the Provincetown Monument reflect a long history of outside governments' concern for Provincetown as a strategic location. In the 1700s beach grass was first planted to prevent silting of the harbor from encircling dunes. In the 1800s, also to prevent silting, dikes were built at the eastern and western reaches of the harbor. To thwart invading navies, two Civil War batteries were erected on Long Point, with barracks for a company of soldiers. Provincetown was never in jeopardy during this war, so these citadels were dubbed by natives as "Fort Useless" and "Fort Ridiculous." Today the remnant mounds are called Twin Hills. Throughout Provincetown's history, each successive governing body has treated it as a protectorate: the Plymouth Colony, the Massachusetts Bay Colony, the Commonwealth, and the Federal Government. Not until 1893 did the Commonwealth of Massachusetts relinquish its claim on Provincetown; for three centuries residents were regarded as squatters. Today the town is confined to a sliver of land facing the harbor, surrounded by the lands under the jurisdiction of the Cape Cod National Seashore.

CHAPTER FIVE

Greenwich Village:
Creating the Scenarios

IN THE DECADE BEFORE WORLD WAR I, rebellious young intellectuals left their restrictive, provincial hometowns and migrated to the artistic mecca of Greenwich Village. Behavior that was outrageous in Davenport, Amherst, or Portland was hardly noticed in Washington Square. Women bobbed their hair, drank and smoked in public in defiance of the local Sullivan ordinance, and the Lucy Stoners kept their maiden names after marriage. Outfitted in a flannel shirt, to identify with the working class, the emancipated man enjoyed an open relationship with the sexually liberated woman. Margaret Sanger's new birth control methods were practiced by the new sophisticates. Unmarried couples freely co-habitated, and if they subsequently married, frequently concealed the fact. The demand for sexual freedom was only one part of these intellectuals' revolt against the status quo.[1]

There was a religious fervor connected with change as America moved into the Twentieth Century. America had transformed quickly from a bucolic, politically innocent nation to an industrialized, imperialistic power. Technological invention and change came rapidly: railroads, automobiles, electricity, the telegraph, and the telephone. Einstein's special theory of relativity had added a new dimension to the fervor. As Neith Boyce commented, "the 'new science' is marvelous and fairylike—all those things about light, and getting rid of matter, time and space (which only religious people could do before!)"[2]

With both reverence and exuberance, Americans had attended the 1893 Columbian Exposition, which displayed acres of illuminated technical marvels. This Exposition reinforced the prevailing belief that all things were possible. The feeling of *annus mirabilis* (literally "year of miracles") continued into the first two decades of the next century. Not only scientists and inventors but also artists, writers, and reformers experimented. All expected miraculous, immediate changes in science, politics, and art. For America's intellectual and artistic vanguard, Greenwich Village became a primary laboratory.

This was an era in American politics during which Progressive reform overlapped with the more radical solutions of Socialism and Marxism. Progressive politics was concerned with material change as well as its social consequences. "To call a man 'progressive' was to label him a reformer, a man determined to improve his society, revise its laws, purify its politics, rearrange its economic awards and invigorate its morals."[3] Although reformers were only a small segment of the population, they captured a wide audience. They were prolific writers, primarily well-educated, middle-class men and women from New England and the Middle West. Progressives sought a solution within America's capitalist system; those who wanted more radical change embraced Socialism, Marxism, and anarchy. Politically, the Provincetown Players were Progressive reformers; the exceptions were Mary Heaton Vorse and Jack Reed, who turned to radical activism.

"The fiddles are tuning as it were all over America" is John Butler Yeats's oft-quoted 1912 comment about America's intellectual renaissance. Bohemianism, which had started in Montmartre in the Gilded Age, began to infiltrate America at the turn of the century, and flourished in a relatively concentrated period, from 1912 to 1917, diminishing after America's entry into World War I. Alfred Kazin called this period "The Joyous Season."[4]

America's young intellectuals, who had reveled in the artistic and sexual freedoms of Europe, demanded the same freedoms at home. They congregated in Greenwich Village, with Washington Square as a symbolic hub. Sanford White's new marble arch looked like the Napoleonic monuments of Paris, while the sedate Georgian houses on the north side of the Square had a London look, enough even to entice Henry James for a time. Early in the century, the south side of the square housed a series of famous boarders: Willa Cather, Theodore Dreiser, O. Henry, and Stephen Crane. One rooming house, dubbed the House of Genius, served as a reminder to the new generation that the Village had literary progenitors in the Gilded Age.

Beyond the tree-lined geometric tranquility of Washington Square lay the crooked streets that housed the bohemian pioneers of the Village. Here, in cramped, cold, unlighted flats, aspiring artists and intellectuals found social freedom away from their middle-class families. "Most of us were from families who had other ideas—who wanted to make money, played bridge, voted the republican ticket, went to church, thinking one should be like every one else," Susan Glaspell related in *Road to the Temple*. Their neighbors were Italian, Irish, and Jewish immigrants. While the bohemians, predominately Anglo-Saxon, were struggling to design a new

America, the new immigrants were struggling to survive. This cultural discrepancy, for the most part, allowed the two groups to distance themselves despite the crowded conditions. The religious immigrants, nevertheless, found the bohemians, with their raucous parties and lewd costumes, offensive, and their sometimes patronizing attitude, demeaning.

Staid American sensibilities had been realigned in Europe. Women painters had been admitted to male-dominated Parisian art schools and occasionally had been permitted to sketch nude male models. American poets abandoned rhyme after hearing the French symbolists; painters restructured space after seeing the Fauves and the cubists. Those wanting to learn the new stagecraft—the fusion of acting, lighting, and setting into a dramatic whole—went to Max Reinhardt's theater in Berlin. It was there that Robert Edmond Jones, the Provincetown Players' first stage designer, learned about simplified scenic designs.[5] Some Americans stayed in Europe, notably T. S. Eliot, a Harvard classmate of Bobby Jones and Jack Reed. Eliot eventually became an English citizen. Among others who did not return to America were Henry James, Ezra Pound, and James McNeill Whistler.

The new American creativity first found significant expression in a Chicago renaissance. There, in 1912, Harriet Monroe published *Poetry: A Magazine of Verse,* and Maurice Browne started the Little Theatre. Floyd Dell and George Cram Cook wrote exciting articles for the *Friday Literary Review,* which stimulated writers to experiment with new forms of expression. In 1913 the Chicago vanguard began their migration to Greenwich Village, joining other restless youth coming from America's cultural wastelands. It was a syncopated march to the tiny village at the foot of Fifth Avenue. There they danced to new music, W. C. Handy's "Memphis Blues" and to ragtime, called cubist music.

* * *

ONE NATIVE NEW YORKER, Eugene O'Neill, stood apart from the noisy migration. In 1912, recovering from an overdose of veronal, he lay in squalor above Jimmy the Priest's saloon, far to the west of Washington Square. Shortly thereafter, he entered a sanatorium for the treatment of tuberculosis. It was during his six-month confinement that he decided to become a playwright. O'Neill, who became one of the most renown Villagers, always stayed on the fringe of bohemia, scoffing at its political pretensions and social frivolities. He sat among them in informal haunts like the Golden Swan Saloon (nicknamed the Hell Hole) but shrank from formal meetings until the Provincetown Players were formed. Never was he among the intellectuals and reformers who gathered for the evening either at Mary Heaton Vorse's radical cooperative house or in Mabel Dodge's Fifth Avenue salon.

While O'Neill, the solitary novice, was writing plays in New London and at Harvard, and trying unsuccessfully to get them produced, events were taking place in Greenwich Village that were significant to the development of the Provincetown Players. It was the persuasive efforts of two former blue-serge women who were now social activists that brought it all together, namely, Mary Vorse O'Brien and Mabel Dodge. Mary coaxed the Village crowd to go to Provincetown, and then she provided them with a stage for their theatricals. Mabel, on the other hand, furnished them with a Manhattan salon where they could experiment with ideas and plan media events, such as the Paterson Pageant. Moreover, her love affair with Jack Reed was the scenario for *Constancy*, the Provincetown Players' first production.

When Mary and Bert Vorse left Provincetown in 1907, they wintered in a cooperative house at 3 Fifth Avenue. It accommodated eighteen people who shared radical interests, from Communists who had helped with the 1905–1907 Russian Revolution to liberal reformers such as the Vorses. Mary had been apolitical until 1904, but that year she had participated in the sandola (work boat) guild strike in Venice. The co-op was facetiously named the "A Club" until 1907, when Maxim Gorky—in America on a lecture tour—stayed there. The press then called it the Anarchist Club. In 1913 it was succeeded by the famed Liberal Club.

Whether in the Village or in Provincetown, Mary Heaton's house was always a bustling center of social and political activity. In 1913, when she married Joe O'Brien, a free-lance reporter and political activist, her life became even more hectic. In 1914 their Village brownstone was the staging center for Wobblie activities. "My days were very long," wrote Mary "for I had the support of the huge household on my hands." Mary was a charter member of the Liberal Club, of the feminist Heterodoxy Club, and both she and Joe were editors of the radical magazine *Masses*.[6]

While Mary Vorse O'Brien, as labor journalist, was covering the news, the activities stemming from Mabel Dodge's Evenings were making news. In was in Dodge's Fifth Avenue salon that plans were made for such media events as the Armory Show, the Paterson Strike and Pageant, and demonstrations in support of New York's homeless. Mabel, as an independently wealthy socialite, was able to serve lavish dinners in her elaborate apartment. On one occasion she served pheasant to two hundred Wobblies, and she often donated the services of her chauffeur and limousine for fund-raising events. As a rule, she drew more attention to herself than she did to the radical causes she supported. In contrast, Mary Vorse routinely served spaghetti to the activists meeting in her crowded apartment and sacrificed time from her professional writing to cover strikes and demonstrations.

* * *

FROM THEIR FIRST MEETING, Mabel Dodge and Mary Vorse were rivals. Dodge thought Vorse "small and domestic"; Vorse thought Dodge "a woman of shallow curiosities about the things in which I was most interested."[7] During the winter of 1914, Mabel had been active in social causes such as the Labor Defense Committee, whose purpose was to make the public aware of the condition of the unemployed and the unfair treatment of labor. This Committee was a mixture of all types—writers, liberals, and socialites like Mabel Dodge and millionaires such as her friend Sam Lewisohn. Mary Heaton Vorse, who was housing the unemployed, resented what she considered tokenism on Mabel's part. "Polite up-town rich ladies mingling with . . . us poor wage slaves of the slums." Mary recalled later that when she attended the uptown meetings she had to borrow "a good coat from Mabel Dodge, for mine was shabby."[8]

For many bohemians who frequented her salon, Mabel Dodge was an intellectual muse. By 1913 most of those who were to become the Provincetown Players were in the Village. Jack Reed, touted as the Village's golden boy, arrived there soon after his graduation from Harvard in 1910. Robert Edmond Jones, a classmate of Reed, was lodged in Mabel Dodge's Fifth Avenue apartment, accepting her patronage while trying to break into stage designing. Jig Cook and Susan Glaspell, early in 1913, had left their homes in Iowa and were living in Provincetown and the Village. Hutchins Hapgood, who in 1897 had gone to New York to work on *The Commercial Advertiser,* and later the *New York Globe,* became a devoted and spiritual companion to Mabel, and successfully promoted her Evenings. For many years he was her primary admirer, mentor, and confidante. He called her a "promoter of the Spirit."

Mabel Dodge has been characterized by others and by herself as vain, self-centered, and manipulative. Her intimates indulged her; acquaintances, especially women, deeply resented her. Few were indifferent. She was married four times. Her first husband was Karl Evans, a wealthy dilettante from her hometown, Buffalo; her second, Edwin Dodge, a proper Boston architect; her third, Maurice Sterne, a Jewish artist; and her fourth, Tony Luhan, a Pueblo Indian. Mabel Dodge preferred to marry her lovers. Jack Reed resisted successfully. In her memoirs, Dodge talked about two seductions she attempted that failed, namely, that of D. H. Lawrence and Gertrude Stein. Mabel was intrigued with power and dangerous liaisons. An only child, Mabel had been raised by quarreling, neurotic parents; she learned early that love was a war of wills. In *Intimate Memories,* her four-volume memoirs, she candidly talks about herself. "I was never much to look at, ever, I am sorry to say." But during her first adolescent flirtation she learned how to attract lovers. "I knew how to make myself wanted as much as I wished, to be wanted and appreciated."

Her Manhattan salon began in January 1913, and was quite well attended for the first three years, then tapered off, and finally ended in 1917 when she moved to New Mexico. Mabel's Fifth Avenue salon became as legendary in its own time as Gertrude Stein's rue de Fleurus salon. Dodge first modeled her salon after Stein's casual gatherings; she later added prearranged topics for discussion. While Stein limited her salon primarily to painters and writers, Dodge opened hers to all the movers and shakers of America's radical, artistic, and intellectual world. Her salon was usually packed with a cross-section of New York society, dressed in ball gowns and shirtwaists, pleated shirts and flannel blouses. On Wednesday evenings they tramped into Dodge's plush apartment at 23 Fifth Avenue—Marxists and capitalists, avant-garde painters and muckrakers, millionaires and the homeless. Politics and art mixed about in a frothy cauldron, at times blending into spectacles and media events. Mabel Dodge described the mix:

> In time there came Steffens and Emma Goldman and Berkman, that group of earnest naive anarchists—Reed, Walter Lippmann, Bobby Jones, Bobby Rogers and Lee Simonson, these but lately out of college: Max Eastman and Ida [Rauh], Frances Perkins, Gertrude Light, Mary Heaton Vorse, and the Sangers—and all the labor leaders, poets, journalists, editors and actors.[9]

If nothing else, Mabel Dodge was willing to experiment: with new ideas as well as fads and fancies, such as peyote, Buddhism, psychoanalysis, and automatic writing. And she was a promoter of the activities of the avant-garde: the cubist writings of Gertrude Stein, the neo-Grecian dance of Isadora Duncan, and the anarchism of Emma Goldman. She is now regarded by some as a prototypical New Woman of the Post-Victorian Age; however, by strict definition she was not one of the New Women who had gone to college or who supported themselves in a profession. Both of Mabel's parents were from rich Buffalo banking families; as their only child and sole heir she was financially independent, and always did pretty much as she pleased.

Her European experiences prepared the way for her successful American salon. From 1903 to 1912, Dodge was an energetic hostess in her luxurious Villa Curonia outside of Florence. She entertained artists and aristocrats and had the prerequisite travelling entourage, her *jeunes gens assortis*. She invited Gertrude Stein to stay at the Villa, and while there

Stein wrote a dedicatory verse-profile, *A Portrait of Mabel Dodge at the Villa Curonia*. In her memoirs Dodge says that while Gertrude was in one room writing "the days are wonderful and the nights are wonderful and life is pleasant," she was sexually teasing her son's twenty-two-year-old tutor in an adjoining bedroom, loud enough for Stein to hear. Dodge further alleged that Alice Toklas so objected to "the electricity" between Mabel and Gertrude that social contacts abruptly ceased. Stein later described Dodge as having "very pretty eyes and very old fashioned coquetry."

The American media first took significant note of Dodge in 1913, when she helped launch the famous New York Armory Show, the International Exhibition of Modern Art. New York City was electric with a sense of scandal—free love, anarchism, psychoanalysis, and now Modern Art. Dodge predicted the long-range effect of the event when she wrote to Gertrude Stein on January 24, 1913: "There will be a riot & a revolution & things will never be quite the same afterwards."[10] The Armory Show was chaotic. While it is not known how many works were shown, the catalog lists 1,300, in 18 rooms. Brassy trumpets heralded the opening on February 19, 1913.

Dodge was appointed vice-chairman in recognition of her new role as patron of the arts. She received literary acclaim for her interpretation of Gertrude Stein's prose, for she intuitively sensed, as no one else had, that Gertrude Stein was "doing with words what Picasso is doing with paint. She is impelling language to induce new states of consciousness." Dodge posited a conceptual link between Marcel Duchamp's explosive, cubist painting, "Nude Descending a Staircase" and Gertrude Stein's fragmented, imagist prose. Mabel's perceptive critique of Stein, published in the magazine *Arts and Decoration,* was widely touted. Gertrude was upset that

Mabel had received more press than she had—not quite what Gertrude, in her own search for recognition, had expected.

During the Evenings' intense debates Mabel Dodge was usually impassive, acting as a catalyst. Max Eastman, in *Venture,* his novel about the Paterson strike, depicted Dodge as an emotional and cultural incubator. In his autobiography he commented:

> For the most part she sits like a lump and says nothing . . . There is something in Mabel's head or bosom, something that creates a magnetic field in which people become polarized . . . Many famous salons have been established by pure will power. And it was no second-rate salon; everybody in the ferment of ideas could be found there.[11]

Following Lincoln Steffens's suggestion, the salon had no fixed organization except a requirement that controversial topics be discussed. Dodge maintained a studied distance, which paradoxically stimulated the furors. One of Dodge's steadfast admirers was Carl Van Vechten, a self-styled arbiter of the new aesthetics who chronicled the era in fiction, musical and theatrical reviews, and in his artistic photographs. He nicknamed Mabel "Aunt Mike" and depicted her as Edith Dale, whose face was "a perfect mask," in his novel *Peter Whiffle.*

Van Vechten and Hapgood filled the Evenings with their intimates and associates: intellectuals, anarchists, Bohemians, blacks, and Suffragists—individuals who seemingly were worlds apart. Topics were chosen that would shock and stimulate argument: prison reform, free verse, free speech, housing for the unemployed, anarchism, psychoanalysis, and Cubism. Wobblies in work clothes and debutantes in evening clothes ate together and argued issues.

Mabel Dodge coolly sat wrapped in a long white dress, amid fragrant white lilies, against a backdrop of white linen draperies, white fireplace, and white woodwork. White was Dodge's stylistic signature, a startling decorative style attributed to Whistler. In 1914 she even decorated the Peaked Hill Station at Provincetown in white. Mabel Dodge said she painted her apartment white to shut out the ugliness of New York and to re-create the elegance of Europe. She lined her white walls with contemporary American art—the vivid, colorful paintings of Marsden Hartley, Andrew Dasburg, Charles Demuth, and John Marin—somewhat in the manner of Gertrude Stein, who skied her atelier walls with Matisse and Picasso.

Mabel Dodge was squat, plump, and impassive; these characteristics prompted contemporaries to call her a "sphinx" and a "brown bear." She would watch dispassionately as her starved guests ravaged the turkeys and hams served by her Florentine butler, Domenico. In 1915, when Dodge had tired of Jack Reed and the radicals—whom she now called the "dangerous people"—she lost interest in her Evenings and turned her full attention to art and the painter Maurice Sterne. While they lasted, Mabel Dodge's Evenings served as a fulcrum for Village intellectual activities.

While Mary Vorse resented Mabel Dodge's involvement in social causes, she was even more resentful of Dodge's incursions into her carefully cultivated circle of friends and associates, which included fellow journalists Hutchins Hapgood, Lincoln Steffens, Jack Reed, and Max Eastman. Despite the antagonistic undercurrents, the two ambitious women avoided open conflict until Mabel Dodge and her entourage rode into Provincetown in the summer of 1914.

Mary Vorse resisted Dodge's intrusion and gathered the support of her Provincetown intimates. Hutch Hapgood stated in his autobiography that Vorse was Provincetown's "historical pioneer," and that he sided with her against

Dodge. With the attendant back-biting and malicious gossip created by the warring coteries, Provincetown became, in Hapgood's words, a "poison-distributing center." When Dodge returned in 1915 and 1916, Hapgood again intervened on Vorse's behalf. These were the summers when the Provincetown Players staged plays on Mary Vorse O'Brien's fishing wharf, which Dodge called "a barn on the shore." Two of these plays openly satirized Dodge, who confined her activities to the outskirts of Provincetown, particularly Peaked Hill.

THE PROVINCETOWN PLAYERS began with the portrayal of the grand passion of Mabel Dodge and John Reed. Their stormy relationship is the comic scenario of *Constancy*. Throughout the two-year, passionate, and—at times—ludicrous affair, Neith and Hutchins Hapgood had served as Mabel Dodge's confidantes. Mabel's professed anguish provided the script for *Constancy*. Hutch recalls one incident when Mabel kept them awake all night, weeping as she repeated, "I want Reed back! I want him now!"[12] The real-life affair of Jack and Mabel, with its exaggerated posturing, might well have been written by an 18th-century dramatist; it was a comedy of manners, played out across the Atlantic twice, with scenes at the Mexican border, in Greenwich Village, and in Provincetown.

It had begun in the Village, where Reed and Dodge met and planned the Paterson Strike Pageant. The Pageant was staged June 1913 in Madison Square Garden to benefit the striking silk workers in Paterson, New Jersey. Although Dodge frequented uptown events and Reed lower-Manhattan haunts, their meeting was inevitable, for in their close-knit community everyone was in each other's pockets, sharing ideas and often bedrooms. Hutch, who claimed responsibility for introducing Mabel and Jack, described the electric meeting:

As Reed was speaking, a look of concentrated passion that I had never seen equaled, came into Mabel's face . . . When I saw that look on her face, I knew it was all over for Mabel, for the time being, and also probably all over for Reed.[13]

THE PATERSON STRIKE PAGEANT prepared the way for the Provincetown plays. It was a mixture of art, politics, and social intrigue, as were the first plays. Robert (Bobby) Jones directed and designed the Pageant sets so successfully that he decided to make theater design his profession. With a fund subscribed to primarily by Reed and Dodge, he was able to spend a season (1913–14) at Max Reinhardt's *Deutsches Theater.* Jack Reed wrote the Pageant's scenario and was its cheerleader, ushering the strikers into Madison Square Garden and shouting directions with a megaphone. Behind the scenes was another future Player, Hutchins Hapgood, who wrote laudatory newspaper articles. Jig and Susan Cook attended the Pageant, which Susan called a "labor play." While the Pageant was organized by the Village intellectuals and artists, the strike was the serious concern of the Industrial Workers of the World. Mary Heaton Vorse and Joseph O'Brien, active union supporters, campaigned directly for the strikers. The Pageant was a theatrical success but a financial failure. Critics claimed that the Pageant trivialized the serious concerns of the strikers.

Jack Reed, just three years out of Harvard, was eight years younger than Mabel Dodge. When they met, Mabel Dodge was separated from but still married to Edwin Dodge. Reed, born in Portland, was the prototypical, ebullient Westerner, a mixture of the derring-do's of the popular Western novelist Jack London and the rough-and-ready exploits of President Teddy Roosevelt. He was an apparent paradox—a political radical and a lyrical poet. He believed that with effort and industry the world could be changed, and he was trying to change everything all at once. In his first years in the Village he was unfocused and perpetually in motion. Lincoln Steffens acted as Jack's protégé, at the request of Jack's father, Charles Reed, who had been a U.S. Marshal in Oregon. Steffens thought the elder Reed's counsel was wise: "Don't let him get a conviction right away or a business or a career, like me. Let him play."[14]

Hutchins, envious of Jack's relationship with Mabel, saw Jack as having a "three-dimensional self-confidence," which, in his opinion, landed Reed in a Paterson jail when he demonstrated on behalf of the silk workers. Hutchins quipped: "Reed, emerging from the jail at Paterson, was put in jail by Mabel—a far more difficult prison to escape from."[15] Both Jack and Mabel were capricious about love, often confusing infatuation with passion. Jack was a strong proponent of free love, while Mabel insisted on her lover's constancy and confessed to being guilty of manipulation to keep a lover's undivided attention.

After the Paterson pageant, Mabel arranged for de-luxe accommodations aboard the German steamship *Amerika* and set out for her Italian villa with a prerequisite entourage— Jack Reed, her ten-year-old son John, the boy's nurse, and Bobby Jones. Jones wrote: "I've just been invited to join a party of congenial rich folks including Jack Reed to sail on the 19th for a motor trip through Provence and along the Riviera ending up with a month's loaf in the Villa Curonia in Flo-rence."[16] Jones left the entourage in Italy and made his way to Berlin. While there he began to dress in theatrical garb. He let his hair and beard grow long, giving him a saintly look, "such as one sees on Jesus Christ in a certain type of painting," as Mabel commented in her memoirs.

One of Mabel's tactics to heighten passion was to keep her lovers "at the threshold of things."[17] So Reed was not invited to join her in her cabin, but was kept waiting on the decks of the steamship. There he wrote amorous verse. At midnight he slipped under Mabel's door sentiments like this: "but the speech of your body to my body will not be denied." Not until Paris did the honeymoon begin. According to Mabel the threshold device worked, for she describes her body as "a Leyden jar, brimful to the edge, charged with a high, electrical force." And Reed melodramatically whispered: "I thought your fire was crimson but you burn blue in the dark." The intense fires of passion quickly dissipated. Mabel languished in bed and Jack took to the streets of Paris, cavorting with friends and colleagues. Jack did not meet the test of respectability Mabel had hoped for when she showed him off to her friends in Paris. His raw Western boyishness was considered gauche, especially in the cultivated Old-World salon of Gertrude Stein.

Reed was equally uncomfortable and restive in Dodge's villa. "I feel like the fisherman caught up by the Genie's daughter and carried to her place on the mountaintop."[18] Outside were ancient cypress trees and white peacocks on the lawn. Inside were bickering guests amid the majestic surroundings. Mabel wrote to Neith Boyce on July 29, 1913: "The house is full of 20th century Beardsley stuff—pianists, pederasts, prostitutes, painters, and peasants. The last tremendously outweighing all the others in the persons of Reed and myself . . . We are red geraniums among black and mauve orchids."[19] Mabel settled Jack in Edwin Dodge's bedroom, which was decorated in crimson and gold with medieval furniture, situated above her own bedroom. A test she set for her lovers was that they had to climb gracefully down a silken ladder to her sumptuous bed, decorated with four golden lions at the corners. Her husband Edwin had failed the test. "As he climbed down toward her bedroom, she noted that his coat rode up and shoes looked too awfully modern on the silk rungs."[20]

Back in America, Jack moved into Mabel's apartment at 23 Fifth Avenue, a daring concession for the outwardly respectable Mabel. Despite her flamboyance, she strove for Victorian respectability by elaborately camouflaging her affairs. The new lovers began in earnest their emotional scenes. Mabel sulked when Jack left the apartment, no matter the reason. He objected when she objected. One day, to goad her, Jack recounted a long talk he had had with a beautiful prostitute. Mabel collapsed on the floor in a near faint. On such occasions Mabel ran to the Hapgoods for comfort.

Jack planned an escape from Mabel by taking a writing assignment for the *Metropolitan* magazine to cover Pancho Villa's revolutionary activities in Mexico. However, right after Jack left New York, Mabel impetuously took the next train, catching up with him in Chicago. Locked in Mabel's compartment, they traveled in style to El Paso. Reed facetiously wrote to a Harvard classmate that "We start with caviar and go right through to nuts." The letter continues: "I think she expects to find General Villa a sort of male Gertrude Stein, or at least a Mexican Stieglitz." Eating breakfast in the Austin railroad station restaurant, Jack visualized how incongruent and ridiculous he and Mabel looked: "With me in my bright yellow corduroy suit and Mabel in her orange hat and satin-lined tiger-skin hunting jacket . . . an expense account and a roll of blankets . . . We shall descend upon El Paso."[21] Jack left Mabel at the Mexican border.

Reed's coverage of the Mexican War was the beginning of "a great, new day" for him. His powerful, well-balanced accounts of the war appeared first in newspapers, then in the magazines *Metropolitan* and *Masses,* and later were gathered together in a book, *Insurgent Mexico*. It was then that Reed focused his career on social revolution. When Jack returned to Greenwich Village in April 1914, he found himself a celebrity. Mabel thereupon devoted her Evenings to Jack and his successful reporting of the Mexican Revolution. Again Jack grew restive and escaped on assignments to southeast Colorado to cover the massacre of the Ludlow coal miners by the state militia and then to Washington, D.C., where he interviewed Secretary of State William Jennings Bryan and President Woodrow Wilson.

Early in the summer of 1914, Mabel and Jack went to Provincetown, described by Mabel as "just a double line of small, white clapboard cottages along a silent street."[22] Mabel arrived in a chauffeur-driven Pierce-Arrow touring car, accompanied by servants. She rented a cottage near her confidantes, the Hapgoods, who, with their four children, were staying in the Atkins shore property in the East End. While Jack wrote, Mabel decorated her rented cottage and explored the recently abandoned Peaked Hill Bars Life-Saving Station.

The Station was up for sale. At first Mabel proposed to buy it, but coaxed Sam Lewisohn, a millionaire friend, to buy it so she could decorate it. Throughout the Fall and into the Winter, she arranged for the decoration and renovation of the old station by long distance, sending instructions from her Croton, N.Y., home to John Francis in Provincetown. John Francis, grocer and realtor, was the bohemians' East-End ombudsman, the local provider of services, accommodations, and loans. Before she left town, Mabel placed an advertisement in the July 9, 1914, issue of the *Provincetown Advocate*: "Wanted old paintings and models of sailing ships. Please write before July 8th to Mabel Dodge, Provincetown, giving price and description."

At the beginning of their Provincetown stay, Mabel

was happy because Jack was exclusively hers. She reported blissful days of bathing and love-making and perhaps, as Mary Heaton Vorse later claimed, an overnight stay in a silken tent at Race Point. Mabel was even pleased when Jack ungraciously saved her from drowning. She and Jack were out in a dory when it sprang a leak. She was wearing a Peter Thompson, a "two-piece costume of middy blouse and long flannel skirt, usually of navy blue." Mabel's heavy skirt became waterlogged and dragged her under. Reed told her to take off the skirt; when she refused he tore off the garment. When help arrived, Mabel refused to get into the boat of her rescuers and had to be towed ashore hanging onto the stern of the dory. On shore, Reed covered her with a blanket. Mabel remarked, "So much for the emancipated woman."[23]

Reed spent his time in Provincetown preparing his book on the Mexican War and writing an article on the Ludlow strike. Jack invited Fred Boyd, an English socialist, to act as his secretary. He also invited Harvard classmates Bobby Jones and Robert (Bobby) Emmons Rogers, an M.I.T. English professor, to join him. Mabel bristled at this invasion. She said nothing at the time, but got even in her memoirs. She described Fred Boyd as an unspeakable cad; and Bobby Rogers as "fat and wore spectacles . . . very facetious and breathless." Mabel secretly planned to end the affair—on her terms, of course. She left Jack in Provincetown and sailed to her Villa in Florence, taking along her son, Neith Boyce, and two of Neith's children. She had tired of camping out in Provincetown's rustic and uncomfortable cottages; she had tired especially of Reed and his absorption in things other than Mabel. Neith, on her part, was happy to leave Hutch and his infidelities. Hutch at the time was writing *The Story of a Lover,* his rationalization for an open marriage.

There were two more real-life scenes in the Mabel–

Jack romance. A critical episode occurred in Paris, the denouement months later in Croton. World War I broke out shortly after Mabel and Neith arrived in Europe. Neith returned to the States with her children and Mabel's son. Mabel went on to Naples to wait for Jack's arrival. When Mabel met him at the wharf, she was dressed in a "long, white ruffled dress" and a parasol to match. From there they went to Rome and Paris, where Jack suffered from dysentery, as he had on their honeymoon. On their earlier trip Mabel had loved nursing a submissive Reed, but not the second time around. After the histrionics and love-making, boredom set in. Jack was gloomy about the war and not writing well. Mabel sulked in her "dreary" hotel room while Jack went out to search for stories or colleagues. Mabel returned alone to America. Jack stayed in Paris, drinking and smoking heavily, and promptly fell in love with and proposed to a married woman, Freddie Lee, the wife of sculptor Arthur Lee.[24] This was not out of habit for Reed who had an affinity to married women. Mabel was married and did not divorce Edwin until June 1916, after her affair with Reed. Moreover, at the time Jack fell in love with Louise Bryant, his future wife, she was also married.

Mabel and Jack exchanged transatlantic cables, mainly in French. He alternated between saying goodbye and professing true love. These telegrams, and attendant confusion, comprise the main dialogue of *Constancy*. Jack was vacillating between Mabel and his new fiancée. He broke his engagement after he was introduced to his fiancée's parents, and then returned to the United States to play out in Dodge's Croton home the final scene of their farcical romance. Jack assumed Mabel would ignore his inconstancy; he brought with him two gold rings. Mabel, who had waited a long time for revenge, prolonged the evening. There was a long dinner, long conversations, keeping her courtier on the threshold, and then an abrupt ending. "It's all finished for us," she said as she pushed him out the door. Mabel claimed she later destroyed all of Reed's letters as a gesture of her love for Maurice Sterne, her next conquest and third husband.

IN THE PROGRESSIVE 1890s, when the New Woman movement began, colleges as well as new careers opened up to women. The 1905 New York City census, for example, reported a large number of women professionals: 73 clergy, 78 dentists, 76 bankers and brokers, and 78 lawyers. While most women workers were sub-professionals, employed as maids and shop girls, surprisingly there were 48 women carpenters, 37 masons, 45 plumbers, and 67 electricians. Actually, the percentage of physicians who were women was 8.6, which exceeded the 1970 proportion of 7 percent.[25]

The rapid proliferation of newspapers and magazines, and of high-school graduates to read them, had also created writing opportunities for women. Susan Glaspell, Mary Heaton Vorse, and Neith Boyce were of this generation—all were fiction writers with newspaper experience. Each cultivated an audience of female readers who enjoyed stories that were sincere and sentimental and also had a high moral purpose. Of the three, Glaspell was the only college graduate. As her writing matured, Glaspell developed beyond her early style as a local colorist and became more of a realist, with broader themes.[26]

Ironically, what Neith Boyce, Susan Glaspell, and Mary Heaton Vorse wrote about—conventional family trials and triumphs—was for the most part antipodal to their bohemian life. However, they were not fully liberated women but rather a lingering part of the blue-serge, conservative society. "The heroines of Neith Boyce's fiction were often martyr-like sufferers, women who were victimized by their husbands but who endured humiliation and deprivation."[27] They put their husbands' careers before their own and at the same time assumed financial responsibility for the family. Susan Glaspell was successful enough as a novelist to support herself throughout her lifetime; when she married Jig, she supported him. Mary Heaton Vorse was the main breadwinner for both her husbands, Albert White Vorse and Joseph O'Brien. Neith Boyce's writings supplemented Hutch's diminishing income. In time Neith's earnings, plus money from Hapgood's father, supported the family.

In 1914 the Hapgood marriage and finances were in jeopardy, for Hutch had replaced his zeal for newspaper work with a zeal for women and drink. As Max Eastman commented: Hutch had "a natural impulse toward sin."[28] Hutchins Hapgood, at forty-five, was the oldest member of the group and was at the end of an esteemed career in journalism. On the other hand, Neith, a short-story writer, was trying to launch a new career, in playwriting. Following his master's degree from Harvard, Hutch Hapgood began his journalist career in 1897 with the *New York Commercial Advertiser*. Lincoln Steffens, the City Editor and renowned journalist, encouraged Hutch to write investigative feature articles about life in New York City. One series of articles became a classic, *The Spirit of the Ghetto* (1902), which depicted the culture of the newly arrived Jewish immigrants. Hutch followed this with studies of radical labor leaders and social anarchists. In many cases, he became friends with the people he interviewed. One was Terence (Terry) Carlin, whom Hutch made a labor hero in *An Anarchist Woman* (1909).[29]

Eugene O'Neill immortalized Terry Carlin as Larry Slade, "the old foolosopher," in *The Iceman Cometh*. After leaving Professor George Pierce Baker's English 47 playwriting class at Harvard, O'Neill made his way back to his old haunts, the waterfront dives in Greenwich Village. He first encountered Carlin in the rear room of the Hell Hole, which had been set aside for heavy drinkers. The room was described by the poet Maxwell Bodenheim as furnished with cheap prints of race horses and nude women, with spotted tables and a blaring nickelodeon. Carlin was the prefect drinking buddy for O'Neill: Irish, nihilistic, and a spellbinding talker. Such were Carlin's talents that he was given free drinks, and room-and-board at the Hell Hole. Despite the difference in their ages—Carlin was 61 and O'Neill was 26 when they met—the two men became lifelong friends. It was Carlin who accompanied O'Neill to Provincetown in 1916 and introduced him to his Village friends who were staging summer theatricals.

Hutch's zeal about "far-reaching revolutionary tendencies of the labor movement" faded as he became increasingly involved in artistic and bohemian circles, in romantic entanglements and late-night philosophical discussions. Hutch, a basso-profundo, tireless talker who groped for the right thought, was trained in philosophy at Harvard and Heidelberg. Hutch, like Jig Cook, who had also studied philosophy, believed the theater should be an ideal community. Hutch conjectured that the Players' zealous activity was a reaction to World War I, "a social effort to live again—spiritually, to recover from discouragement and disappointment."

While Hutch was only marginally involved with the Players, he delighted in long, rambling dionysian discussions with Jig about the theoretical import of theater. When Hutch was an assistant to George Pierce Baker, the Harvard dramatics professor, he first realized that as a performer he had "absolutely no spark of theatrical imagination." His short career with the Provincetown Players convinced him that he was "hopelessly bad," a too self-conscious actor.[30] In the summer of 1916 he acted in *Enemies,* the play he co-authored with Neith. This was the beginning and end of his career as a Provincetown Player.

Hutch had fallen in love at first sight with Neith Boyce, a redheaded young woman new to the staff of the *Commercial Advertiser.* Neith's aloofness and self-possession both intrigued and tormented the garrulous Hutch. His pursuit of the "slim, pale, silent woman," as Max Eastman described her, led to a traditional Victorian church wedding with music, flowers, and bridesmaids. In 1898, when Hutch courted Neith, Greenwich Village was a mixture of Victorian manners and bohemian outlandishness, the latter newly imported from Paris. Washington Square was quiet and gracious. Hutch recalled: "There were no motors, the horse-cars jingled along Eighth Street, the old two-horse stages with imperial atop crawled up Fifth Avenue, where hansom cabs plied and, from the stables in Washington Mews emerged victorias with high-stepping horses, coachman and footman on the box, and enthroned elegant ladies."

Against this Victorian backdrop Neith Boyce, a New Woman, learned to drink, to smoke, and to frequent places previously reserved for men. Hutch, in his autobiography, recalls a humorous, yet telling, incident when he accompanied Neith to a Bowery saloon on Eight Avenue "where women were admitted to drink and where rough conduct was not frowned upon. She took a glass of beer and lit a cigarette. The bartender came over to our table and indignantly said to her: 'Say, where do you think you are? The Ritz?'"[31]

After 17 years of marriage and four children, Neith and Hutch were airing their marital difficulties on Lewis Wharf. Together the Hapgoods wrote *Enemies,* a one-act play that was a therapeutic attempt to reconcile the tensions stemming from their open marriage. Hutch wanted an open marriage. For his late-Victorian generation this usually meant that the husband but not the wife could philander. Such was the case for Hutchins Hapgood, as well as the other Victorian husbands, Albert Vorse and Jig Cook. When wives engaged in extramarital affairs, husbands rebelled and invoked the double standard. Neith reluctantly took a lover at Hutch's feigned insistence; he thereupon became uncontrollably angry. Neith suffered a nervous breakdown.

What disturbed Neith was not just Hutch's extramarital intimacies, but that he had kept secret a long-time affair with Lucy Collier, who also had an open marriage. *The Story of a Lover* was Hutch's attempt to explain his philosophy of marriage and love. It was more a complaint about Neith's not understanding him. In the winter of 1915 Neith became infuriated when Hutch took this manuscript, presumably dedicated to Neith, to Lucy Collier to read. Mabel Dodge told Neith about the Lucy–Hutch affair. Hutch never forgave Mabel for what he regarded as her indiscretion in the matter.

GEORGE CRAM COOK AND SUSAN GLASPELL finally gave in to their suppressed desires. In 1913 they made the bold decision to abandon their Midwestern roots and start over in places where there was sexual freedom: Provincetown and Greenwich Village. For five years they had been in love and knew it was impossible to live together in their native town of Davenport, Iowa. Jig, at the time, was married to Mollie, a second wife who bore him two children while the affair was going on. Jig and Sue inopportunely fell in love just after Jig had left his first wife and became engaged to Mollie. Jig's letter of December 10, 1907, to Sue records the start of their affair: "You don't know how good it was to me to sit and talk last night . . . Weren't we all scared when we found out the time? Guilty wretches!"[32] Jig's newest infatuation exasperated his long-time friend and confidante Floyd Dell: "How many times are you going to ask me to believe in your eternal love for some girl?" Floyd was not completely unbiased in his scolding, for he was smitten with Mollie. In 1911 Jig left Mollie and moved to Chicago. In two more years he was on his way East to prepare the way for a third marriage.

In his capacity as editor of the *Chicago Evening Post's Friday Literary Review*, Jig became particularly attuned to experimentations in poetry and drama. Floyd Dell and his first wife, Margery Curry, were at the social center of the Chicago bohemians, who resided in shabby buildings near the site of the 1893 Chicago World's Fair. Here, in the Dell's salon, free verse was first discussed in America. At the time, Midwest poets, such as Carl Sandburg, Edgar Lee Masters, and Vachel Lindsay, wrote in the vernacular for the common man. The few esoteric, intellectual poets were published in Harriet Monroe's *Poetry* magazine. Monroe had been poet laureate of the 1893 World's Fair. Through the transatlantic efforts of Ezra Pound in London, Imagists poetry and T. S. Eliot's *Prufrock* were first published in *Poetry*. Also started in Chicago was Margaret Anderson's *The Little Review*, which introduced the works of the cutting-edge writers James Joyce, Ben Hecht, T. S. Eliot, and H. D.[33]

Throughout his life Jig was fascinated with the theater, especially classic Greek drama. His enthusiasm was ignited when the Irish Abbey Players performed in Chicago. Jig was especially intrigued with Maurice Browne and his Chicago Little Theater, which drew parallels between ideal Christian societies and ancient Greek festivals. Browne experimented with "creative creation," allowing actors in the *Passion Plays* to add dialogue. To Jig's delight, Browne staged Euripides' *The Trojan Women,* which later inspired Jig to write *The Athenian Women*. Bror Nordfeldt designed the set for *The Trojan Women*.[34]

Maurice Browne, an Englishman, is recognized as a prime leader in America's Little Theater movement, and was the inspiration for other little theaters, particularly the Provincetown Players. In the decade before World War I, the Little Theater movement spread rapidly in America. Constance Mackay stated that, by 1917, there were fifty such organizations. In Europe, hired halls were engaged, but in America all types of structures were used, "a stable, the chapel, the art museum, the masonic temple . . . even the saloon . . . While an abandoned fish house in a picturesque Massachusetts town has been so Metamorphosed that Stanislavsky himself would applaud it."[35]

Jig Cook made a histrionic entrance into Greenwich Village, garbed in the trappings of an artist—sweeping black cape, walking cane, a long gray beard, and a wide-brimmed hat that topped a leonine head of hair. His towering figure attracted attention even in the Village, where everyone was costumed. In many ways Jig Cook was an older version of Jack Reed: both were energetic, broad-chested, and emotionally volatile, falling in and out of love easily. Reed, however, was not a heavy drinker, as was Cook, who rationalized his drinking bouts as a necessary bacchanalian, inspirational ritual. Furthermore, Jig never received the immediate fame bestowed on Jack, whose martyrdom to Communism immediately elevated him to hero status. It was because of Jig's and Jack's combined enthusiasm that the Provincetown theater was launched. It was Jig, however, who kept the Players going in their early years, for Jack left for Russia in 1917 and never returned to the Playhouse.

In February 1913, when Jig arrived in Greenwich Village, it was at its peak of avant-garde activity. The Armory Show, with its cubist, impressionist art, was the riveting event. Village intellectuals were crusading for the striking Paterson silk workers; demonstrating in support of Margaret Sanger and birth control; attending and planning little theater productions; and talking incessantly about the newly published translation of Freud's *Interpretation of Dreams*. Jig, a forty-year-old with a checkered career, was not startled by what he saw in the Village. He was nevertheless intrigued by the heated debates on art and psychoanalysis, manias which had not yet reached the Midwest; on the other hand, he was sorely disappointed by the theater. Jig was unemployed and looking for a way to harness his typically unfocused energies. He decided to write plays that spoofed the Village bohemian manias about art and psychoanalysis. "You could not go out to buy a bun without hearing of someone's complex," recalled Susan Glaspell.[36]

For six years, 1916 to 1922, Jig Cook spearheaded and inspired the Provincetown Players. This was as close as Jig ever came to his visionary "new Athens," his abiding life-long passion. Jig had been educated at the University of Iowa, Harvard, Heidelberg, and Geneva, and had taught for short periods at the University of Iowa and Stanford. In 1903 he decided to devote himself to writing and to socialism, supporting himself by truck-farming and raising chickens on the family farm in Davenport. In 1911 he left the farm for his editor's job in Chicago.[37] He also left behind a second marriage and two children.

To please Jig, Susan set aside her career as a novelist to write plays. In retrospect she may have regretted this decision. "I gave up practically everything else, though I had an established position as a novelist. I wanted to do this, and I'm glad I did."[38] This bitter-sweet assessment of her years with the Provincetown Players was written in 1929 to Eleanor Fitzgerald (Fritzie), who was trying to hold the Players together while they were reorganizing. They wanted to revert to the original name, Provincetown Players; Susan strenuously objected to exhuming the past name, for she equated the name with the singular accomplishments of Jig. "An organization, as much as an individual, has a right to have its decision, its death respected."

Susan's memorial to Jig, *Road to the Temple,* in part recounts the story of the Provincetown Players. At that time she was living with a younger writer, Norman Matson, in a common-law marriage. *Road* is a sentimental tribute to Jig; at times, resentment surfaces for she had sacrificed her time, her energies, and her reputation for the theater, the focus of Jig's enthusiasm not hers. Despite these regrets, Susan, in learning dramatic techniques, improved the structure of her short stories and novels. *A Jury of Her Peers* is considered her finest short story; it was adopted from *Trifles,* a play she wrote for the 1916 Provincetown summer season.

ONE IMPETUS FOR WRITING PLAYS was the emergence of the Washington Square Players. This little theater group started with an impromptu performance in the back of the Boni bookshop adjoining the Liberal Club, in a makeshift theater arranged for Lord Dunsany's *The Glittering Gate.* Two future Provincetown Players were part of the opening performance: Robert Edmund Jones, who designed the set, and Ida Rauh, a lawyer and Max Eastman's wife, who took one of the two roles. The group quickly outgrew its makeshift space; on February 19, 1915, the Washington Square Players opened in its new home, the Bandbox Theater on East 57th Street. They advertised for new plays, preferably American; the only restriction was that the "writing must be sincere, truthful, and effective." The response was overwhelming.

Two of the first plays staged were by the founders, Edward Goodman, future director and theater critic, and Lawrence Langner, a stage-struck patent attorney and later founder of the Theater Guild, which was an offshoot of the Washington Square Players. John Reed's play, *Moondown,* was produced on the second program. The Cook's *Suppressed Desires* was rejected as being too esoteric. Mary Heaton Vorse indicates that the Cooks had thought their play was to be produced by the Washington Square Players: "Jig and Sue have written a very funny one-act play on psychoanalysis which they are going to bring out."[39] Jack Reed's play *Freedom* was also rejected, as most likely was Neith Boyce's *Constancy.* In a January 20, 1915, letter, Neith wrote: "I have been doing some plays—one was accepted and would probably have been produced this winter—only, alas! the manager has just failed—so it's out in the cold again."[40] Plays from *Thirst* and a manuscript, *Bound East for Cardiff,* were submitted by Eugene O'Neill; they were also rejected. Jig said later that he was not pleased with the plays selected by the Washington Square group for they were neither experimental nor predominately American.

Those plays that the Washington Square Theater had rejected—*Constancy, Freedom,* and *Suppressed Desires,* as well as *Bound East* and *Thirst*—were mainsprings for creating the Provincetown Players. During the summer of 1915, with their rejected scenarios in hand, the first of the Provincetown playwrights moved from Greenwich Village to Provincetown. What followed was the beginning of a new art theater.

CHAPTER SIX

Provincetown:
Finding a Stage

I N 1915 IT SEEMED THAT EVERYONE was looking for a
stage—all across the country, from Los Angeles to New
York. Theatricals were the newest craze, and little theatres
proliferated, set up in barns, churches, bookstores, and even
in a fishhouse on a wharf. Productions were as varied as the
locales: some were amateur, others commercial; most revived
classics and European masters; only a few experimented with
new American plays and new scenic art. The original Provincetown Players were exclusively American and exclusively
experimental.

Nothing grandiose marked the beginning of the Provincetown Players. The first productions were impromptu summer entertainment set in the cramped living room and
adjoining veranda of a waterfront cottage. Neith Boyce
Hapgood invited her vacationing neighbors—artists and writers from Greenwich Village—to see her one-act farce *Constancy* (originally titled *The Faithful Lover*), a dialogue
re-enacting the love affair of Mabel Dodge and Jack Reed.
Neith played the part of her friend Mabel; Joe O'Brien played
Jack. Bobby Jones set up a makeshift stage on the small porch,

arranging the audience in the adjoining living room. The crowd loved the play for they already knew the plot. The love affair was the talk of the Village. That same evening Jig and Susan Glaspell Cook performed their one-act play, *Suppressed Desires*. Bobby Jones moved the audience onto the porch, and staged the second play in the living room. Jig and Susan portrayed a bohemian couple obsessed with psychoanalysis and dream interpretation.

Two new one-act plays, also dealing with current issues, emerged: *Change Your Style* by Jig Cook satirized the warring painting styles, avant-garde versus traditional; and *Contemporaries* by Wilbur Daniel Steele, which was a serious allegorical drama about demonstrations for the homeless in New York City. For the second bill that summer (a reprise of the first two plays plus the two new ones) Mary Heaton Vorse was persuaded to relinquish space in her fishhouse on Lewis Wharf.

The four plays of the first season (see Appendix) closely reflected the bohemians' private lives, their intimacies, and the issues they talked about in their Village coteries: free love, Freudianism, avant-garde art, and radical politics. In *Constancy*, the first scenario, Neith Boyce reworked the actual contents of Mabel and Jack's often-absurd letters and conversations. Susan and Jig Cook, fresh from the Midwest, were intrigued by the new Village crazes; they parodied the conversations they heard in the Village streets and clubs about Freudianism and avant-garde art, respectively, in *Suppressed Desires* and *Change Your Style*. Using reportorial information given to him by Mary Heaton Vorse, Wilbur Daniel Steele dramatized in *Contemporaries* the incident in which reformer Frank Tannenbaum was jailed for staging a protest for the homeless in a New York church.

Likewise, the next summer, the produced plays reflected personal conflicts and *au courant* themes. Jack Reed, who had managed to get arrested while reporting on the striking Paterson silk workers, wrote *Freedom,* a satire about idealists in prison. Neith and Hutch Hapgood dramatized their troubled marriage in *Enemies* and *Winter's Night.* Steele spoofed free love in *Not Smart,* which contrasted the bohemian attitude with that of the Provincetown Portuguese. Louise Bryant's *The Game,* an abstract morality play, dealt with social consequences of behavior. To counteract some of the gossip about Bryant's affair with O'Neill, Reed quickly composed *Eternal Quadrangle,* a parody about triangular love affairs.

The exceptions to this light and topical fare were the plays of Susan Glaspell and Eugene O'Neill. While their 1916 productions stemmed from personal experiences, they reached back for a longer view. With *Trifles,* Glaspell produced a feminist classic, a story line based on a murder trial she had covered earlier as a newspaper reporter in Iowa. O'Neill staged two sea plays that he had written three years earlier, *Bound East for Cardiff* and *Thirst,* which wrestled with universal themes about death and fate. O'Neill's and Glaspell's psychologically riveting plays added a new and serious dimension to the activities of the summer theatricals.

For these versatile bohemians, writing plays was just another experiment in trying to change the world. They also wrote for other, more personal reasons: for the dedicated O'Neill playwriting was his lifework; Glaspell did so initially to please her husband; as for Steele, under financial duress, he was tapping another writing market; and as for Reed, about to embark on his own personal heroic stage in sacrifice to communism, he wrote plays to please his friends. Lewis

Wharf was similar to Mary Heaton Vorse's "A" house and Mabel Dodge's salon, a place where the volatile crowd exploded into activity. Experimentation seemed so easy for the ragtime generation; it was that kind of decade.

EUROPE WAS A NIGHTMARE during the summer of 1915. Germany and Austria were storming the Eastern Front and invading Poland, the Balkans, and Russia. Russia had lost a million men. On the Western Front, the trenches were scenes of carnage: thousands of soldiers died from poison gas, shrapnel, and bayonet wounds. German submarines menaced the seas, randomly sinking neutral merchant ships and ocean liners. In May 1915 the *Lusitania* was sunk by a German submarine off the coast of Ireland, with a loss of 1,198 civilians, including 139 Americans. The United States came perilously close to entering World War I.

When war was declared in Europe in the summer of 1914, the bohemians in Provincetown went on a rampage. First they drew up a list of formal resolutions protesting the war, then they got drunk, skinny-dipped in the harbor, quarrelled with one another, and raged up and down Commercial Street. The Englishman Fred Boyd went berserk. Ranting incoherently and brandishing a gun, he went from cottage to cottage and then into Provincetown's telegraph station and tried unsuccessfully to cable the joint resolutions to the Kaiser, the President of the French Republic, the Czar, and the Emperor of Austria.[1]

American foreign correspondents were scrambling about on all the European fronts. Mary Heaton Vorse, after attending the Women's International Peace Conference in The Hague, was forcefully held in Europe following the sinking of the *Lusitania*. She, along "with many American delegates . . . [were] unwillingly detained in England by the refusal of the

British government to permit the sailing of any steamer for Holland." Jack Reed was on assignment for *Metropolitan* magazine on the Eastern Front. He was likewise detained, in Russia, where he suffered a serious kidney ailment. In covering the war he stepped on mass graves and witnessed disease, famine, and grisly corpses. In his book, *The War in Eastern Europe,* Reed described the carnage.

> Between opposing lines of trenches were huge earth mounds from which protruded parts of ten thousand human beings—skulls with draggled hair, white arm bones with rotting flesh, bloody limbs sticking from worn army boots . . . We walked on the dead, so thick were they—sometimes our feet sank through into pits of rotting flesh, crunching bones.[2]

In spite of these hardships, a seemingly buoyant Jack returned to America with a sentimental attachment to Mother Russia, an attachment that eventually destroyed him. He described Petrograd almost as he had Greenwich Village in his *Day of Bohemia*, that is, in terms of community spirit.

> Our streets are narrow . . . We live in houses crushed up against one another . . . Houses are always open; people are always visiting each other all hours of the day and night. Food and tea and conversation flow interminably; every one acts just as he feels like acting, and says just what he wants to. There are no particular times for getting up or going to bed or eating dinner, and there is no conventional way of murdering a man, or of making love.[3]

Mary Heaton Vorse, on the other hand, returned home visibly depressed: "a strange thing happened to me. I could not communicate what I had been through to the people

I met . . . I was different. A revolution had occurred within me."[4] She had left behind her three children, Heaton, Mary Ellen, and infant son Joel, in the care of her husband Joe O'Brien. On finally returning home and when catching sight of Provincetown from the train, Mary expressed her relief:

> I had seen so many lovely little towns destroyed that I had the fear that Provincetown wouldn't be there. There it was across the bay from North Truro. My home, that gray long town with its monument. It was untouched. War hadn't been near it. Suddenly, at sight of it, I burst into tears.[5]

Excluding the radicals, the bohemians in Provincetown in 1915 were subdued and not overly anxious. America had not entered the war; patriotic fervor had not yet turned the country into ferociously splintered groups. "I Didn't Raise My Boy to be a Soldier" was constantly being played on phonographs and on the piano. Conscription had not as yet become a divisive issue with the radicals. Provincetown remained untouched until 1917, when America officially entered the war. Then the town was kept on edge by rumors of lurking German submarines and spies. In 1915, however, the artists and writers in the protected harbor of Provincetown escaped into dramatic fiction and hoped the war would end quickly. Out of their initial hysteria came calm and a new beginning.

During the summer of 1915, there were enough Villagers in the East End of Provincetown to support two transplanted Village restaurants, Polly's and Christine's. Carrying on the role they had in the Village, they became gathering places for the radicals, as well as for artists and writers who were summering in Provincetown. These restaurants were as much the heart of Village activities as the Liberal Club, the Brevoort, or the Boni Bookshop. Polly's was established earlier than Christine's and was located beneath the Liberal Club. Hippolyte Havel—cook, fiery revolutionist, and sometimes lover to Polly—would serve food and denounce customers as "bourgeois pigs!" Christine first worked as Polly's cook, then later opened her own restaurant atop the Provincetown Playhouse on MacDougal St. in the Village. Eugene O'Neill was especially attracted to Christine and portrayed her several times in his plays as Earth-Mother and generous prostitute; once, when drunk, he called her "the female Christ."

Polly had opened her Provincetown restaurant in 1914 at 484 Commercial Street; in 1915 Christine started "The Oaks" at 264A Bradford. Heaton Vorse recalled that as a child he had collected kitchen scraps from The Oaks to feed his chickens. These restaurants were more like speakeasies, for they served illegal whiskey that had been distilled in Truro. O'Neill called it "tiger piss." On September 30, 1915, the *Advocate* reported an incident at The Oaks.

> Officer Kelly about 11 P.M. on Saturday was called to quell a disturbance at "The Oaks" building owned by grocer John A. Francis . . . used as a restaurant by the . . . renters, out of town parties. Four people ran away but two were caught, John W. Joffrey and wife Margaret of Brooklyn, N.Y. They were locked up overnight . . . fined $25 to a plea of guilty to being drunk. Mrs. Joffrey was not found guilty; the law excuses a wife when she commits a misdemeanor in the presence of her husband; it is presumed that she committed the crime under coercion of the husband.

"I HAVE BEEN STIRRING UP THE PEOPLE HERE to write and act some short plays. We began the season with one of mine," wrote Neith Boyce Hapgood to her father-in-law. On July 15, 1915, at ten o'clock at night, Bobby Jones decorated the Hapgood's veranda in orange and yellow and staged Neith

Boyce's *Constancy* against the backdrop of the darkened Provincetown harbor and sky. Neith acted the part of Moira (Mabel Dodge) and Joe O'Brien took the part of Rex (Jack Reed). Bobby Jones, with the same ingenuity that he had used to improvise a stage in 1914 in the Boni Bookshop (marking the beginning of the Washington Square Players), created an illusionary theater with minimum sets and minimum lighting, "a candle here and a lamp there." For the second play, *Suppressed Desires,* Jig and Sue took the roles of Stephen and Henrietta. It is not known who played the third part, that of Mabel.

Compared with their experience in Chicago, Jig and Sue had found the New York theater "dull and lifeless," except for the Neighborhood Playhouse's production of *Jephthah's Daughter.* "Full of a strong inherited religious feeling," Glaspell wrote in *Road to the Temple,* "the tribal religious feeling of the ancient Jews still a living thing to some of the Jews of Henry Street. That night, before the glowing grate in Milligan Place, we talked of what the theatre might be." Jig envisioned a "dream city" of artists working in the theater without concern for commercial success and a community project such as the Paterson Pageant.

When Jig and Sue began to write plays, nevertheless, they settled on comedy. They produced neither the "tribal religious feeling" of *Jephthah's Daughter,* nor the stark realism staged by the Abbey Players, nor even the social message of John Reed's Paterson Pageant, but a drawing-room satire, a spoof on Freudianism entitled *Suppressed Desires.* The names of the two main characters are puns traceable to a childhood story of Jig's that he outlined in an autobiographical sketch dated 1914.[6] Jig wrote the story when he was ten years old; it is about visiting the Brewster family in Far Rockaway on Long Island. One of the young Brewsters was named Stephen (Jig called him "Step-Hen"). This word-play on the name

Stephen is the central pun. In the play, Henrietta (Hen-rietta) Brewster's amateur attempts at Freudian analysis compel her husband Stephen and her sister Mabel to visit a psychoanalyst for help in interpreting their dreams. Stephen discovers that he wants to get out of his marriage and Mabel discovers that she desires "Step-Hen" and also wants to get rid of "Henrietta." Thereupon Henrietta decides to suppress her desire for Freudian analysis. Despite the thinness of its plot, *Suppressed Desires* even today is an effective satire on parlorroom Freudianism. It remains popular with small amateur theater groups.

CHARLES DEMUTH, the fastidious avant-garde artist from Philadelphia, was "portraying a yellow sand dune at Provincetown by industriously painting what appeared to be large pink and blue worms on his white canvas."[7] At the same time, street artist Arthur V. Diehl was drawing and selling three hundred pictures of sand dunes to the delight of tourists.[8] Diehl, with his English accent, mobile face, and dark eyes, talked incessantly as he painted. "I paint pictures to sell . . . I will paint them as cheaply or as expensively as you want them. I have little ones for $1.25 and larger ones for larger prices." Demuth the cool cubist and Diehl the commercial traditionalist were at opposite poles; in between the two ranged a host of artists with conflicting art styles, all scrambling for attention. During World War I Provincetown was a concentrated artistic battle zone.

The Provincetown Art Association had been founded in 1914 amid controversy. Modernists (called, among other things, "futurists") warred with the traditionalists (also called "academics"), a controversy that is still going on. Futurists were allied with the new European art, especially the cubists and post-impressionists who were the scandals of the New York Armory Show. The modernist Ambrose Webster, who had exhibited in the Show, was appointed honorary vice-president of Provincetown's Art Association, as was his opposite number, Charles W. Hawthorne, the pioneer leader of the Provincetown academic school.

In its second year the Art Association held its first exhibit in Town Hall, opening on July 3, 1915. This attracted a reporter from *The Christian Science Monitor* who was not quite ready to appreciate the new art. He wished for a "fine, high, sober standard, avoiding the pitfalls of futurism." Much preferred by the *Monitor* reporter was the academic art that was dominant in Boston. Even Charles Hawthorne's classic "The Sun Bath" was criticized for its seeming departure from academic standards: "so interested did the painter become . . . in his color scheme that the drawing was neglected." Futurists like Oliver Chaffee and Tod Lindenmuth were but reluctantly admired. The reviewer hoped that the "false tendencies" of the new art, like "ragtime melodies," would disappear and that America would soon awaken from these nightmares.

Boston Globe reporter A. J. Philpott also covered the art exhibit at Town Hall in an August 9, 1915, article, "The Modernists." He was not as tactful as the *Monitor* reporter. "The pictures by Mr. and Mrs. Zorach are way beyond me. I don't get 'em." William and Marguerite Zorach became active with the Provincetown Players the following summer. In 1915 Marguerite Zorach was earning much-needed expense money by teaching women to embroider samplers.

> Under the watchful eye of Marguerite Zorach, high priestess of the ultra-modernists, a class of some 30 women artists are sitting day after day close by the sea, with stout wooden frames and balls of many colored yarns, embroidering away at samplers of their own design. The designs vary from conventional to the most excruciating cubist and vorticist designs.[9]

The article further stated that these embroidered samplers were the "new craze" in Provincetown, some selling for as much as $200 or $300 each.

Another artist who became a Provincetown Player was B. J. O. Nordfeldt.[10] He was an archetypical artist for his time, that is, peripatetic and rebellious. Born in Sweden, reared in Chicago, and well-traveled in Europe, he experimented widely with new media and new concepts of art. He exhibited in Paris, Milan, and Chicago; learned Japanese wood-block printing in England; and to support himself taught art, rendered magazine etchings, and painted portraits. In 1907 he lived at the "A" Club in Greenwich Village, where he met both Mary Heaton Vorse and Margaret Doolittle, his future wife. He accompanied Vorse to Europe to illustrate a series of drawings for her travel articles in *Harper's* and *Outlook*. From 1914 to 1917 he wintered in New York and summered in Provincetown.

Nordfeldt is noted for his unique "white-line" wood-block prints. Japanese wood-block printing, popular with Art Nouveau artists, was difficult and taxing, sometimes requiring five separate blocks for a finished print—one for line, three for color, and one to print tone. In 1914 Nordfeldt developed a simplified single-block process by cutting grooves in the wood to separate each color. This left white lines, which he integrated into the overall design of the prints. Watercolors were applied directly to the carved block to create, at one printing, a multi-hued print. Nordfeldt's technique was adopted by a group of wood-block print-makers in Provincetown. The white-line print became an artistic signature of the Provincetown movement.

Nordfeldt played himself, as an artist, in Jig Cook's play *Change Your Style*. Jig staged this play on the second bill, September 1915, on Lewis Wharf. All the characters were easily identifiable; in *roman à clef* style, real names were thinly disguised. Bordfeldt (Nordfeldt) was "Head of a Post-Impressionist Art School"' Crabtree (Hawthorne), "Head of an Academic Art School"; Myrtle Dart (Mabel Dodge), "Lover of the Buddhistic"; and Marmaduke Marvin, Jr. (Fred Marvin, Mary Heaton Vorse's half-brother), an artist. The "beneficent landlord," Mr. Josephs, represented John Francis, the Provincetown grocer and real estate agent who long endured and at times subsidized the bohemian group.

Charles Demuth played the lead role of avant-garde artist. Jig was intimately aware of Demuth's futuristic art style, for Demuth had painted an upstairs wall of the Cook's Provincetown home by rubbing "orange into old plaster, sensitively as if it were a canvas." In *Change Your Style*, Demuth portrayed a young artist in conflict with his banker father (played by Jig Cook) who, according to the script, wanted his son to follow a "sane" academic style rather than an "outrageous" post-impressionistic one. When the young artist makes a sale (albeit later withdrawn) to wealthy Myrtle Dart, who sees in his painting "the spiritual form of the navel," the banker father is converted. "The tide is turning. You mustn't change your style now, my boy." A recent reviewer found the play still interesting "despite its heavy-handed humor . . . the issues have hardly changed, and the clichés (e.g., the artist corrects a painting that was hung upside down)" are nevertheless fresh.[11]

In staging his play *Change Your Style*, Jig Cook began to realize the beginning of his dream—theater as a community of creative talents in which "The arts fertilize each other."[12] Demuth shared this philosophy and had written plays himself as a means of integrating the arts. Painters were a substantial, enthusiastic part of the first audiences. It was an exciting summer for the artists, because their inaugural art exhibition and their costume ball were being held in Town Hall. The Art Association's first costume ball was a smashing success. The eight hundred participants, dressed in mandatory costume, danced to the music of the Social Orchestra.

A SERIOUS DRAMA WRITTEN BY a serious young man ended the 1915 theater season on Lewis Wharf. Wilbur Daniel Steele, a Methodist minister's son, re-created in *Contemporaries* the 1914 arrest of Frank Tannenbaum who—in defiance of the law—led a group of homeless men out of the winter cold into a New York church. Tannenbaum, a young Wobblie organizer, "had won a day of front-page glory and six months in jail."[13] His case became a cause célèbre for union activists who protested widespread unemployment. *Contemporaries* dramatically re-enacted Tannenbaum's arrest, drawing parallels with the life of Christ, who was also portrayed as a victim of social injustice. In the sense that victims of social injustice are united throughout time, Steele viewed Tannenbaum and Christ as contemporaries.

Mary O'Brien's house in Greenwich Village was the staging center for Wobblie activities in support of Tannenbaum. Mary had originally encouraged Wilbur to take up writing and further encouraged him by providing an account of Tannenbaum's imprisonment and release in a letter dated March 15, 1915, that she sent to Wilbur in Provincetown:

> Joe and I rose in the dawn and got up to 53rd Street a little after 9 to meet Tannenbaum, who came out of jail. There were . . . Wobblies, a couple of dozen anarchists . . . moving picture men, photographers and newspaper reporters, one hundred and twenty-five. All united in singing "The Red Flag Forever" to the tune of "My Maryland" as the Department of Correction barge hove to. Frank is in really fine shape . . . and utterly unembittered and told me with a

smile that he was not feeling quite as well as he had been since he had been in solitary and the cooler for the last month with only three minutes out a day for a wash, no exercise, no work, no literature, no letters even and no sight of any friendly face . . . Last week Joe and Lincoln Steffens went down to Wadhams' Court and talked over the case of Tannenbaum . . . [to release him] because of the social service rendered by him to the community through his activities of last year . . . a great number of bread lines and soup kitchens had been opened throughout the city and the public at large made for the first time to realize seriously the problem of unemployment.

So, having got home from meeting Tannenbaum and seeing Dolly Sloan about Pat Quinlan who is serving [a] jail sentence . . . I am now writing you instead of earning my living, before I go over to Polly's to sell tickets for Tannenbaum's dance to-night . . . Polite up-town rich ladies mingling with free and democratic spirits with us poor wage slaves of the slums.[14]

Wilbur Daniel Steele,[15] having been raised in a Methodist parsonage, was quite comfortable writing a religious parable like *Contemporaries*. While a supporter of some advanced social causes, he was never part of the Village vanguard of radical revolutionists. His socialism was tempered by a Progressive's continuing belief in the American ideals of democracy, faith, and service. Although he was born in North Carolina and raised in Colorado, Steele's ancestry was New England Puritan. One ancestor, Stephen Hopkins, had signed the Mayflower Compact when the Pilgrims' ship lay at anchor in Provincetown Harbor. In 1913, when Steele achieved some success as a writer, he married Margaret Thurston, the painter who was graciously evicted from Lewis Wharf the summer of 1915 to make room for a theater.

136

At the time of the Tannenbaum trial in 1915, Steele bought a former whaling captain's home in Provincetown's oldest section, the West End, away from the Village bohemians in the East End. "We all went up to have tea with Wilbur yesterday—way out in the suburbs," commented Susan Glaspell.[16] Steele's biographer, Martin Bucco, calls this the period of Steele's suffering apprenticeship, because he was struggling to earn a living as a writer and to support a wife and infant son. His marriage was undergoing a great deal of stress. In a September 1915 letter to Joe, Mary describes the unhappiness surrounding the Steeles' move to their new home: "We ate gloomily of the ham which we felt had been baked in tears and blood. She and Wilbur were moving into their new home with sighs and tears, with gloom and nervous exhaustion, with dark foreboding, with suspicion that the house would be cold in winter with sadness, pessimism, and nervousness." This report reflected Mary's negative feelings toward Margaret, as well as her own depression, for Joe at the time was terminally ill and Mary was facing gloom in her own house.

Steele wrote one other play for the Provincetown Players, *Not Smart,* a light comedy about the Portuguese in Provincetown which was given in July 1916, the same night as the premiere of O'Neill's *Bound East for Cardiff.* Steele wrote to his parents about the play and declared that "I'll never do another." However, after a second marriage to actress Norma Mitchell, he did write a few other one-act plays and in 1938, in collaboration with Norma, wrote a successful Broadway play, *Post Road.* He is remembered not for the theater but for the twenty years (1915–1935) when he was one of America's best-known short-story writers. While the preponderance of his nearly two hundred published stories followed the popular magazine format of his time—consisting of melodramatic ad-

ventures, coincidental twists, and surprise endings—there are a
few with naturalistic themes that are still anthologized, such as
"The Man Who Saw Through Heaven" and "How Beautiful
With Shoes." Martin Bucco rates Steele's stories highly.

> Between World War I and the great depression, the radiant
> stories of Wilbur Daniel Steele won so many prizes and ad-
> mirers that even after Sherwood Anderson and Ernest
> Hemingway drove melodrama and plot out of vogue,
> Steele's champions considered him to be still one of the
> greatest masters of the short-story form.[17]

WHILE HER FRIENDS WERE SPOOFING HER on stage in the village of Provincetown in *Constancy* and *Change Your Style,*
Mabel Dodge was spending her time across the dunes at
Peaked Hill. When in 1914 the abandoned Peaked Hill Bars
Life-Saving Station was offered for sale, the possibilities of
ownership had fired the imagination of the summer colony. In
1915 the bohemians' interest had shifted instead to the summer theatricals.

Mabel deliberately distanced herself and concentrated
on the painter, Maurice Sterne. At the time she met Maurice
Sterne, Mabel had lost interest in many of the *au courant* social causes and was returning to her former interests, art and
literature. It was Jack Reed who temporarily had redirected
her interests. To Jack's mortification, Mabel once took him
on a tour of the ghetto and the Bowery in a chauffeured limousine. After the Reed affair, Mabel began to support the
dance schools of Isadora Duncan and her sister Elizabeth
Duncan and was particularly delighted by Bobby Jones and
his theatrical productions. She retreated from her Fifth Avenue apartment, gave up the Evenings, and spent much of her
time in the country at Croton, N.Y. There, in her garden,
metaphysically and aesthetically transported, she pitied the

New York women who "hurried to check the population, or to raise wages, or to swing more urgent affairs."

Mabel first became interested in the Station in 1914, a time when she was bored with Jack Reed, who was spending his summer days and nights writing about the Mexican War. Her other friends and acquaintances in Provincetown were artists or writers who also were working. Another problem that added to Mabel's alienation was that the "literary folks" in Provincetown were Mary Heaton O'Brien's property, a congenial, close-knit social group, not easily splintered by Mabel. And her former close confidante, Hutch, had withdrawn his support after Mabel told Neith about the Lucy Collins affair.

Mabel had planned to buy the old Peaked Hill Bars Station. Instead she donated her money to the dancing schools of Elizabeth Duncan. She persuaded Sam Lewisohn, a millionaire who invested in copper mines, to purchase the Station, with the agreement that she would decorate and renovate it for him. According to Mabel, Lewisohn paid all the costs—$1,000 for the buildings and $1,000 for the furnishings—and he even contributed $500 to the dancing school. Mabel used the renovated station once in 1915, and Lewisohn used it once in 1916. In 1919 it was bought by James O'Neill and given to his son Eugene as a wedding present.

When Mabel first saw the old Peaked Hill Bars Station in 1914, it was forty-two-years-old, well-weathered but sturdy. It had been abandoned because the ocean was eroding the sand on which the building sat. It lasted seventeen more years, finally sinking into the sea in 1931. Over the years winter storms had eroded and washed away the sand, part of a long process that moves sand in this portion of the Atlantic Coast in a northwesterly direction, sculpting and resculpting the outer beaches of Cape Cod. Erosion and sand transport are the two forces that built and are still changing the sandspit on which Provincetown rests. In 1914, a new Peaked Hill Bars Station was completed, set back from the sea, one-quarter of a mile southeast of the abandoned station.

At the time of her 1915 Provincetown trip, Mabel was still married to Edwin Dodge. Although she had lived openly with Reed, she was elaborately discrete in her arrangements with Sterne. She rented two houses in Provincetown: one cottage was on Commercial Street near the Hapgoods, and the other two miles away across steep sand dunes. To further camouflage her affair, she invited as house guests Bobby Jones and Hazel Albertson, an acquaintance from Newburyport. She installed Maurice and his art materials in an outbuilding at the Peaked Hill Bars Station and then placed Bobby Jones on Commercial Street as guardian for her twelve-year-old son, John Evans. Either she or Maurice would trudge across the dunes for their daily tryst.

Sterne was an able antagonist for Mabel; he was two years older, had a reputation as a womanizer, and did not object to being supported by women. As her first power play, Mabel bought one of Sterne's paintings, proclaiming that "Nothing stimulates an artist's interest . . . as [much as] having one buy something of his." To forestall Maurice's philandering, Mabel married him just as he was ready to leave for New Mexico. She did not follow him west. It was a perfect "no-fuss" honeymoon for Mabel.

In 1915, accompanied by Maurice, Mabel entered Provincetown in her leather-upholstered Pierce-Arrow car, chauffeured by her servant Albert. Rather quickly Mabel alienated the Hapgoods by quarreling with Neith, accusing her of flirting with Maurice, and sent Hazel home for returning Maurice's glances. Mabel became irritable and depressed as a result of her self-made isolation. In her memoirs, Mabel attributed jealousy as the cause for her distancing herself; what she does not mention are the plays. She stayed on her veranda overlooking the sea and read Hindu poetry from the *Upanishads* to Maurice. She expended her energy trying to stem his roving eye, increasing his financial dependency on her, and changing his artistic medium from painting—from a "muddy" [her word] palette—to sculpting. She succeeded in changing everything, except his compulsion to seduce women.

The Sterne love affair was not the romantic, drawing-room light farce that the Reed affair had been; it was manipulative, often cruel, and burlesque. In his autobiography, *Shadow and Light,* Maurice admitted to playing a love game with a profit motive in mind, while perhaps succumbing to love somewhere along the way. When Sterne was much older and living in Provincetown, he often commented to his neighbor, Mary Lewis, that he had never had more fun than he had that summer when Mabel chased him over the dunes.

Time had sifted out and discarded the worst moments. For instance, there was the harrowing and bizarre incident that occurred at Peaked Hill. On the afternoon of Sunday, September 6, 1915, Maurice Sterne, Mabel's son John Evans, and Bobby Jones went swimming in the surf at Peaked Hill bars. Knowing that this was dangerous, the three had tied a single rope about their bodies, as a safety measure, but the rope became entangled about their legs and arms hampering them badly. Maurice nearly drowned and was rescued by the Coast Guard at Peaked Hill Bars Station. The *Provincetown Advocate* reported on the rescue: "Maurice Sterne, aged 38 of New York, was under water for the third time. He was grasped by the hair and hauled into the dory. Sterne was near death." The Coast Guard worked on Sterne for 20 minutes before there was any sign of life.

What could have been a tragedy instead became ludi-crous. At the time of the incident, Mabel had been walking toward the swimmers, over a quarter of a mile of loose sand, skirting swampy areas, when she heard the cries for help and saw three dark heads bob up and down in the water. She was wearing high-heeled slippers, "my foolish French heels"; openwork socks that burned into the flesh of her feet; and long, full, lace and muslin skirts that tangled about her ankles.

She watched as two surfmen in partial dress rescued Sterne: "one was clad in undervest alone, and the other undervest and drawers from start to finish of the affair." (Regulations at the time specified that guardsmen should "di-vest themselves of all clothes" to prevent being dragged un-der.) With revulsion, Mabel described the scene:

> The body of Maurice, as it lay swollen and shapeless over a barrel with its discolored face and swinging arms, had lost its charm. Feeling, then, coldly embarrassed and detached from that scene of resuscitation I turned and walked away home.[18]

After the initial shock, Mabel became furious. Actu-ally, she had started out angry because the three had left her alone to go swimming; her anger apparently turned to fury when the three had nearly drowned. When Bobby and her son John were safely on the way home, she left Maurice at the Coast Guard Station, where he remained for two hours under Coast Guard observation. The theatrical Bobby Jones often retold the incident, emphasizing the macabre humor and the spectacle of Mabel with her white lace dress and long chiffon scarves, holding a ruffled white parasol over her head, and with "the most horrible face I ever saw in my life." There was no humor that evening, however, as Mabel made Bobby and John spend the night at Peaked Hill rather than return to town

Earliest view of Provincetown Harbor. Drawn by John Warner Barber, first published in 1839, *Massachusetts Historical Collections*, Worcester.

Sand dunes, part of three sand ridges that separate Provincetown from the Atlantic Ocean. In the 18th century, when these dunes were deforested and unanchored, the Town was nearly buried in sand. *Collection of Cape Cod Pilgrim Memorial Association.*

Trap fishermen in Provincetown Harbor, c. 1900. *Courtesy of Reginald Cabral.*

Railroad Wharf, looking south, c. 1890. *Courtesy of Lee Feroba.*

Unloading fish from dory to horse-drawn jigger. Provincetown Harbor, c. 1900.

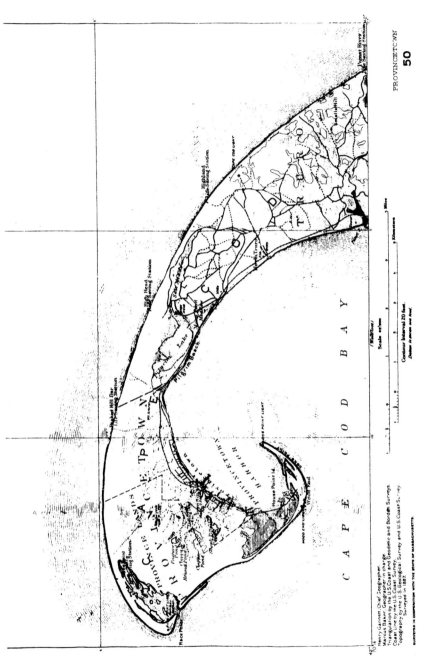

1917 map of Provincetown. Note location of Peaked Hill Life-Saving Station, northeast of Town.

Charles Hawthorne and class on Town beach, c. 1920. *Courtesy of Frederick Hemley.*

Eugene O'Neill (to right in raingear) in *Bound East for Cardiff*, Wharf Theatre, Provincetown, Summer 1916. This production was O'Neill's premiere as a playwright. *Museum of the City of New York.*

Bound East for Cardiff. Playwright's Theatre, New York City, Fall 1916. (O'Neill to left on ladder.) *Museum of the City of New York.*

Wharf Theatre (Lewis Wharf). Site of Provincetown Players, 1915–1916.

THE

Provincetown Players

WILL GIVE

Two Special Performances

Friday, September 1st
Saturday, September 2d
at 8:30 P. M.

AT THE

Modern Art School Wharf

Tickets, - - 50 Cents

Three Plays will be presented at each
Performance

"Thirst"---by Eugene O'Neil

CAST:

A dancer...Louise Bryant
A gentleman.....................George Cram Cook
A Negro sailor.......................Eugene O'Neil

"The Game"---by Louise Bryant

(Decorated and staged by the Zorachs)

CAST:

Death ....Jack Reed
Life.....................................Judith Lewis
Youth..............................William Zorach
The Girl............................Helene Freeman

"Suppressed Desires"

By George Cram Cook and Susan Glaspel

CAST:

Henrietta Brewster ....Susan Glaspel
Stephen Brewster ....Robert Rogers
Mabel (Henrietta's sister).........Margaret Nordfeldt

Tickets on sale at the Arequippa 571 Commercial Street,
Adams' Pharmacy and Francis' Store 577 Commercial St.

Playbill, The Provincetown Players, Provincetown 1916. *Henry W.
and Albert A. Berg Collection, The New York Public Library,
Astor, Lenox and Tilden Foundation.*

Eugene O'Neill, in American Line sweater, c. 1912. *Beinecke Library, Yale University.*

Eugene O'Neill (in bathing suit) and Charles Demuth in Provincetown, 1916. *John Reed Collection, Houghton Library, Harvard University.*

John Reed and Louise Bryant, c. 1917. *John Reed Collection, Houghton Library, Harvard University.*

Louise Bryant, Provincetown, 1916. Bryant sent this photograph to Reed, who was on assignment, writing on the back: "This is to remind you of 'the Dunes' & all the nice months after the Convention." *John Reed Collection, Houghton Library, Harvard University.*

Robert Edmond Jones,
c. 1916. *Theatre
Collection, Harvard
University.*

Mary Heaton Vorse,
c. 1912. *Archives of
Labor & Urban Affairs,
Wayne State University.*

Joe O'Brien and Mary Heaton Vorse, c. 1914. *Archives of Labor & Urban Affairs, Wayne State University.*

Susan Glaspell, c. 1913. *Henry W. and Albert A. Berg Collection, The New York Public Library, Astor, Lenox and Tilden Foundation.*

George Cram Cook, c. 1913.
*Henry W. and Albert A. Berg
Collection, The New York Public
Library, Astor, Lenox and Tilden
Foundation.*

Neith Boyce, "The Cigarette
Girl," c. 1897. *Library of
Congress.*

Mabel Ganson Dodge, 1911.
*The Beinecke Library, Yale
University.*

Wilbur Daniel Steele and wife,
Margaret, c. 1914, Provincetown.
*Department of Special Collections,
Stanford University Libraries.*

Peaked Hill U.S. Life-Saving Station, c. 1907, Provincetown.

O'Neill's home, former Peaked Hill Station, falling into the Atlantic Ocean, 1931.

Harry Kemp in Pilgrim costume, c. 1950, commemorating the Landing of the Pilgrims in Provincetown Harbor.

Hazel Hawthorne, c. 1920, on beach at Peaked Hill.

The Provincetown Theatre, MacDougal St., Greenwich Village. *Franz Kline, linoleum cut.*

as they had wanted to. She admitted "It was as bad as drowning—all tied on the same string."[19]

What should have been a triumphant summer for Mabel ended in a fiasco. She had labored all winter over the details of remodeling the Peaked Hill Bars Life-Saving Station, a locale coveted and romanticized by those who summered in Provincetown. By the early 20th century, the surrounding wind-swept beach and the tapestry of the dunes had become legendary; the beauty of the setting had been chronicled by Thoreau in *Cape Cod* and his descriptions were often quoted. Renovating the abandoned Station became a challenge for Mabel, a way to fight her depression. Moreover, Provincetown's white clapboard cottages, with their inadequate heat and furnishings, were not Mabel's style of living. She was accustomed to more sumptuous quarters, such as her villa in Florence and the elegant appointments of her Fifth Avenue apartment, each filled with servants and social distractions.

In the January 21, 1915, issue of the *Provincetown Advocate,* three items relate to Peaked Hill. These establish the fact that the first owner was Lewisohn and not Dodge, as has often been alleged; and they also give the reason for the government's abandoning the structure. First, there is a description of new storm damage to the old Peaked Hill Bars Station, with the result that at high tide the sea was within 13 feet of the buildings. "In a little time, it is believed the land on which the deserted buildings stand will have been swallowed up by the sea." The next item reported that John A. Francis placed a bid for the Peaked Hill Bars Station that was accepted; he was acting for Sam Lewisohn, 91 Broadway, New York City. The final item mentioned the passing of the Congressional bill that created the Coast Guard by combining the Life-Saving Service and the Revenue Cutter Service.

In February, the crews of the Life-Saving Stations gave allegiance to the new Coast Guard service. That same week, Sam Lewisohn was reported to have visited the old Peaked Hill Station, which he was to use as a "summer camp." According to the *Advocate,* the two-horse rig carrying Lewisohn between the old and the new stations was "caught without warning in a quicksand . . . one of several similar traps in the hollow of the beach." It was hours before the Coast Guard could free the rig. Not until April were workmen able to begin renovation. In less than three months, the patient yet exasperated John A. Francis, with long-distance instructions from Mabel, supervised the completion of the extensive changes. For his extraordinary efforts, according to Mabel and at her suggestion, Francis was given a gold watch by Lewisohn.

It was the winter of 1914–1915; Mabel was in New York and John Francis in Provincetown acting as her agent. Mabel was depressed; for her an antidote to depression was decorating. She had elaborately decorated her Villa Curonia in Florence when she was bored with her husband Edwin Dodge; she had decorated her Fifth Avenue apartment in New York when she was depressed about being in New York, that "ugly, ugly" place as she described the city in 1912 when she arrived from Italy. And now she turned her attention and talent to Peaked Hill Station and layered the walls in white, her signature. She had whitened her walls both in Florence and in New York and would do the same later on in Taos. She customarily dressed in white so that she would blend into the white walls. Mabel craved to be invisible but in control.

The Peaked Hill Bars Stations, old and new, were an active part of the life of the town. Between the town and the Stations was a well-travelled path traversing the width of the Cape at its narrow end. The distance from Peaked Hill Bars Station on the Atlantic side south to Cape Cod Bay is

1½ miles; about a mile or so west is the center of town. Before 1915, when it was under the Life-Saving Service, the crew of from five to seven men were local residents appointed by the Station Keeper. They worked seven days a week and were allowed to come home only 12 hours each week; they were on duty ten months of the year, off the months of July and August.

When the Coast Guard was established, the former leave time of 12 hours was extended to 24 hours. Even so, there was little time at home; so the path to town was well-worn by families and friends. Tourists were encouraged to visit the Station, and horse-drawn carriages were available for hire to take baggage and passengers across the dunes. The Coast Guard made a daily trip into town, and routinely would take messages and perform errands for those staying at the old Peaked Hill Station. In 1915 telephone wires and poles connected Peaked Hill with Provincetown and the other eight stations on Cape Cod.

When O'Neill lived at Peaked Hill, he took advantage of the Coast Guard's courtesy of delivering messages and packages. He was only by choice isolated from visitors and from the town, for the walk from Peaked Hill to the center of town takes between 25 and 45 minutes, less time in cold weather because the sand is firmer. Even for Mabel in her "foolish French heels," it was manageable walk.

Mabel's summer camp, the renovated Peaked Hill Bars Station, was commodious by Provincetown standards of the time. It was a two-story, fully shingled building approximately 36 feet wide and 42 feet long. One room was large enough to have housed two large life-saving dories that were 16 and 18 feet long. Another room was for the keeper (the head of the station), and a large room on the second floor sheltered survivors of shipwrecks. There was also a kitchen and many storage lockers. Among the improvements Mabel made was the building of a two-story, brick fireplace, a lookout on top of the roof, a gasoline-powered pump for water, an indoor bathroom, and a modern kitchen. The only convenience lacking, and still rare at the time, was electricity; kerosene lamps were used for lighting.

Mabel energetically engaged in the Station's renovation and decoration, with perhaps some minimal guidance from Bobby Jones. The walls and ceilings that were painted with coat after coat of white paint created a luminous effect as they reflected the sun and the refracted light from the sand and water. Hazel Hawthorne Werner, a longtime Provincetown resident, who lived at Peaked Hill for two seasons, called the large living room, a sea chamber. The building was made tight to withstand the howling wind, the sea spray, and the eroding sand that etched patterns in the casement windows. Peaked Hill was the ideal home for O'Neill, the tragedian of the sea. In the spring of 1919, four years after Mabel had decorated it, Eugene O'Neill moved in.

Peaked Hill, with its secluded dunes and panoramic oceanviews, was an essential part of the inspirational life of the Provincetown Players, the setting for fictional stories and plays and for real love affairs. For O'Neill it was the focus of his life for six years (1919–1924); it was where he ended his apprenticeship with *Beyond the Horizon,* which won him the first of his four Pulitzer prizes.

WHEN THE RAGTIME GENERATION GREW OLDER and wrote their memoirs, they generally confused the two summers when the plays were staged on Lewis Wharf, melding 1915 and 1916 into one continuous summer. They confused the two because they were in many ways alike: many of the same people were in Provincetown for both summers, and the four plays staged in 1915 were again staged in 1916. What happened on Lewis Wharf in 1915 was talked about all through the Fall, Winter, and Spring; the Summer of 1916 was actually an elaboration of the previous summer.

A sentimental mist gradually enveloped the tales of the two summers as they were told over and over again and were embellished as folklore. The close-knit colony of writers and artists was intensely aware of its place in history, for they preserved much. In archives scattered throughout the country there are scraps and scribbles, as well as lengthy manuscripts. For example, Mary Heaton Vorse's papers at Wayne State University comprise one of the largest collections there. It encompasses not only her published writings—for she was prolific—but also volumes of private papers, even scraps of papers, such as "pillow notes" that were left by her departing lovers. Housed in her archives are also the literary manuscripts of her husbands, lovers, children, mother, and all who were close to her over the years. Jack Reed's Harvard scrapbook is filled with the juvenile minutiae of his undergraduate life. Mabel Dodge also saved great quantities of documents that were not published in her memoirs, *Intimate Memories.*

Jig Cook's manuscripts are mostly in fragments and at times are incoherent, mainly because he drank for inspiration. After his death, Susan Glaspell pulled together some of Jig's writings and published them in two volumes. In one book, *Greek Coins,* there is a collection of Jig's poems as well as memorial tributes to him. In the other book, *The Road to the Temple,* there is Glaspell's first-person account of Jig's life, told in a sentimental fashion, as well as excerpts from his novels, plays and other writings, even ideas he wrote on scraps of paper and in margins of books. Glaspell never wrote her own memoirs.

Hutchins Hapgood strove to have the last word

among his peers. In his autobiography, *A Victorian in the Modern World,* he attempted to refute or clarify, in his philosophical style, the prior accounts of his peers, especially Mabel Dodge, whose own memoirs were not as sympathetic to Hutch as he would have liked. Hutch was especially vicious toward feminists, blaming the movement for his marital difficulties.

Steele was the most reticent of them all. He wrote no memoirs and his letters were generally non-committal and unrevealing. O'Neill's Beinecke Library archives are a storehouse of materials, some just recently released from restrictions set up by his third wife, Carlotta Monterey.

PROVINCETOWN'S SUMMER "COLONY OF LITERARY FOLKS" stayed on after the summer crowds left. The *Advocate* reported on September 23, 1915, that some were to stay on— the Hapgoods, the Steeles and others— "to learn that Provincetown is a far better place of residence in the winter [than] in the summer . . . the town's people find the maximum of enjoyment in winter (not summer) here, after the noise and dust and bustle of the short summer, and it is then that the town's fishermen do the mass of the work that brings in the dollars by whose aid the town lives and has its being." The Hapgoods remained the winter because of the whopping cough epidemic; they were especially worried about the health of Beatrix, the youngest child.

Provincetown was becoming home to some of the Players. For Jig and Sue it was a struggle, for they missed Iowa. At the time of Jig's father's death in 1914, Sue poignantly told of the loss, as she recalled in *The Road to the Temple:* "We felt anew how strange it was that we would be there, on this tip of land far out to sea—this farthest point, we who were from deep in the land."

On October 28, 1915, the *Advocate* reported Joseph O'Brien's death: "Word was received yesterday of the death that day of Joseph O'Brien, writer, at a hospital in New York City." Aside from her grief, Mary was confronted with being the sole support of three children. She was faced with debts on the Provincetown properties incurred during her short marriage to Joe, as well as long-outstanding debts of Joe's. To meet these financial obligations, she had to take assignments outside her career interests, such as writing war propaganda documents. During World War I the popularity of her sentimental fiction declined. So even her "lollipops," as she called them, her quickly written stories for profit, were no longer a source of income. Although she returned to Provincetown for the 1916 summer, she participated but minimally in the theater.

The fierce winter storms of 1915 drove the crowd, excepting the Hapgoods, back to New York. On November 19, as the *Advocate* reported, a gale wind wrecked the tree in the door-yard of Mary Heaton O'Brien; the large willow fell against the front of the dwelling; on the east side, the neighbor's chimney fell in on her property. Another fierce storm hit Provincetown the end of December: "The wind came with a sound as of innumerable freight trains and with violence. Trees were uprooted, windows blown inward, chimneys razed, and signs, etc., ripped from their moorings and sent flying." Winds were clocked at 73 miles per hour. The summer colony of "literary folks" thereupon left and did not return until April.

CHAPTER SEVEN

That Remarkable Summer:

Provincetown, 1916

PRACTICALLY EVERY DAY DURING THE SUMMER OF 1916,
1,650 passengers—many of them drunk and disorderly—
jammed the four decks of the iron excursion boat *Dorothy
Bradford,* which left Rowe's Wharf in Boston at 9:00 A.M.
and arrived four hours later at Railroad Wharf in Provincetown. One afternoon in June, a twenty-seven-year-old,
gaunt, darkly handsome man, dressed in sailor's clothes and
carrying a knapsack, disembarked. Eugene O'Neill had come
to Provincetown for the first time. On approaching Provincetown, O'Neill did not see it as Thoreau had, as a "filmy
sliver of land," nor as Vorse had, rising in "magic fashion"
from the sea, for he was depressed and possibly drunk.

He was with his Irish drinking companion, the self-
proclaimed anarchist, sixty-one-year-old Terry Carlin, who
had been to Provincetown before and was well known by the
Greenwich Village crowd. Hutchins Hapgood had met Terry
Carlin in Chicago in 1907, had written about him in *The
Spirit of Labor* and *An Anarchist Woman,* and over the years
had provided him with money and liquor. Hutch claimed in
his memoirs that in 1916 both Terry and Gene arrived broke

and that Terry, with Gene, went directly to Hutch's house and asked for a $10 loan that was never repaid.

Gene and Terry had come from the Hell Hole, Gene's favorite bar in the Village (his "No Chance Saloon"), where they had spent the winter and spring drinking, philosophizing, and negating existence. As a key character, the "old Foolosopher," in *The Iceman Cometh,* Terry Carlin proclaims "to hell with the truth!" O'Neill had come to Provincetown hoping his plays would be staged by Carlin's friends, for they had already been rejected by the Washington Square Players and ignored by Broadway producers. O'Neill arrived by sea— a symbolic entry for the Poet-Dramatist of the Sea—while the other Provincetown Players had come by train.

Many of the significant shifts in O'Neill's life were sea-related. Six summers before, in 1910, O'Neill had sailed out of Boston Harbor aboard the *Charles Racine,* a Norwegian windjammer. He sought escape from the emotional aftermath of a clandestine marriage and the recent birth of his first son, Eugene, Jr., whom he would see as an infant and then not again until Eugene, Jr. was eleven years old. Particularly upsetting had been a recent newspaper account that disclosed the marriage and birth, given by his mother-in-law in an attempt to reconcile the couple. In 1910, he impetuously left his make-work assignment with his father's play, *White Sister,* and—with his father paying the bulk of the fare—booked passage for a combined work-cruise aboard the windjammer. He was an aimless twenty-two-old and the despair of his doting father.

Six years later, still dependent upon his father's support and indulgence, O'Neill found himself once again in the Port of Boston, now waiting for the Provincetown ferry. This time he was not running away; he was bound for somewhere, for Provincetown, in his determination "to be an artist or nothing," as he had written two years before to Professor

George Pierce Baker at Harvard as part of his request to enter Baker's playwriting course, English 47.

For more than a year before his acceptance at Harvard, O'Neill had been writing one-act plays; in 1914, he persuaded his father to finance—at a cost of $450—the vanity publication of five one-act plays, a slim volume entitled *Thirst*. While at Harvard, O'Neill periodically checked at a Cambridge bookstore to see if *Thirst* was selling. The book was not a commercial success; the publisher later offered to sell copies at 30 cents apiece to O'Neill, but he declined and did not permit re-issue of the volume during his lifetime. *Thirst*, the title play, was staged in Provincetown in the summer of 1916. Gene, with convincing passion, played the mulatto sailor opposite the Dancer, seductively played by Louise Bryant.

O'Neill knew the theater and the impact of theatrical costuming and timing, so—with his flair for self-dramatization—he costumed himself for Provincetown as a well-traveled, seasoned seaman. He wore his favorite seaman's jersey—navy-blue with bold white letters spelling out *American Line*—a souvenir of his last voyage as a seaman. He also carried a sailor's knapsack containing plays stuffed into a Magic Yeast box, according to his own account. Four of the plays dealt with the sea. He arrived in the East End of Provincetown at the height of activity on Lewis Wharf, where the Players were excitedly preparing for the season's opening on July 13. O'Neill entered upon the scene as one darkly handsome sailor with burning eyes and burning ambition, with undiscovered talent and unproduced plays. All that was needed for a dramatic denouement were recognition and possibly romance. He found both that summer.

PROVINCETOWN IN 1916 was similar in spirit to the farm in Charleston, Sussex, England, that served as a summer retreat where the Bloomsbury group of writers and artists gathered during World War I, and a setting Virginia Woolf described in her diary (May 28, 1918) as "teeming, amorous, and creative." Quentin Bell, Virginia Woolf's nephew and biographer, facetiously dubbed Charleston, an inland town, Bloomsbury-by-the-Sea. In these two tightly woven, avant-garde colonies, artists and writers were extremely competitive and highly creative. Amazingly they still had energy left over for fervent socializing and sexual intrigue. Both the American and British coteries were experimenting with new forms of art, new forms of writing, and new relationships. Provincetown painters who had been schooled in the European avant-garde were closer in style to Bloomsbury than were the Provincetown writers. Artists like Charles Demuth, Marsden Hartley, Bror Nordfeldt, and William Zorach were post-impressionists, as were their English counterparts Duncan Grant, Vanessa Bell, and Roger Fry.

Philosophically there were marked differences between the two groups. Bloomsbury consisted of upper-class intellectuals dedicated to aesthetic enjoyment and individual expression, as set forth by the philosopher, George E. Moore, in *Principia Ethica*. The Provincetown Players, on the other hand, were middle-class American idealists, philosophically unfocussed. They linked themselves with social causes and the laboring masses, and bordered on the revolutionary, as in the case of John Reed and Mary Heaton Vorse. O'Neill's artistic philosophy approximated that of the elitist Bloomsbury group. He was a solitary who drew from his own inner resources rather than from social conventions.

The Provincetown bohemians experimented in their sexual relationships, but they were in no way as sophisticated and guilt-free as their English counterparts, whose private liaisons were notorious for their "permutations and combinations." As one critic quipped, "All the couples were triangles and lived in squares." Even that was an oversimplification of their intricate sexual arrangements. In contrast, the most complex, intense, and overt affair in the Provincetown group was the love triangle of O'Neill–Bryant–Reed. This was quite unsophisticated by Bloomsbury standards.

Personal relationships within the Provincetown group were unstable, attributable in part to the uncertainties of World War I. While none of the Players was conscripted, both Reed and O'Neill were evaluated and then exempted for physical reasons: Reed for his kidney ailment and O'Neill because of his tubercular history. Others, such as Hapgood and Cook, were too old. Mainly what caused the Americans' personal turmoil were their uneasy experiments in free love. Everyone, it seemed, had a roving eye—Louise for Gene; Mabel for Jack; Hutch for Lucy; Mary for Don; and Jig for all the women. Even the sedate Neith played at seduction. And all the while these writers were creatively explaining their emotional choices by means of love notes, poems, letters, discourses, novels, and plays. The summer of 1916 was a cauldron of passions acted out in the dunes, along the waterfront, in the living rooms along Commercial Street, and on Lewis Wharf. What was fiction and what was fact blurred together that "teeming, amorous, and creative" summer of 1916.

Night and day the New York crowd, tucked away in Provincetown's East End, bombarded each other with ideas. For years the East End had been referred to as the town's Wasteland, until summer visitors began to populate it. The far West End at the tip of Provincetown (and Cape Cod) had long ago stabilized; it was an older settlement where the Pilgrims had first waded ashore and where longtime residents lived. In the summer of 1916 the East End became an intellectual test site: a proving ground for new ideas and a litmus test for careers. Writers and artists exchanged poems, story lines, and scenarios as freely as they did theatrical chores and roles. They wrote, acted, directed, and designed costumes and scenery, all the tasks demanded by the theater.

In 1916, Provincetown, particularly the East End, was a place that permitted no secrets, as an early visitor, the 19th-century writer, Nathaniel Willis, had astutely pointed out. And as Willis had further noted, "Everybody at Provincetown knows every time everybody goes out, and every time anybody comes in." The East End crowd could not avoid one another. They were locked in by Cape Cod Bay on the south, the Atlantic Ocean on the north, the congested town center to the west, and a wasteland to the east, the sandy entrance to Provincetown. The Players stumbled over each other along the narrow streets of Provincetown, as they did on the crooked streets of Greenwich Village. If not for the geography of Provincetown—an intimate town with narrow streets and one narrow, twenty-two-foot-wide street that fronted the harbor and tied the Players together like insects on a stick—they might not have flourished as they did.

AN EDITORIAL IN THE *Provincetown Advocate* on August 24, 1916, enthusiastically proclaimed that:

> Provincetown is full; Provincetown is intoxicated: full of people; intoxicated with pleasure. As never before . . . inland people have recently come to this old Pilgrim town. As a summer resort, Provincetown's future seems roseate with promise. Many thousands came by steamer, some thousands by rail, while motorcars brought in several hundreds on each of several days, with some scores every day.

Several other editorials that summer echoed these observations as crowds swarmed into Provincetown in unprecedented numbers.

Chroniclers of the Provincetown Players often repeat the cliché that Provincetown during the summers of 1915 and 1916 was "a quiet little fishing village." On the contrary, the summer of 1915 was hectic; that of 1916 was frantic. It is astonishing that any time or space was found for a new theater. Mary Heaton Vorse's son Heaton, who as a teenager took part in the Lewis Wharf productions, clearly remembered those summers. He reacted to the descriptions of Provincetown as a quiet fishing village with the comment: "pure junk . . . fantasy." There were capacity crowds on the excursion boat and on the trains, and traffic jams in the narrow streets. There were well-attended art exhibitions and entertainment in Town Hall. Boston journalists travelled to Provincetown specifically to review the art exhibits and the plays on Lewis Wharf. In 1916, Provincetown was no longer a "quiet little fishing village." It was on the map as "a place to be" and was heady with excitement.

Adding to the commotion was a moving-picture company that came to town, an event the *Provincetown Advocate* reported on in its August 3, 1916, issue. An unnamed motion-picture operator choose as his primary subject George Washington Readey, "town character" and town crier, the "old time bell-ringing town crier . . . a real *rara avis*." Unfortunately, the time for filming coincided with the arrival of the steamboat *Dorothy Bradford*. The reporter observed that "it seemed to me that samples of everything that goes on wheels except railroad locomotives were wending their way along the roadway between Freeman and Carver streets. There were dump carts, and hay carts and jiggers, and baby carriages and miniature swill carts, and bicycles, and motor cycles and automobiles—Lord! automobiles by the dozen. And the sidewalks were full of people: townspeople, artists and hundreds of steamer excursionists."

In the middle of all these wheels and masses of people was a "chap, with a machine mounted on a tripod, standing in the middle of Commercial Street . . . I saw that he was turning a crank rapidly and realized a moving picture machine was busily recording . . . George Washington Readey was supposed to come along from the eastward ringing his bell and shouting . . . some message for the public ear." However, he misunderstood the cameraman's cue and stopped performing. The frustrated camera operator shouted, "Oh, damn! You've spoiled the whole thing . . . [You've caused] "forty more feet of wasted life."

And there were street brawls involving sailors drunk from the local "kill-em-quick" liquor. For most of the summer the U.S. Navy battleships *Ohio, Missouri,* and *Wisconsin* were in port, part of a naval practice squadron that had conducted maneuvers in and out of Provincetown Harbor since 1911. During their first night of liberty, 150 sailors got hold of the bootleg kill-em-quick liquor and terrorized the people living along Commercial Street between Ryder and Winthrop Streets with "filthy language, a free-for-all fight . . . about four o'clock A.M." A ship's officer said that the liberty party "was made up largely of Illinois and Pennsylvania lads . . . reputed to include the worst behaved men in the Atlantic squadron . . . making life unpleasant for all coast communities that have the misfortune to receive them."[1]

Rowdy sailors and mariners were not new to Provincetown. For over 200 years it had been predominantly a seaman's port, harboring renegades and squatters and undisciplined crews, a town slow to embrace the refinements of civilization. In the two decades preceding World War I, however, in order to attract tourists, Provincetown had become somewhat gentrified. To reflect a new image, streets were renamed for *Mayflower* passengers: Bradford, Winthrop, Standish, and

Alden. Town Hall Square was landscaped; the railroad terminal building was painted straw color with bright red trim; passenger buses were put into service on Commercial Street; and the one sidewalk, running on the starboard side of Commercial Street, was being changed from wooden planks to concrete.

Since the turn of the century, Provincetown had joined with the other Cape towns in outlawing drinking, but it did little to enforce the law prohibiting the sale of bootleg whiskey. While public drinking was often epidemic, arrests for peddling liquor were infrequent. The local Temperance groups kept trying to curb drinking by luring sailors into its reading room above the Town Library, which was stocked with magazines, papers and writing materials, and by arranging baseball games on Evans Field. Nevertheless, temptation followed the Navy even to the ball games and vice won out, with the help of professional gamblers and the town's twenty kill-em-quick liquor dealers, who provided floating barrooms.

The *Provincetown Advocate*, on July 20, 1916, gave a colorful account of the mayhem caused by 2,000 sailors on liberty. Gamblers suckered the sailors into shell-and-pea games and craps. "Ship's police got wise to the move and put the nimble-fingered sharpers out of business." "Skylarking" and disruptive behavior were blamed on the "villainous brew" sold "under the guise of whiskey . . . One drink is said to be enough to cause an angel from heaven to lick without provocation his own grandmother, while a full portion produces the most profound anesthesia known to the world."

Drinking and rowdiness aboard the *Dorothy Bradford* were commonplace. Provincetown police usually met the Boston boat and jailed those who had been caught drinking within the three-mile-limit of Provincetown. In July 1916 the local Provincetown judge found two young men from South

Boston guilty of drunkenness and disorderly conduct aboard the *Dorothy Bradford*. For their misconduct the two young men were kept in the Provincetown jail overnight and then sent home by rail because the steamer officials would not honor their round-trip ticket:

> It would appear that the prisoners imbibed freely of liquor and smoked cigarettes in the main saloon; that in passing a liquor bottle some of its contents were spilled upon the dress of a female passenger sitting nearby; that when the female passenger called the prisoners' attention to the fact one of the pair replied, using most obscene language.[2]

On the first Sunday in August 1916, the *Advocate* estimated that "1500 officers, sailors, naval academy men and naval militia," from the battleships crowded the center of Provincetown. The Navy was only part of a record crowd of an estimated 5,000 people who "congregated within the area bounded east by railroad square and west by the post office at two o'clock P.M. . . . It seemed that all the automobiles owned in the Commonwealth had sought rallying place here." Progress had its price. Traffic accidents were frequent; pedestrians were often struck by automobiles and "auto busses" that squeezed past one another, running in both directions on the twenty-two-foot-wide Commercial Street. There were also frequent collisions of bicyclists and walkers. Pedestrians were often injured by bolting horses.

The *Dorothy Bradford*'s whistle blasted, as the boat disembarked its 1,650 passengers, and often frightened horses that ran amuck along the narrow passageway on Railroad Wharf, bolting into the crowd. Residents along Commercial Street complained about the noise and vibration from the big buses, particularly between 10:00 and 12:00 P.M., when the nightly dances in Town Hall let out. Those trying to sleep felt "that they have some rights that midnight joy riders are obliged to respect." Vibration from the heavily laden giant cars had already cracked plaster; according to complainants, ceilings were ready to collapse.

> The entire town population seemed afoot last evening, the streets being thronged with humanity on foot and awheel. Both moving picture houses were filled with patrons and the Town Hall dance of the Socials' drew like a magnet ... [There is] the largest summer band seen here for a dozen years.[3]

Many activities were available to the summer tourist. Especially popular was the Amphion Orchestra, which began its sixteenth season of Friday-night dances in the Town Hall on July 4 and continued throughout the season. The Art Association, in addition to its stereopticon lectures and art exhibitions at the Town Hall, sponsored a costume ball that was thoroughly enjoyed by tourists and townspeople. Furthermore, there were special events: the Beachcombers gave a minstrel show and the Episcopal Mission gave a Garden Party and Sale, complete with fortune telling, donkey rides, and "fancy work" for sale. Band concerts were held on the lawn of the Town Hall, featuring both local bands and Navy bands from visiting ships. There was bathing, hiking on the dunes, sailing, sports fishing, baseball games, and indoor amusements found in pool halls and the bowling alley.

Other than the excursion day-trippers, there were increasing numbers of overnight and summer-long tourists. They found few modern conveniences in Provincetown. In 1916 there were telephones, but they were expensive and limited to businesses; private individuals sent messages by telegram. Electricity had come to town and was being promoted by the local electric company, but few could afford the rates.

Residents were unhappy about the large number of street lights illuminating the center of town, despite the fact that many were furnished free by the electric company. Houses were heated by fireplaces or by kerosene and coal stoves, which doubled as cooking appliances. Indoor plumbing was rare. Outhouses were common in most dooryards and on some wharves, making it quite risky to walk on the beach under the wharves. Slop buckets were carried through the streets on the rear of low-lying horse-carts called jiggers. The town had trouble enforcing an ordinance that required the covering of the slop buckets, as well as restricting honey-dipping (septic-disposal) to off-hours.

Nevertheless, the smell most complained about in the summer of 1916 was that of rotting fish. "Men working under the direction of the board of health, buried great quantities of squid and whiting, that had drifted upon the shore . . . Some of the beach cottage occupants also labored hard and efficiently at the task . . . when pelted by the sun rays, the mass developed an odor the reverse of pleasing." So reported the *Advocate* for the week of July 6, 1916. It was a news item frequently repeated that summer, because fish are often stranded on the beach when chased by larger fish; for instance, blues in a feeding frenzy regularly chase squid and whiting onto the beach. Most of the tremendous litter of fish described in 1916, however, was caused by fishermen cleaning out their weirs and illegally dumping unmarketable species of fish into the water. Incoming tides deposited the fish onto the beaches in vast numbers. Early in the summer Gene O'Neill and Terry Carlin gathered up some of the squid that had washed ashore and made stew. Unfamiliar with the preparation of squid, they overcooked it, making it too tough to chew, so they had to throw it out.

* * *

PROVINCETOWN IN 1916 WAS AWASH WITH PAINTERS. Not since the Portuguese immigration following the Civil War had the town seen such an influx of brightly garbed exotics. Women in brightly colored linen smocks and men in red flannel shirts lined the wharves, crowded into sail lofts, boarded in private homes, and posed and painted on the beach and in the narrow streets.

Phyllis Higgins, a Provincetown native, remembered the female artists who roomed in her family house in the East End. She and her sister were mesmerized by these strange ladies from strange towns like Baltimore and Philadelphia, who carried their easels to the beach and painted seascapes and portraits of one another. Phyllis and her sister would sit all day long and watch the women paint. Then they imitated them, first dressing and posing like artists, then salvaging pigments from the discarded oily rags. To encourage his daughters, Charles Higgins, a Peaked Hill surfman, made them palettes in the Station's workshop. For the rest of her long life Phyllis painted Provincetown scenes, as had the lady artists from Baltimore and Philadelphia.

For the new Players' Club, being surrounded by artists was a windfall, for they were eager to help with productions on Lewis Wharf. They sold tickets, packed the audience, acted in and helped direct plays and, of course, designed scenery. For the Players there were no creative boundaries. As the scenic artist Bobby Jones wrote that summer: "No books to read except free verse, so I shall have to write in self defence."[4] There were writers who were also painters and sculptors, namely, Wilbur Steele and Jig Cook. And there were artists who also wrote, such as Charles Demuth, Marsden Hartley, and Bror Nordfeldt.

During the summer of 1916, Provincetown artists— in addition to painting, stretching canvas, and cutting wood blocks—were organizing art shows with the Art Association and entertainment frolics such as the Beachcombers' Ball and the Artists' Balls. When the Players left in the fall to mount theater productions, some artists followed along, namely Jones, Nordfeldt, and the Zorachs. Many others stayed on in Provincetown for the winter, for the war's duration, and for a lifetime. Painters who were year-round residents bought cottages in every section of the town, and became voters and library members. Writers, for the most part, stayed in their tight East-End enclave and returned to the Village for the winter. After the Navy battleships sailed away, after the day-trippers clambered aboard the *Dorothy Bradford* for its last run to Boston, and after the summer colony of New York writers and Boston professionals loaded their belongings aboard the trains heading off-Cape, there remained the painters, intent on capturing the special light of Provincetown.

"Notable exhibition in Cape Cod town that now has largest summer art colony in the world" was the brazen headline of the *Boston Sunday Post,* on July 2, 1916. There were two exhibits held in Town Hall by the Provincetown Art Association. The first exhibit displayed 175 paintings, block prints, water colors, etchings, and sculpture, and was followed by a second show with an equal number of entirely new works of art. It was a popular show "of youthful audacity and experimentalism." In July 1916 there were 1,050 paid admissions, compared to 704 in July 1915. When the exhibition closed in September, 68 works were sent to the Vose galleries in Boston.

On October 12, 1916, the *Provincetown Advocate* reported that there were more than 600 painters and would-be painters in the town's five art schools. "Artists have, in fact, become so common that the natives no longer stop to gaze at them as they pass them on the single winding street. And the artists themselves have found the place ideal for their work, weather and lighting conditions conducing to the best possible activity." Charles W. Hawthorne, whose classes numbered 110 in July and August, had the largest following. Also available were E. Ambrose Webster's school, which "specialized in color"; George Elmer Browne's classes in "landscape expression"; the Modern Art School (on Lewis Wharf); and George Senseney's etching classes.

The *Boston Transcript*'s October 17, 1916, review of the Provincetown art exhibit in Boston was reprinted in the *Advocate* on October 26, 1916. The *Boston Transcript* commented on the "superiority of Provincetown as a summer camp for painters . . . There is no seaport or fishing town on the Atlantic coast that comes quite up to Provincetown for picturesque material. There is a certain foreign air about that part of the Cape . . . at times like the tropics . . . it has endless color . . . the romance of the sea hovers over it."

Especially noted were Ross E. Moffett's "Along the Shore" and its portrayal of "boats drawn up on the beach, with their blue-black, red and green colors contrasting with the sand colors"; "Winter in Provincetown" by Oscar Gieberich, with its grey tones of winter; and George Elmer Browne's "Seiners," which, in the *Transcript*'s opinion, was the cynosure of the display—a gouache of blue, white and red, a harbor scene in brilliant hues. Other paintings vividly limned Provincetown, with its white houses, green shutters, pinkish roofs, and grey wharves and boatyards. The anonymous reviewer thought Charles Hawthorne's "Boy and Pitcher" was drab: "an indifferent example of his work, depicting a stupid-looking boy with an open mouth and staring eyes." Specially commended were the "wood block prints in color gay and bright . . . immensely clever," especially Ada Gilmore's "A Promenade in Provincetown." After leaving Boston, the exhibition of Provincetown painters travelled on to Springfield, Massachusetts; Columbus, Ohio; Youngstown, Ohio; Syracuse, New York; and Dartmouth College.

In 1916 the artists organized a social club, the Beach-combers. Their clubhouse, called The Hulk, was located on Knowles Wharf, to the west of Lewis Wharf. It was an all-male club; women were allowed to accompany members only for special events such as dinners and dances. Among the charter members were the Provincetown Players Wilbur Daniel Steele and George Cram Cook, both of whom, as noted, were writer-artists. In 1916 women artists formed their own club called the Up-Alongs; later the name was changed to the Sail Loft. At the end of the summer, the Up-Alongs moved down-along to the studio of Miss Blanke of Chicago, located on the Modern Art School wharf, where the Players Club was organizing into the Provincetown Players. Many Sail Loft members who had attended the theater performances also contributed to the Players' First Subscription List.

Bror Nordfeldt headed the Modern Art School on Lewis Wharf. He had been a long-time associate of Jig Cook in Chicago and Mary Heaton Vorse in the Village. He had designed sets for Maurice Browne's Little Theater in Chicago. The languid and aesthete artist Charles Demuth, who had been the lead actor in the 1915 production of *Change Your Style,* deferred to Nordfeldt in 1916. Bror's wife, Margaret Nordfeldt, who acted in *Suppressed Desires* in 1916, became the Players' first secretary. She was quite contentious and caused much dissension among the Players, and eventually was asked to resign. On March 2, 1916, the *Provincetown Advocate* reported that Nordfeldt had left Provincetown and had been taken to Boston for an appendectomy. His homeo-pathic wife had wrongly diagnosed his illness as a gall bladder attack and Bror's condition had worsened. Bror was trans-ported on a delivery wagon to the train, and then to Massachusetts General Hospital in Boston, where an emergency operation was performed.

Jig wrote to Sue on December 13, 1916, about the difficulty of getting Nordfeldt to cooperate in creating a set design. "Mary [O'Brien] asked him yesterday why he was so fierce around the place and told him he ought, when he was in that hospital, to have his spleen removed." During his recovery, Nordfeldt made a series of drawings chronicling the experience, one entitled *Leaving Provincetown in Butcher's Wagon.* The original charcoal drawings were lost, but they have been reproduced in Van Doren Coke's biography of Nordfeldt.[5] By the summer, Nordfeldt was sufficiently recovered to act in *Bound East for Cardiff,* as well as to continue his painting and to produce the now-famous white-line prints from the single woodblock process he had devised in 1914.

William Zorach had expected to instruct in the Modern Art School summer session. According to Zorach, Myra Carr and Freddie Burt, co-directors of the school, had hired him during the winter in Greenwich Village; however, when he arrived at Lewis Wharf he found that Nordfeldt had insinuated himself as the instructor. "It was not as much of a problem as we thought; there were no pupils," Zorach peevishly recalled.[6] Zorach and his wife, Marguerite, had rented a fish loft on the shore in the town banker's backyard. At night the Zorachs swam naked, leaving their bathing suits in boats moored in the harbor. Nude bathing was a favorite pastime of the Village crowd and was usually practiced discretely in the dark, but wine and liquor often led to daytime skinnydipping, still vividly remembered by some locals. Nude bathing, in fact, was a widespread craze. Floyd Dell, a later Player, recalled nude bathing on Staten Island, accompanied by silvery female forms in the moonlight.

Both Zorachs were active in the Provincetown Players, mainly as scenery and costume designers. William also acted, notably in the premiere of *The Game*. According to Alfred Kreymborg, a later Provincetown Player, William Zorach "cavorted like an elephant and could never memorize his lines."[7] The Zorachs preferred to deal in illusions, and designed a stunning set for Louise Bryant's morality play, *The Game*. Marguerite designed the backdrop, an "abstract pattern of the sea, trees, the moon path in the water." The Zorachs' designs were more effective than the play, however, and accounted for what little success *The Game* had. The sketch of the scenery for *The Game* was used extensively in books and posters, and for quite some time as the playbill logo for the Provincetown Players.

IN HIS MEMOIRS, MARSDEN HARTLEY recalled the Provincetown summer of 1916 as "a remarkable summer." Louise Bryant remembered it as "a strange year. Never were so many people in America who wrote or painted or acted ever thrown together in the same little place."[8] Bobby Jones wrote a gossipy letter about the exciting season, saying that "The town is mad over the experimental theater."[9] In addition to the writing and staging of the plays, and despite romantic intrigues and social hyperactivity, an extraordinary amount of other writing was accomplished that summer: magazine articles, books, short stories, and free verse. Most of the Provincetown playwrights were professional writers, mainly journalists. O'Neill was the exception. He had abandoned his various short-lived careers as newspaper reporter, stagehand for his father's productions, and seaman to devote himself full-time to writing plays.

Although twenty-seven-year-old O'Neill was the youngest of the group, he had written the most plays. After early years of dissipation and aimlessness, he decided in 1913, while in a tuberculosis sanitarium, that he wanted to be a playwright. As of 1916, Jack Reed was the only one who had had a play published professionally. His *Moondown* had appeared in the September 1913 issue of *Masses;* it was later produced by the Washington Square Players. Jig Cook, one of the oldest of the Players, was the primary mover, the one who initially organized, publicized, and guided their activities. It was the merging of two passions that made the Players successful: Jig Cook's to create an idealized community and Eugene O'Neill's to be an artist or nothing.

The intimate Provincetown theatricals of 1915 searched for a name in 1916. During its short seven-week season the group changed its identification from a Players' Club to a Toy Theater to a Laboratory of Drama to a Try-out Playhouse, and finally to the Provincetown Players. At the end of the season, in September, they set up a formal organization that agreed on the name. As a concession to O'Neill, the playhouse was to be identified as The Playwright's Theatre.

Five separate bills, comprising sixteen plays, were staged in the theater-on-the-wharf. Of the sixteen one-act plays produced in 1916, nine were premieres, the other seven reprises (see Appendix). There was a children's play, *Mother Carey's Chickens,* written by Dr. Henry Marion Hall, a summer resident. No record exists of this play. It was produced mainly to keep the children busy, as Miriam Hapgood, who was one of the juvenile actors, recalled. Not included in the count of plays are the unknown number read and rejected. It is speculated that O'Neill's comedy, *Movie Man,* about the filming of the civil war in Mexico was one of those rejected. This play was never produced. O'Neill's *Fog* was likely considered, but it was not staged until the troupe reopened in New York.

* * *

O'NEILL'S *Thirst* AND REED'S *Eternal Quadrangle,* both produced on Lewis Wharf in 1916, were blatant statements about
the love triangle of O'Neill–Bryant–Reed. The flamboyant
and magnetic Louise Bryant—born in San Francisco, reared
in Nevada, and a graduate of the University of Oregon—was
professionally ambitious and emotionally reckless. She had
worked as a journalist, and had contributed social news to a
weekly journal in Portland and poetry to *Blast,* a San Francisco anarchist weekly. By all contemporary accounts Bryant
was a classic beauty; she had a slim body, auburn hair, and
riveting eyes. Sixty years after having first met her, both
Miriam Hapgood Dewitt and Hazel Hawthorne Werner recalled that the first thing they noticed about Bryant was her
outstanding beauty. In a 1985 interview, Heaton Vorse remembered that as a teenager he was struck by Bryant's "amazing complexion and brightly colored cheeks."

"We *are* a household," wrote Bobby Jones about the
crowd in Jack Reed's rented cottage at 592 Commercial Street:

> Dave [Carb], of course, Reed, his secretary [Fred Boyd]
> who is just out of Paterson jail for I.W.W.ing around. Our
> cook—a dandy—is a famous slavic anarchist [Hippolyte
> Havel] or words to that effect. Also Marsden Hartley, a
> mad and notable painter of triangles and such. Also Jack's
> latest love, named Louise, a newspaper woman, Irish,
> young, a free-versist and quite intelligent & very pleasant.
> The town is mad over the experimental theatre. We recently
> heard *six* one-actors read at one fell swoop. Nearly passed
> out. And they will all have to be acted or their authors will
> know the reason why. Yes, indeedy.[10]

Reed's cottage had one of the few large living rooms in
Provincetown. It was a gathering place for anyone who wanted
to talk, to eat one of anarchist Hippolyte Havel's meals, or to

read aloud a script to the Players' Club. Jack was a generous host and his place, whether in New York or Provincetown, was always filled. With the seductive Louise living there, it was even more attractive to his non-paying guests. "I lived altogether in a bathing suit, and Jack came and went and did his writing in another little cottage nearby," she wrote in her memoirs.[11] Jack rented the house in late May; in early June he left for a three-week *Metropolitan* assignment to cover the national political conventions in Chicago and St. Louis, with a side trip to Detroit to interview Henry Ford. These assignments did not further his career the way his coverage of the war in Eastern Europe had, but Jack agreed to do them because he needed the money. Because of his pacifist stand, he was finding it increasingly difficult to get assignments.

Louise Bryant, the bohemian's apotheosis of the liberated woman, was the social mistress and only female in the summer cottage. While Jack was away, Louise wrote the letters of invitation, met the guests at the railroad station, and acted as lady-of-the-house. For the sake of outsiders she was referred to as Jack's wife, even though the two had made no marriage plans. Even O'Neill, for reasons of his own, kept up the pretense. He invited Beatrice Ashe, his current love interest in New London, to come to Provincetown, to stay with "Jack Reed and his wife [who] would act as chaperon."[12] Louise claimed that Mary Heaton Vorse had invited her and Jack to stay in Mary's house, but "when we got there she was having one of her love affairs, and greeted us as if she hadn't expected us at all."[13] Mary was actually having a summer love affair with the architect Donald Corley.

Constancy was again on the bill in 1916. This school-for-scandal love affair between Jack and Mabel was re-enacted with both principals nearby. Jack was in Provincetown with Louise; Mabel was on the outskirts of town, waiting to see if his newest romance would last the summer. Jack was still playing the reluctant bachelor. Even though the Jack–Louise affair was only six-months' old and at a high romantic pitch, Jack welcomed the breathing spell provided by travel and the chance to be away from Louise. He wrote her from Detroit on June 18, 1916: "But I'm glad I came alone, and left you there. It gave me a new perspective on us, darling, and a new view of myself, and I think a vacation from each other every now and then is wonderful for two lovers."[14] After receiving this letter Louise turned her full attention to pursuing the talented newcomer O'Neill.

"MABEL CAME TO THE THEATER TO SCOFF and went away in the same mood," quipped Hutch.[15] Mabel was no more interested in the theater in 1916 than she had been in 1915; both times she sequestered herself. In 1916 Mabel came to town without her new lover, Maurice Sterne, having sent him to Monhegan Island, Maine, "to paint rocks." She had recently been awarded her divorce from Edwin Dodge, and said she needed time for personal assessment. In fact she did keep quite busy; that summer she wrote two short stories that were published in the September and October 1916 issues of the *Masses*. The stories were the direct outcome of her analysis with A.A. Brill, the head of the psychoanalytic movement in America and another one of Mabel's sought-after prime movers and shakers. In these two stories, Mabel quite perceptively analyzes her neurotic impulse to devote herself to a male figure, exclusively and jealously. She realized that she first chose a man dedicated to his work and then resented his absorption, thereby experiencing hatred, envy, and "temporary extinction." After she had sent Maurice to Maine, she experienced "The old depressed nothingness, which was all I was without a man."[16]

In August, Mabel joined Maurice in Maine, but not before she had checked out her successor Louise. Mabel's description of Louise was partially inaccurate: "a very pretty, tall young woman with soft, black hair and very blue eyes." (Louise had red hair and green eyes.) Mabel knew of the summer gossip about the Louise–Gene affair. She conjectured that "Reed would be glad to see me if things were like that between him and Louise—but he wasn't . . . He steeled himself against me." "All those people disheartened me," she wrote, especially those in the Reed house, "a white clapboard cottage that had a geranium in the upstairs bedroom window." Mabel thereupon left the "confused cheerfulness of the Hapgood household," where she was staying, and moved into "a tiny wooden house on the bay a little way outside the town." Always the interior decorator, she painted the walls blue and made red-and-white checked gingham curtains, the "first ones to be imported" from England. There, on the outskirts of town, Mabel kept careful track of Lucy Collier, in order to foil Lucy's affair with Hutchins Hapgood. Lucy Collier and her three little boys—who "played all day on the empty beach stark naked"—were Mabel's next-door neighbors. Hutch's secret affair with Lucy was contrary to the Hapgoods' long-standing agreement to discuss openly their extramarital affairs.

In his reminiscences, Marsden Hartley referred to 1916 as "that remarkable and never repeated summer at Provincetown." He was in Maine in June 1916, visiting with the "mysterious thing called family," when he accepted Louise Bryant's invitation to come to Provincetown. He wanted to experience novel things "like dunes and ships."[17] Hartley was a thirty-nine-year-old painter, well-known in Greenwich Village, Berlin and Paris, and a long-time intimate of the poet-doctor William Carlos Williams, who divided his time between his friends in the Village and his family and medical practice in nearby New Jersey. Marsden was also a part-time writer and poet. Alfred Kreymborg observed that "His poetry was old-fashioned . . . but his painting could be wild."[18] Like Jig Cook and Hutch Hapgood, Hartley was an inveterate talker, much to the dismay of the Reed household.

Hartley participated in the social activity of the "budding celebrities," but was only marginally involved in the theatrical activities.[19] He did design a stock-market ticker for Reed's farce, *The Eternal Quadrangle*. Zorach remembered Hartley's "remarkable summer" as quite disturbing. He claimed that Reed enlisted his help in getting Hartley out of the house. Reed supposedly confided to Zorach that "Marsden Hartley has been here a month. He doesn't even contribute anything intellectually and I don't really like him, but how can we move him out without offending him?" Zorach takes credit in his autobiography for somehow doing just that.

Charles Demuth lodged elsewhere but frequented the Reed household. He was a frail and elegant artist, a friend of Hartley, and also a long-time friend—as well as medical patient—of William Carlos Williams. In his autobiography, Williams said he met Demuth in a boarding house "over a dish of prunes,"[20] along with the Imagist poets, Ezra Pound and Hilda Doolittle, when all were students in Philadelphia. Williams treated Demuth for diabetes, a condition that resulted in his early death in 1935. Hartley eulogized Demuth in an essay, *Farewell, Charles*. Hartley recalled that Demuth enjoyed the parties and the "long night sessions" of the Provincetown summers, and that he pursued amusements with "tiger-like stalkings . . . down the course of the night." In his admiration of the *fin de siècle* artist Aubrey Beardsley, Demuth often costumed himself as a dandy.

While casual dress was *de rigueur* in Provincetown,

Demuth most often dressed in "a black shirt, white slacks, a plum-colored scarf tied around his waist, and black-laced shoes, highly polished." One of Demuth's favorite pastimes was to ride Provincetown's large bus—called the accommodation—positioning himself on the board seat alongside the driver and going "hell-bent from one end of the town to the other," waving to his friends. Demuth was part of the Village crowd who were in Provincetown at the outbreak of World War I, when the artist Stuart Davis had "a little studio on the beach where they all danced and drank and went in swimming at night, with Cubist costumes and without them."[21]

During the summer of 1916, Demuth spent time lolling on the beach with O'Neill in front of the Reed cottage. The solitary O'Neill tolerated Demuth because he was an easy companion and did not require a lot of conversation. Demuth—with his black eyes, slender hands, and nervous reticence—somewhat resembled O'Neill. Demuth's artistic style at that time was like Duchamp's: nihilistic and cynical, quite compatible with O'Neill's own personal philosophy. (Louise Bryant referred to O'Neill as that German Schopenhauer.) Demuth concentrated more on painting than theater in 1916, crossing the mosquito belt of the Peaked Hill dunes to paint "dark blue dunes undulating under a blue sunset." Demuth's *oeuvre* include symbolic portraits of William Carlos Williams and Eugene O'Neill. O'Neill, in his play *Strange Interlude,* portrayed Charles Demuth and Marsden Hartley, both bachelors, as one combined character, Charles Marsden, the "prim, mother-dominated" writer who is afraid of women.[22]

Miraculously, Robert Edmond Jones was able to juggle his friendship with Mabel Dodge while living in Reed's house with Louise Bryant. He wrote: "To add to the fun Mrs. Dodge is down, at the Hapgoods, but seems making up her mind to stay all summer. She's very nice to me when we meet, though the houses aren't near."[23] Mabel was at that time a patron of the arts, and Bobby Jones was one of her protégés. She was generous in providing housing for him in her Fifth Avenue apartment and at Finney Farm near Croton, New York. She also arranged to have a group of sponsors send Jones to Zurich for analysis by the famed therapist Carl Jung. Jones credited Dodge as a positive influence in his life, both professionally and socially. Jones was one of the few who was immunized against Mabel's fickleness. She found him delightful and he devotedly reciprocated her affection. Lincoln Steffens recounted Mabel's generosity toward Jones.

> She gave "Bobbie" Jones a back room in her flat to play in. . . . There he slept, worked, and played with the miniature stages and stage accessories he gathered to develop his childlike gift for stage-making and decorating.[24]

FOR MARY HEATON VORSE O'BRIEN, the summer of 1916—the landmark season for the Provincetown Players—should have been an extremely happy time. On the contrary, it was a most desperate time. For nearly a decade she had encouraged her Greenwich Village friends to come to Provincetown. Her persuasive campaign began in 1907, when she and her first husband, Albert White Vorse, bought their Provincetown home. Gradually over the years, with Mary Vorse's encouragement, her coterie expanded from its nucleus—the Hapgoods, the Steeles, and the Cooks—to a host of Village friends and associates. But during the summer of 1916, she virtually ignored them.

After the death of Joseph O'Brien in October 1915, Mary O'Brien was in a severe depression, a condition that had begun in the spring of 1915 when she confronted the war in Europe first-hand. "A revolution had occurred within me. . . . All that summer I was cut off from other people. I had a sense of a transparent barrier between me and them."[25] By the summer of 1916 things had worsened. She was numbed by Joe's death, by the awesome responsibility of providing for three children, and by a shrinking literary market for genteel fiction, which was her one economic mainstay. Further, she was experiencing writer's block and was worried about the accumulated debts that had been incurred by two profligate husbands.

"Mary! Mary! Why didn't you come with me?"[26] This plea came from Griffin Barry in Moscow in the fall of 1916. In the summer and into the winter of 1916, Mary turned to Griffin for solace after her break-up with Don Corley. Griffin was a thirty-two-year-old free-lance journalist, a friend of Corley, and was in Russia covering the war. Griffin's letter of September 12, 1916, from Russia indicated that he had received six of her letters at one time. They documented her mercurial moods during the summer, from "contentment that sits in your soul" to "the last . . . a farewell note before beating it to the trouble belt in Minnesota." Don had married by the time Griffin received her letters. He asked that she "Give Don my very real love and good luck. I don't know the lady but I hope she can deliver Don out of the gloom."

Heaton Vorse remembered Griffin Barry as one who "had the egotism of a person of short stature." Barry sired two children for Dora Russell while she was still married to Bertrand Russell. Dora Russell, in her biography, *The Tamerisk Tree*,[27] described Griffin as having a "pleasing male Irish-American voice" and the "deepest blue-grey eyes." She was attracted to him because of his Soviet leanings and his permissive attitude toward love, although later she did complain of his indifference to their children, Harriet and Roderick. Griffin never became the great writer he had hoped to be, but continued as a free-lancer covering politics and war, and finally writing travelogues until his death in England after World War II.

John Dos Passos, a later Provincetown resident, met Griffin Barry in Paris through Mary O'Brien. Dos Passos was initially impressed with Barry and his radical politics but, like most people who knew him, grew tired of his braggadocio and his crassness. According to Dos Passos, Barry claimed to have slept with every woman a person might mention. Edmund Wilson, on the other hand, characterized him as "exactly like a woman and yet not exactly like a fairy."[28] In 1916, just before his graduation from Harvard, Dos Passos visited Provincetown. He took the train from Boston to Chatham and from there walked to Provincetown. He returned for a brief visit in 1925 and again in 1929, when he married the writer Katherine Smith and settled into her house, formerly Mary Heaton Vorse's Arequipa cottage, at the foot of the site of Lewis Wharf.

Dos Passos in 1916 was enthralled with the Continental air of Provincetown, and described the residents as "Yankees with hard looking hatchet faces and Portuguese and Canary Islanders—dark and marvelously good looking—The contrast is amazing." Dos Passos was sensitive to his Portuguese heritage. He had been born out of wedlock to John R. Dos Passos; not until 1912 did he learn that his guardian and new stepfather was actually his natural father. John Roderigo Madison had been using the name John Dos Passos for only four years when he wrote about the good-looking Portuguese in Provincetown. He would spend the rest of his life sorting out his Portuguese ancestry.[29]

Mary Heaton Vorse maintained contact with Griffin Barry over the years because of their mutual left-wing learnings and, sentimentally, because Griffin had been the one who had introduced Joe to Mary. As early as 1914, Griffin became unemployed because of his radical politics. Joe O'Brien wrote in the fall of 1914 to Mary: "I had Griffin to lunch with me today at the Brevoort. He is blacklisted by the newspapers, and can't get a job, but he doesn't seem unhappy."[30] In the fall of 1916, Mary's letters to Griffin were frequent, venting her problems about continuing debts, her indecision about her career, and whether she should live in New York or Provincetown. "If the war lasts through the winter I'm wondering why you can't cache Heaton in school and bring Ellen and Joe to Moscow," wrote Griffin.

To Griffin's credit he understood Mary, in terms of both her characteristic resiliency and her vacillation between what he called her "scarlet sins" and "domestic virtues." While she was devoted to her house, she disliked housekeeping, and therefore engaged servants. While she was devoted to her children, she found single parenting a burden. While she enjoyed being a writer, she dreaded the endless, arduous hours of writing. Griffin had trouble deciphering Mary's vague and rambling letters. "I feel sad and puzzled because you are so emotionally up in the air and the events at the bottom are hidden from me." He was shrewd enough, however, to finally discern that she was recovering from an affair. "Your last letter . . . left me figuring you having had a thumping good fling on the primrose path and your face only newly turned to virtue." Mary's moods were volatile. There was a sad, short letter, "full of debts and bustedness." "How well I understand your wandering out of yourself and getting lost," wrote Griffin with insight, "only you like it out there beyond the tide."

Mrs. O'Brien's wharf had been changed from a fishing stage to a theatrical stage: for Mary it meant the passing of a romantic, refined era. It also signified the displacement of her generation. The future looked grim. Out of her depression came a short story: *The Mirror of Silence,* a bitter rendering of her feelings. In that story Mary's harsh comments were directed toward women: "There was between them the free-masonry of predatory women whose paths do not touch." Mary, in real life, had alienated her female rivals, women such as Louise Bryant, Mabel Dodge, and Margaret Steele. Mary's salvation, as expressed in the story, stems from an understanding man who encourages Virginia [Mary] and whose observation ends the story on an optimistic note: "'You could find some way out of it, if you feel like it. You always do,' he insisted." The female protagonist, Virginia, had lost her tradition-steeped house to a "swift-moving, nouveau riche" woman, Crystal (probably Mabel Dodge), who defied social decorum, that is, "The social surface without which society cannot exist." Crystal and her friends represented the bohemian group invading Provincetown with harsh sounds of "macabre ragtime," destroying the silence of the past.

These "parvenus" staged a "masque, Midsummer Madness" with "half-naked girls, bacchantes and dryads." Shocking to Virginia was not so much the nakedness of their bodies but the "nakedness of . . . emotion." Mitzi (perhaps Louise Bryant) was depicted with unusual bitterness and harshness, "her gutter-snipe soul," "a common little comedian," who said "I and my friends are here in your great house, and what are you going to do about it?" Beautiful, talented, sensuous and young, Louise Bryant had indeed taken over Mary O'Brien's house, that is, her domain, Provincetown. In contrast, another character, an older woman who had taken care of the house, represented tradition. "Age and dignity and grief were in her face, and there was the lassitude about her of someone whose heart had been broken and whose body suffered with its heart."

It is clear, in analyzing this short story, that Mary Heaton Vorse was not honest about her own "scarlet sins," her extramarital affairs. In affairs of the heart, she was reacting—

as a blue-serge, late-Victorian—to the need for discretion, in much the same way Mabel Dodge did. Mary was especially offended by the indecorous, sometimes brutal, public dialogue rendered in the theater on her wharf. The scurrilous parlor dialogue of Reed and Dodge as portrayed in *Constancy,* the Freudian and blunt word-games of *Suppressed Desires,* the frank discussion of illegitimacy in *Not Smart,* and the naked thespian display of lust in *Thirst* were themes that Mary Heaton Vorse O'Brien thought should not be publicly flaunted.

An acting role she accepted illustrates her bias. On July 13, 1916, in Neith Boyce's *Winter's Night,* Mary played a minor role, the part of Sarah, whose shriek of horror ends the play. In this scenario the male protagonist had the decency to commit suicide rather than openly face his sexual desire for his sister-in-law. One must consider Mary's bravery in taking part in this play, for the action takes place following a funeral and Mary had recently been widowed. According to Mary's own report years later, her shriek as Sarah caused quite a stir. Another minor role she had was in Steele's *Not Smart.* "Margaret is the leading lady . . . Mary is another character,"[31] he wrote to his parents on June 28, 1916.

Mary may have been something of an actress, but never was she successful as a playwright. By November 1916 she had recovered sufficiently from her aversion to things theatrical and to Don Corley's presence in the theater to read her play *Tomorrow* to the Provincetown Players in New York. It was not accepted for staging nor was her *In the Fishhouse,* read by her in December 1916. Not until 1924 was a play of hers staged; it was produced by the Wharf Players in the West End of Provincetown (not to be confused with the Provincetown Players), under the direction of writer-publisher Frank Shay. According to a local reviewer, the play *Wreckage,* adapted by Colin Campbell Clements and taken from a short story by Mary Heaton Vorse, "was technically unsuited to the stage." Her son Heaton Vorse volunteered his opinion that the play was a "mistake" and "horrible."

Despite what she wrote later in life, Mary O'Brien was but marginally involved in the activities of the Provincetown Players during the summer of 1916. Like Mabel Dodge, Mary distanced herself both psychologically and geographically. In August she left Provincetown on a writing assignment for *Outlook* to cover the miners' strike on the Mesabi Range in Minnesota and then the oil strike in Bayonne, New Jersey. In the fall of 1917, Mary Heaton Vorse turned momentarily from reporting about strikes to writing a successful sentimental serial in the *Metropolitan* on life in Greenwich Village's bohemia, *I've Come to Stay, A Love Comedy of Bohemia.* Her picture of the Village does not describe the raucous artists' balls, drinking parties, and midnight escapades that made the Village a legend, but portrays the "innocent tea-shop, kept by nice young girls." Her story is about the conventional people in the bohemian Village, those "children of the righteous" with a "Blue Serge Past." Mary's white-glove view of the Village was the antithesis of the fare presented by the Provincetown Players.

A printed card announced the 1916 season:

The Provincetown Players
Open their season, Thursday, July 13, 1916
at Mrs. O'Brien's wharf
with two new one-act plays:
Neith Boyce's "Winter Night"
and Jack Reed's Freedom[32]

"We gave a brilliant performance at our theatre last night—my *Winter's Night,* a play by Jack Reed, and one by Jig Cook! This bill (our first this season) ran for three nights to crowded houses . . . We give our next bill in two weeks and are all working like beavers." This letter of Neith Boyce to her father-in-law, dated July 16, 1916, corroborates the dates of the opening of the 1916 season on Mrs. O'Brien's wharf.[33] Neith's play was given first, as a tribute to her play *Constancy,* which had inaugurated the Players in 1915, followed by *Freedom* and a reprise of *Suppressed Desires.*

Winter's Night deals with death, rejection, and suicide. Its significance is its similarity to O'Neill's later play *Beyond the Horizon,* in which a brother gives up his beloved for his brother. The action follows Daniel Wescott's funeral. Daniel's brother Jacob, a bachelor, who has been a member of the household, confesses his love to the widow Rachel. "I loved you before he did," said Jacob. Rachel rejects him, stating: "And your brother hardly cold in his grave." Jacob shoots himself and is found by the third character, Sarah, poignantly played by the recent widow, Mary O'Brien, whose piercing scream ends the play.[34]

Neith Boyce wrote *Winter's Night* during the previous winter in Provincetown. She asked her friend, the writer Carl Van Vechten, for assistance: "I'm working on a scenario! Can you tell me where to get a book or something giving technical directions about it?"[35] While Neith was writing one scenario, Hutch was secretly pursuing Lucy, which gave rise to another scenario, *Enemies.* Neith and Hutch both wrote and acted in the two-character play *Enemies,* a frank and open discussion of their infidelities. Neith's lines in the play confront Hutch about his affair: "I didn't separate from you when you were running after the widow last winter—spending hours with her every day, dining with her and leaving me alone, and telling me she was the only woman who had ever understood you." When Hutch challenges her about her relationship with "Hank," saying that she is more alert and sociable with him, she counters with "He and I spend hours together looking at the sea—each of us absorbed in our own thoughts—without saying a word." Both realize that going their separate ways has caused "a gulf between us . . . We have destroyed one another—we are enemies." There is talk of divorce and separation but *Enemies* ends with a reconciliation. So too did Neith and Hutch come to a reconciliation in their marriage, for it lasted until death.

In early December Hutch had taken their daughter to New York City for a medical check-up. He wrote to Neith in Provincetown that he had seen Lucy Collier, who was "much in love" with her husband John, who nevertheless believed in open marriages. Hutch wrote that they talked about Neith: "[Lucy] thought you disturbingly beautiful—that when you walk it is like music to her—and that she wants to look at you all the time." A week later Hutch wrote to Neith: "I have fallen in love with Lucy Collier but not in the way I am with you! I'll tell you all about it when we meet." But Hutch took his time returning to Provincetown. Neith insisted that he return by Christmas. They quarreled, but they reached some understanding, as Hutch explained to Mabel: "Neith and I have had a very emotional time. Perfect frankness has brought us nearer together."[36]

The Lucy Collier affair was only one of a long line of infatuations for Hutch, who fell in love with women who were unhappy in their marriages, such as Mabel Dodge and Mary Pyne. He was Mabel Dodge's adviser when she was struggling to separate from Edwin Dodge. He was a sympathetic counselor to Mary Pyne when she was ill and virtually neglected by her husband, Harry Kemp. Susan Glaspell aptly characterized Hutch's ambivalence about love: "Hutch, who loves us when we are unhappy, and will make us unhappy in order to love him."[37]

Neith wrote in December: "So you confess to being 'in love' with Lucy. Suppose I told you I was 'in love'—oh, what thunders—sighs, sobs and curses you would emit." Neith's letters to other correspondents that winter were restrained and veiled like her fiction, exhibiting the Victorian womanly traits of long-suffering but steadfast devotion to caddish husbands. When Lucy Collier and her children came to Provincetown in 1916, Mabel Dodge claimed she stayed nearby Lucy so she could be a guardian of Hutch's morals. That summer the Hapgoods once again settled into their long, rocky, companionate marriage.

Jig Cook categorized *Enemies* as one of the genre of personal therapy plays. "He saw the theater as a 'laboratory of human emotion' and ran it so that the Players might be helped and developed personally by the work they performed."[38] *Enemies* was one of the plays that Mary O'Brien found excessively frank, along with *Constancy* and Jack Reed's *Eternal Quadrangle* (a discussion of free love). Hutch viewed Mary's isolation as part of a conspiracy and he personally set out to rectify the situation. In his opinion, the group was filled with "suspicion, bitterness, disappointment, and a certain instinct to destroy each other's personalities."[39]

Enemies and *Winter's Night* were subsequently staged in New York by the Players during their first two seasons, as was a new play by Neith Boyce, *The Two Sons*. In 1916 both Neith's and Hutch's careers were winding down; Neith at forty-four and Hutch at forty-seven were the oldest of the Players. "Two old people like us, we can't be thinking of such things."

Neith's words in *Winter's Night* alluded to their love affairs, but could well have applied to their waning creativity. Hutch was a journalist whose only association with the Wharf Theater was *Enemies*. "My only appearance on the stage of the Provincetown theatre was that one in the fish-house, when, in spite of careful drilling and the fact that I had written my lines myself, I could not remember them but was forced to read from the manuscript."[40] Hutch described his mood when he wrote to Mabel from Provincetown on July 1, 1916: "I am trying to compose a book on Religion, a social novel, a one-act play and an essay. Mostly preliminary brooding."

Hutch never did work regularly after World War I, except on his autobiography, which was published in the Thirties. Aging, disillusionment, and particularly the death of his first son during the 1918–19 influenza epidemic sapped his drive and enthusiasm. In his autobiography, Hutch blamed world conditions and other people, especially strong women, for his failures. A man who had started his career as a champion of rights for laborers, minorities, and women became in his later years a bitter anti-feminist.

During World War I, Neith's career was at its ebb, as were those of most women writers of popular fiction that depicted family trials and triumphs. She was momentarily inspired by the activities of the Little Theater Movement and may have continued as a playwright, had not she been devastated by the untimely death of her son. Jig Cook's appraisal was that "Neith was not of the theater, but we shall do nothing without Neith or her equivalent."[41] With commendable fortitude she published, in 1923, *Harry,* a paean to her son who—enamored with the West, and resisting education and career—died while working as a cowboy at seventeen years of age. Both Hapgoods died in their home in Provincetown: Hutch in 1944, Neith in 1951.

SUSAN GLASPELL WROTE *Trifles* in a matter of days. It was not only her best short play but also the best-crafted play presented on Lewis Wharf. The Players were running out of plays, so—with typical bravado—Jig turned to his wife: "I have announced a play of yours for the next bill." Forty-year-old Susan Glaspell, an accomplished novelist, short-story writer, and journalist—in order to placate her husband—turned her talents to an unfamiliar genre. Ten days after she had protested that she "did not know how to write a play," *Trifles* was ready for rehearsal.

For the story line, Glaspell reached back to her days as an Iowa reporter and created a murder mystery based on an actual court trial she had covered for the *Des Moines Daily News*. Glaspell recalled her moment of inspiration:

> So I went out on the wharf, sat alone on one of our wooden benches without a back, and looked a long time at the bare little stage. After a time the stage became a kitchen . . . then the door at the back opened, and people all bundled up came in . . . When I was a newspaper reporter out in Iowa, I was sent down-state to do a murder trial, and I never forgot going into the kitchen of a woman locked up in town. I had meant to do it as a short story, but the stage took it for its own.[42]

In *Trifles*, Glaspell takes a cold, disquieting look at the desperate pain of isolation. On the surface, *Trifles* is a suspenseful murder mystery about a farmer's wife who strangles her husband. On a deeper level, it depicts a lonely woman's humiliation and desperation after years of marital abuse. The story is told sympathetically from a woman's viewpoint. The male characters, a sheriff and a county attorney, in a search for clues, overlook the trifles—the accusatory details that implicate the distraught wife. The men are blind to the trail of clues that point to motive: dirty towels, unbaked bread, neglected sewing, and the final trifles—a mangled bird cage and—in the wife's sewing box—the bird with its neck broken. It was the husband's final brutality, the killing of the bird, that precipitated the murder. What subtle clues the men had ignored, the sheriff's wife intuitively sensed, and, to protect the farmer's wife, she hides the conclusive evidence, the dead bird. Parallel to the feminist theme is the exploration of the cause of the woman's madness—the devastatingly harsh and lonely Iowa farmland, characterized as "a lonesome place and always was."

Glaspell later rewrote *Trifles*, with few changes, as a short story retitled *A Jury of Her Peers*. Among her fifty or more short stories, this is considered her best. Glaspell had a long, disciplined writing career. She told a reporter, "I work every day with regularity from nine till one, unless I am all keyed up, and then I am afraid I forget about time." In addition to her short stories, Glaspell wrote nine novels and fourteen plays. *Allison's House,* a play based on the life of Emily Dickinson, won a Pulitzer Prize in 1931. Lawrence Langner described her as a "delicate woman with sad eyes and a sweet smile, who seemed as fragile as old lace, until you talked with her and glimpsed the steel lining beneath the tender surface."[43]

Susan Glaspell understood isolation and loneliness. After her marriage and the resultant self-imposed exile from her family, Glaspell poignantly wrote of separation from her native Davenport. Although she lived thirty-five years by the Atlantic Ocean, she never left her native landscape. As a nostalgic reminder, she kept in her Provincetown parlor the spinning wheel of her grandmother, who had made the trip from Maine to Iowa in a prairie schooner.

Glaspell's attachment to inland America is reminiscent of Thoreau's attachment to inland Concord. When Thoreau wrote "I have travelled a good deal in Concord," he affirmed his attachment to his native landscape, his inspiration. Most of Glaspell's novels are set in the Midwest, with the exception of *Judd Rankin's Daughter,* which takes place both in Provincetown and in the Midwest. She wrote in this novel that "The Cape was a narrow strip of land out in the sea and she came from land that was wide and deep." In 1948 Glaspell died alone in her Provincetown house, a house that is sited facing away from the sea.

Susan Glaspell's house still stands on Commercial Street, while across the street only a few pilings remain of Lewis Wharf. Although the Players continued on until 1929, Glaspell believed that it was in 1922 that "The Provincetown Players ended their story." Sue and Jig frequently walked to the end of Lewis Wharf and sat in the evening, looking out over the harbor. One evening after the 1916 play season, Jig sat on the wharf and said that he "was thinking about raft boats on the Mississippi."

Jig missed his homeland as well as his farm. As Glaspell wrote: "[Provincetown] was outermost land, was sparse. But out there growing was taken for granted and here was always the wonder that things should be growing at all." The first thing Jig did in Provincetown was to plant a garden, despite the old Cape Codder who warned him that only beach grass grows on the shore. Glaspell jubilantly wrote on May 8, 1913 to the O'Briens in Europe: "Do you think we are going to offer you lettuce picked up off a vegetable wagon? Oh, not so. Out of our own kitchen door will we step . . . and from our own beautiful garden pluck the choicest offerings . . . The cauliflower is already up, and so are the peas."[44]

What Provincetown meant to the Cooks, in Jig's words, was a "place of great erotic freedom."[45] Jig sculpted a sundial base with four nude female figures, representing

Dawn, Noon, Sunset, and the North Star, and boldly placed it in his yard. This sundial is featured in the Cooks' collaborative play, *Tickless Time*. Provincetown meant friendships and parties but, unfortunately—according to Jig—distractions and "petty jealousies." The Cooks bought another house, ten miles away in Truro, where Jig had his farm and Sue a quiet place to work. She eventually built a shack "for work, and work alone. That kind of thing is good, especially for women. . . . A maid will feel she can interrupt a woman where she wouldn't dream of interrupting a man."[46]

Although Glaspell wrote plays reluctantly, she quickly became a remarkable craftsman. She also directed and acted in many of her own plays. William Zorach recalled that she was a "marvelous actress . . . she had that rare power and quality inherent in great actresses. She had only to be on the stage and the play and the audience came alive."[47] *Trifles* has been widely translated and has remained over the years one of the most popular one-act American plays, a particular favorite with small theater groups. In texts on dramatic technique, it is considered a model of a well-crafted one-act play.

For her love of Jig, Sue had relinquished Davenport and her status as "Davenport's leading novelist." In regard to the Provincetown Players, she wrote, "I gave up practically everything else, though I had an established position as a novelist."[48] Nevertheless, she did her best writing while married to Jig. Her previous fiction stories were sentimental, the type popular in women's magazines, and the kind that Mary Vorse and Neith Boyce also wrote. Susan's best short stories were written between 1916 and 1919, during the same period of time she was writing plays for the Provincetown Players. She wrote only one novel, *Fidelity*, while married to Jig; it dealt with falling in love with a married man, a venting of her ambiguous feelings about Jig. When she resumed writing novels in the late 1920s, her technique had improved, with better characterization and dramatic plot, while her settings and themes continued to deal with the Midwest. Her fiction, however, was never as experimental as her plays.

O'Neill's plays, *Bound East for Cardiff* and *Thirst,* and Glaspell's *Trifles* differed from the other 1916 summer fare presented on Lewis Wharf. Theirs were realistic plays that dealt with universal themes; the others were bohemian spoofs and didactic social dramas. With *Trifles,* Glaspell joined O'Neill in a new, exclusive movement toward realism in the theater. She, however, recognized the limitation of this type of theater, as she wrote: "In the theatre there is unquestionably a desire for the best. Yet the things of the mind and spirit will never have the same popularity as the bedroom farce."[49] Significantly, when Glaspell sat on Lewis Wharf and looked for inspiration, she did not turn to the romantic past of whaling nor to bohemian sophistry but to a grim assessment of loneliness, the theme of *Trifles:* "It's a lonesome place and always was."

As a Provincetown Player, Glaspell was second only to O'Neill in introducing innovative themes and techniques to American drama. When O'Neill's success in 1920 took him to Broadway, Glaspell was the mainstay of the Provincetown Players. Glaspell offered early guidance and inspiration to the young O'Neill. One of the reasons O'Neill moved to Provincetown was to take advantage of the professional resources that Jig and Susan Cook provided. In the beginning, Gene spent so much time consulting with Susan that his new wife, Agnes Boulton, became jealous: "She seemed to me an ethereal being, detached and yet passionate." Susan's quiet, intellectual competence appealed especially to men. O'Neill, who never forgot much—whether it was an insult or praise—later paid a small tribute to Glaspell. In an dedicatory inscription to her in a 1931 edition of *Mourning Becomes Electra,* he wrote: "For Susan Glaspell, Congratulations on winning the Pulitzer Prize. An honor long overdue!!"[50]

AS THE LEGEND GOES, Susan Glaspell met Terry Carlin on Commercial Street near Snow's boathouse, where he and Gene were staying, and asked him if he had a play to bring to her house for an 8:00 P.M. reading. After the first bill, which consisted of *Winter's Night, Freedom,* and *Suppressed Desires,* the troupe had nearly exhausted their repertoire and were searching for new plays and playwrights. Carlin replied that he did not write, but that his friend O'Neill had a trunk full of plays. Gene took *Bound East for Cardiff* to the meeting, and—in Hutch's version, as related in his autobiography—gave the play to Neith, who in turn took it to Jig and said, "We have got to do this play." As the actor, Teddy Ballantine, read the play, Gene sat on the floor in an adjoining room, perfectly silent, and listened. In *The Road to the Temple,* Glaspell recalled that when the reading had finished, the group enthusiastically descended on Gene; "then [we] knew what we were for."

Less than two weeks elapsed between the reading in the Glaspell house and the premiere of *Bound East.* During that time O'Neill was writing daily to his love interest, Beatrice Ashe, who was in New London, and also was writing love poems to Louise Bryant in Provincetown. In addition, he had started the comedy, *Now I Ask You.* In his letter postmarked July 25, 1916 (Beatrice had asked Gene not to mail his daily notes, but to send a weekly letter), he said that *Bound East* was to be produced next Friday and Saturday nights. "The cast is good—several professionals are summering here . . . The theatre is a delightfully quaint place—an old storehouse on the end of a long dock owned by Mary Heaton

192

Vorse, the writer. Of course, we make all our own scenery, music, costumes, etc. Have people in the Players who are up on all those things."

Wilbur Daniel Steele's letter of July 28, 1916, to his parents establishes the date of the premiere of O'Neill's *Bound East for Cardiff.* "It has been the most terrible spell of muggy, rainy weather . . . Today the wind has shifted and the sun is out." The fog that rolled in that night to heighten the ambience for O'Neill's sea play contributed nothing to Steele's farce. "The crowd is putting on three one-act plays tonight at a place on the wharf, and I have one of them."[51] Steele's own play, *Not Smart,* was a light, didactic comedy. The other two were Louise Bryant's *The Game* and O'Neill's *Bound East for Cardiff.*

That Friday night on Lewis Wharf was not a particularly momentous event for Steele, as it was for O'Neill. Steele's letter continues: "I've been up to my topknot in business—finishing a story to send off, etc." Steele grudgingly took time from his main business, writing short stories, for he was struggling out of his apprenticeship. In the words of his protagonist in *Not Smart:* "My affairs are in a delicate condition . . . It's a confounded precarious period in my career." Steele's first story had been published in 1910, his first novel in 1914, and he was on the threshold of establishing himself as one of the best-known short-story writers in America. Theater for him was then incidental.

Steele was not at all happy about the rehearsals: "I've been busy seeing that it got rehearsed and all. Margaret [Steele] is the leading lady, and is doing well. Mary [O'Brien] is another character, and Margaret's cousin Nani Bailey is the third. Teddy Ballantine of the Washington Square Players of New York is the only male actor. And he doesn't understand the part, and the whole thing falls flat (it's a comedy supposedly) and I am in despair. I'll never do another."

Not Smart was presented twice more, in 1918 and 1919, by the Provincetown Players in New York. It was viewed as "somewhat dated and shopworn"[52] by that time, especially so because it was on the same bill as *Aria Da Capo,* an innovative play by Edna St. Vincent Millay. The setting of *Not Smart* is Provincetown, a locale frequently used by Steele in his early fiction. The title itself was a local euphemism for being pregnant out of wedlock. The play criticizes the hypocrisy of bohemians who preach free love and unlicensed morality until faced with its consequences. The male lead character describes the maid, a native, as a "splendid, deep-bosomed ox-eyed, earth-woman" until he himself is suspected of being the father of her unborn child; then, conversely, the "not smart" maid becomes "the coarse, heavy, dull-witted *animal*!"

Steele was a naturalistic writer, much like Vorse, and resisted the trend toward realism. While Steele rarely wrote about himself, there are autobiographical elements in *Not Smart:* the main character is a struggling artist on the threshold of a successful career, torn between the new liberal behaviors and older ethical mores. Steele never really stopped being a minister's son. His stories are didactic and moralistic. He became an extremely popular author, but never gained literary recognition because his stories lacked originality in structure and content. His appeal was to the middle-class reader who liked escape stories with aphoristic endings.

Steele, unsuccessfully, tried to model his stories after those of Joseph Conrad, who was also an early model for O'Neill. A typical Steele melodramatic story about Provincetown fishermen, *A White Horse Winter,* was published in 1912. It was filled with shipwrecks, drownings, and poverty-level struggles for survival. Despite his moralistic stance, Steele was like many of his contemporaries when it came to holding patronizing attitudes toward the new immigrants.

"I seem to be pretty much the common or garden variety person . . . My main desire is to have the moon." Steele was the ideal of American manhood—ruggedly handsome, athletic, charming, responsible, and successful. Whatever slight bohemian leanings he started with were discouraged by his aristocratic Boston wife, Margaret Thurston. She particularly disliked the amatory hi-jinks of the East End crowd. On one occasion, when rebuffed by Margaret, Jig sent Wilbur an explanation of his behavior: "Tell Margaret that the night the Spring busted uptown I wrote her a forty page letter of gratitude for remembering my savage love."[53] In 1923, the Steeles were driven out of Provincetown by their distaste for the illegal activities during Prohibition, to them a time of unlicensed behavior and "Flaming Youth." The most rebellious thing Wilbur ever did was to defy his parent's wishes by changing from his early career as an artist to that of a writer. His son Peter remembered him as shy, non-political, and loving a party.

JACK REED'S SATIRE, *Freedom,* was first staged on July 13 on Lewis Wharf, then on August 24 in Town Hall, as part of the Beachcombers' entertainment. (It was not staged on Knowles Wharf in the Beachcombers Club, as has usually been reported.) *Freedom* was the only play of the 1916 season not staged on Lewis Wharf. The other plays—which the *Advocate* called futuristic—dealt with cannibalism, extramarital sex and pregnancy, Freudianism, and religious satire, themes that would hardly have been acceptable fare at Town Hall.

Freedom is a satire of romanticism, particularly romantic poseurs. There are four prisoners in the play (Poet, Romancer, Smith, and Trusty). After years of plotting to escape, each character finds reasons not to leave prison. The

Poet, who has won his reputation as a prison-poet, paradoxically says, "For God's sake, how can I write about freedom when I'm free?"[54] Although the cast was not named in the newspaper article, there is a strong possibility that, in addition to Reed himself, some of the joint members of the Players Club and the Beachcombers Club acted in *Freedom:* Bror Nordfeldt, Jig Cook, Freddie Burt, and Wilbur Daniel Steele. Nordfeldt did the staging for the New York production of *Freedom* and may have also done the same for the Provincetown productions.

Freedom, with its subtleties and paradoxes, may not have been fully understood by the Town Hall audience. The only comment made by the *Advocate* reporter was that it was "well received," hardly a rave notice. Lines in *Freedom,* such as, "a block of stone heaves out of the wall, falling silently on the bed" and "I was trying to break into a padded cell so I could be free" were oxymorons, no doubt lost on the audience, already pumped up by a preceding minstrel show and a marathon evening of entertainment. "In addition to the minstrel [show and] numerous songs . . . there will be a one-act play entitled *Freedom* by Jack Reed. Then Harold Browne and Domingo Zamorra, of Spain, will dance some Spanish dances . . . There will also be a Grand Finale Scene, which is being kept as a surprise."[55] The minstrel show was directed by Frederick Burt, a sculptor in the Modern Art School and actor for the Players. There were jokes and solo musical performances by the artists; for example, the artist George Elmer Browne sang "Camptown Races" and Charles Hawthorne sang "Old Folks at Home."

After intermission and an interlude by the Provincetown Symphony Orchestra, *Freedom* was presented.[56] "The Beachcombers minstrel show of last Thursday evening's presentation was hailed with delight by a crowded house.

High praise for orchestra and singers (soloists and chorus members) is still resounding and folks are still talking of the clean cut quips and jokes of end men and their brethren of the semicircle. 'Freedom,' Jack Reed's play was well received. In fact, every number of the long program 'took' with the audience."[57]

The *Boston Globe* (August 12, 1916) covered both the Players' Club and the Beachcombers Club in one article, "Laboratory of the Drama on Cape Cod's Farthest Wharf," commenting that the Beachcombers Club "meets for fun," while the Players are a "pretty serious group."

> The art colony here, which includes several hundred painters of all grades, a few sculptors, about a dozen etchers, and a number of writers, actors and playwrights have two clubs— the Players' Club and the Beachcombers—both unique and decidedly unconventional . . . the theatre of the Players beats anything that even a Western mining camp in the freshness of a boom could boast, and the clubhouse of the Beachcombers . . . is not many steps in advance of the theatre.

In 1916 Jack Reed was reassessing and trying to restructure his life. He was overworked, severely in debt, having nightmares about his war experiences, and despondent over an impending kidney operation. He was also mourning the death of the poet Alan Seeger, a Harvard classmate, who had been killed on the Western Front. Reed was helping with a memorial edition of Seeger's poems, which included the famous "I Have a Rendezvous with Death." "Fog," a poem written in 1916 in Provincetown, illustrates his morbidity, an unusual mood for the buoyant, optimistic Reed:

> Death comes like this, I know—
> Snow-soft and gently cold . . .

And yet I know beyond the fog is naught
But lonely bell across gray wastes of sea.[58]

Jack reacted in an erratic, manic way to stress. Within a three-month period, he bought two properties in Truro, a house in Croton, New York, and married Louise Bryant—all the while going further into debt. "He was always coming or going. He would enter a room, hitching up his trousers, rough and ready—with big eyes, and he-man shoulders—which he would shrug with an amusing coyness."[59] That summer Reed was "coming and going" at an accelerated rate, but he had lost some of his "three-dimensional self-confidence" and "Gargantuan gall."[60] He was travelling, writing articles on the political conventions and on Henry Ford, and turning out several potboilers for *Collier's* and *Metropolitan* to help support his family in Oregon. It is amazing that he also found time to write serious poetry and participate in the summer theatricals.

In *Freedom,* Reed satirized the poet-poseur, a way of exorcising his own poetic self. Reed had become, in a remarkably short time, one of America's best-known war correspondents. He had reported brilliantly on the Mexican war (1913) and the war in Eastern and Western Europe (1914–15), yet he lamented his loss of poetic grace. "But please God I intend to get back to poetry and sweetness, some way."[61] There was no turning back. Susan recalled the last time she saw Jack Reed at his house in Truro:

> Once more, after we knew Jack would not return to this house, we took the old road, sat under his big tree, and thought of one evening we sat there with Jack, talked with him for the last time. "I wish I could stay here," he said. "Maybe it will surprise you, but what I really want is to

write poetry." We said it didn't surprise us, and "Why don't you?" I asked. But he shook his head, at once troubled, saying he had "promised too many people."[62]

Mabel Dodge paid homage to Reed's abandoned dream in 1936 when she dedicated her *Movers and Shakers* to his memory, "For Jack Reed the Poet." Greenwich Village's Golden Boy saw Russia, as he had first seen the Village, through a magic casement. In Russia, "Houses are always open; people are always visiting each other at all hours of the day and night." Jack Reed searched for the ideal community, found it, and then lost it in the Soviet experiment.

Jig Cook also searched for an ideal community, a Hellenic one, and for a while found it with the Provincetown Players, which for him represented a revival of the Greek spirit. When Jig became disillusioned with the Players, he essentially exiled himself to Greece, as Jack had exiled himself to Russia. In their self-imposed countries of exile, both died prematurely: Jack in Russia of typhoid, Jig in Greece of glanders. Overwork contributed to Jack's death, while excessive drinking hastened Jig's. Both were given honorable burials by their adopted countries. Jack was interred in the wall of the Kremlin that is reserved for a select few non-Russian heroes, and Jig was buried in a graveyard in Delphi near the temple of Apollo. But for the summer of 1916 and part of the winter of 1916–17, Jack and Jig shared the same dream of community, the Provincetown Players. Both were enthusiasts and expediters. Neither realized his ultimate dream of achieving poetic greatness or of creating an ideal community.

IF ANYONE HAD ANY DOUBT on that Friday evening, September 1, 1916, that Eugene O'Neill and Louise Bryant were lovers, all doubt was erased after their explicit, passionate performance in *Thirst*. O'Neill's second premiere was part of the final bill, along with reprises of Bryant's *The Game* and the Cooks' *Suppressed Desires*. Although O'Neill's lines were few for his role as a West Indian mulatto sailor, it was his largest part ever as an actor. Bryant had urged the extremely withdrawn O'Neill to take the role. Physically he was well cast, for it was the end of the summer and he had tanned to his usual deep mahogany. The other two characters—a Dancer performed by Bryant and a Gentleman acted by Cook—were white. Bryant claimed that her inspiration for the dancer's bangled costume came from suggestions by the local Portuguese.[63]

Although *Thirst* had been written three years before its staging, art copied life in the enactment of a seduction on Lewis Wharf. The O'Neill–Bryant affair began that summer and lasted for nearly two years, even after they had married other people. *Thirst* was written a year after the sinking of the *Titanic*. Likewise, in the play, the ship sinks "with a horrible dull crack." The action of *Thirst* takes place on a life raft that carries three survivors who are plagued by thirst, exposure, and lurking sharks. Although melodramatic, with stilted dialogue and gestures, O'Neill's one-act play did break new ground in that it dealt with unusual themes—cannibalism and interracial sex. After the dancer dies, the mulatto tries to devour the corpse: "We will live now . . . We shall eat." He is stopped by the gentleman; they struggle and both fall into shark-infested waters. There is a seduction scene in which the dancer (Louise) tries to entice the sailor (Gene) to give her water, which he doesn't have: "I have promised to love *you*— a Negro sailor—if you will give me one small drink of water." In addition to pretentious dialogue, there are melodramatic gestures: "his body grows tense and it seems as if he is about to sweep her into his arms."

Edna Kenton, a long-time colleague of Jig Cook, who persuaded her to come down from New York for the final bill, recalled in *Greek Coins* that the backdrop for *Thirst* "was a simple shift—a mere throwing back of the two great doors at the rear; and, behold, the living sea dancing with light, its sound and space and all but its waters pouring in through the height and breadth of the stage." From all contemporary accounts, Louise and Gene overplayed this overblown melodrama. Mabel Dodge recalled that Louise had offered to play her role of the Dancer in the nude. There is no record of any subsequent production of *Thirst,* nor any record of its being reviewed. The volume, *Thirst and Other One Act Plays,* containing the eponymous play *Thirst,* was, however, reviewed by Clayton Hamilton in the *Bookman,* April 1915, with the comment: "This writer's favorite mood is one of horror."

Louise Bryant was a handsome, vivacious Irish girl from Oregon. She claimed kinship to Oscar Wilde, and married, in turn, John Reed and William Bullitt, a U.S. ambassador to Russia. Bryant aggressively pursued O'Neill, as she had Reed six months before. Louise Bryant was bold, bright, beautiful and ambitious; she wanted it all—success, money and passion. The summer of 1916 she had it all: the security provided by Jack Reed; the professional recognition gained from the staging of her play, *The Game;* the publication of her poems and articles in the *Masses;* and the passionate love of Eugene O'Neill.

Louise Bryant was still married to Paul A. Trullinger, a handsome, liberal and wealthy dentist in Portland, Oregon, when she boldly staged a meeting with Jack Reed on his trip to Portland in December 1915. Daring and emotionally ruthless, Louise made demands that her lovers usually met. Even after her marriage to Trullinger, she kept a separate studio in downtown Portland, with a separate directory listing herself as an editor and artist. Louise had contributed her poetry to *Blast,* a San Francisco anarchist weekly, and was trying to insinuate her writing into the radical Greenwich Village magazine, the *Masses.* What better way than to enlist the help of Jack Reed, the celebrated journalist and the Golden Boy of the Village. After arranging to meet Jack, seemingly by chance, on the streets of Portland, she persuaded him to visit her studio to hear her poetry. Jack said he fell in love again, instantaneously and—he thought—safely with a married woman, as was his habit.

Jack perceived Louise as a female version of himself: "I think I've found her at last . . . She's two years younger than I, wild and brave and straight, and graceful and lovely to look at . . . Refuses to be bound . . . an artist, a rampant, joyous, individualist, a poet and a revolutionary."[64] (Actually, Louise was nearly two years older than Jack.) After two passionate weeks in Portland, Jack left for New York. Louise wrote him torrid, explicit love letters, and then followed him to the Village less than two weeks after his departure. She left Portland wearing a corsage of fresh violets from her husband.

Louise moved into Jack's apartment at 43 Washington Square South and into his life, eschewing the separate room Jack had rented for her. Jack took Louise for extensive walks in the Village, and introduced her to his friends, Max Eastman and Floyd Dell, editors of the *Masses,* who shortly thereafter published her articles and poems, as she had intended. With typical generosity, Jack opened up his wallet. In her unpublished memoirs, Louise recalled her time with Jack. "He was one of the most popular writers in America . . . one of the highest paid . . . We used to spend it as he made it. There was a common familiar purse. I could always go to it and take what I wanted and no questions were ever asked."[65]

When Louise was confronted with the ultimate choice

between Jack Reed and Eugene O'Neill, she chose Reed, for O'Neill was impoverished and was living off an allowance from his father. He had promise, but no income. Jack, on the other hand, was near the peak of his earning power. Louise's other husbands were also financially well-off; Paul Trullinger was from a wealthy family, as was William Bullitt.

In her memoirs, Bryant describes the summer of 1916 at 592 Commercial Street. She rejected the first summer cottage she looked at: "I couldn't live in [it] because of the wallpaper . . . finally found another on the seashore with its own little beach, in an excellent location, and all furnished." Across the street from the Reed cottage was a beach access, and east of that was Snow's boat house, "a shack where the fishermen hung up their nets, that no one was using," recalled Bryant. There, in June, O'Neill and Terry Carlin encamped and "lived like sailors, slept in hammocks and lived most of the time out-of-doors, with their door open wide to the sea."

Louise lounged about day and night in her bathing suit, sometimes sleeping in it, rarely changing into her one other outfit, white linens and a red cape. Much of her time on the beach was spent with Gene. According to Louise, Hippolyte warned her against associating with "those two bums," but Louise fed them and took it upon herself to keep O'Neill sober. Bryant was then one of the few teetotalers in the group. Perhaps it was because her father had been an alcoholic. Later, she herself became an alcoholic and died as such in Sevres, France, alone and rejected by her divorced husband, William Bullitt.

Bryant's conquest of O'Neill may have begun as an attempt to pique Reed. Though in love with Bryant, Reed was again forestalling commitment. Louise was writing him frequent letters and enticingly included in one a nude photo of herself, taken in Provincetown on the sand dunes. She inscribed on the back: "This is to remind you of the Dunes & all the nice months after the Convention."

O'Neill arrived in Provincetown about June 15 or shortly thereafter, for on this date the *Dorothy Bradford* made the first trip of the season from Boston. This was approximately a week before Jack Reed's return to town on June 21. However slight the interest Louise may initially have had in Gene, it doubtless blossomed after the enthusiastic reception in July of *Bound East for Cardiff*. So while Jack Reed dictated to his English secretary, Fred Boyd, about political conventions and the meaning of war, Louise took Gene under her wing, fed him, encouraged his sobriety, and promoted his acting, his poetry, and his interest in her.

Any woman with social aspirations toward the summer crowd in Provincetown had to contend with Mary O'Brien, in Hutch's words, the "historical pioneer." Margaret Steele and Mabel Dodge had both lost out to Mary O'Brien and were in virtual exile—Margaret located way-up-along, to the West End of town, and Mabel miles away over the dunes at Peaked Hill. Wisely enough, neither Neith Boyce nor Susan Glaspell tried to compete. To Mary's dismay, Louise set up a coterie of male admirers in the East End of town. Louise's beauty was her best leverage. William Carlos Williams, in his autobiography, describes Louise's arresting, sensuous look:

> [She] had on a heavy, very heavy, white silk skirt so woven that it hung over the curve of her buttocks like the strands of a glistening waterfall. There could have been nothing under it, for it followed the very crease between the buttocks in its fall.[66]

Louise Bryant's unpublished memoirs were written toward the end of her life when she was dissipated and often irrational. Her comments were in part exaggerated. She said that *Thirst* "wasn't much of a success . . . I put on *The Game* which was the first modern play in America. Marguerite and William Zorach made the setting. Jack played the part of Death. Zorach the part of Youth, Kitty Cannell played the part of Life. Jack was a fine, rollicking Death." She did not comment on the reception of her morality play, which paled next to Gene's psychologically tense *Bound East for Cardiff*. *The Game* was staged twice on Lewis Wharf, in July and September.

The Game is a stilted morality play in which the game of dice is played by Life and Death for the lives of Youth and Girl. What is remembered about the play is not the script, but the cubist sets and costume designs created by the Zorachs. Actors in costume looked like Egyptian reliefs, while "the backdrop was a decorative and abstract pattern of the sea, trees, the moon, and the moon path in the water designed by Marguerite."[67]

To the west of the beach where Gene and Terry camped out was the rented summer cottage of Max and Ida Eastman, where they stayed "in a small white house that turned its back on the main street in order to face the bay." From outward appearances the Eastmans, who recently had marked the birth of a son, seemed content; in reality, they were on the verge of separating. Max was in love with a younger woman and was not fully in touch with the activities of the summer.

In his autobiography, *Enjoyment of Living,* Eastman recalled that his contribution to the Provincetown Players was "willfully slight." "In Provincetown I did little but pay my dues and stroll around the wharf sometimes at rehearsals." His personal bitterness colored his perceptions of the Village crowd. He was highly critical of the anarchists Terry Carlin, "a thin, dark, handsome, hawklike type," and Hippolyte Havel, a "long-haired, owl-eyed, irrepressibly intellectual" man, who exploited their anarchistic beliefs to justify loafing, in Eastman's opinion. He was also uneasy with Louise and her coterie. [She] was "no housekeeper, and their place was barnlike," with "a large assortment of interesting males." Eugene O'Neill was "darkly handsome but somber and sallow as a down-and-outer brought to Jesus by the Salvation Army."

As part of her amorous pursuit of O'Neill, Bryant tried to get O'Neill published. She began with Max Eastman, then chief editor of the *Masses,* whose summer cottage was conveniently located just across the street. He was indifferent to O'Neill's and Bryant's poems, so she sent them on to New York to Floyd Dell, the assistant editor, who was captivated by Louise. Floyd liked Louise's poems: "Those six poems hit me hard. I think they are almost terribly beautiful—like Greek fragments." Gene's poems he rejected, ostensibly because they were dated. Floyd wrote, "I don't think people who date their poems are very much."[68] Bryant's poems were published in the October 1916 issue of the *Masses.*

Eastman's "Provincetown" appeared in the same October 1916 issue of the *Masses.* It is a testament to his depression.

> A summer town where all the folks are old.
>   The fishers old with labor, and the rest
>   With Life, or Art, or some exotic thing.
> A simple child who loved to run and laugh
> And look among the pebbles, and play ball,
>   Were lonely-hearted here. The gulls cry sadly
>   As their shadows drift across the sand.

The poems that Louise and Gene wrote that summer chronicled their affair, for they resounded to the same incidents.

Bryant's "To a Swimmer":

Ah me!
When sun and wind
And the water . . . caress you
How can I who am flesh, withhold
My love?[69]

O'Neill's "On the Dunes":

Your body is warm and undulating
As the sand dunes
Eager with tremulous heat waves.
Beneath the kisses of my desire
Your passions reach upward
Their quivering fingers.
I shall come to you
In the delirium of noon.

Laughter of spray
Dancing on exultant wave-crests . . .
Consummation and peace . . .
When the sea
Becomes one with the sky, . . .[70]

Even the titles of O'Neill's unpublished poems "On the Dunes" and "Tides," as well as Bryant's published "Beach Grass" and "To a Swimmer," strongly suggest that they were sharing a common experience and that their clandestine meetings—like those of other lovers before them—were on the oceanside dunes, away from the crowd. O'Neill's "I shall come to you / In the delirium of noon" echoes Bryant's "Midnight . . . the grey hours / When I cannot touch you or hear your voice."

Max Eastman was perhaps deluded in thinking that

Louise was only interested in Gene because of his writings and because she wanted to help him stop drinking. His assumptions may have stemmed from his conversations with Jack Reed. Jack and Max were close associates and were engaged in the same class war being waged on the pages of the *Masses*. Max admired Jack, his daring and belligerency: he actually liked battle; he liked dust and smoke. In 1917 Jack dedicated his poems *Tamburlaine* to Max. Sometimes their mutual admiration led to good-natured rivalry. Jack "climbed up to the peak of our fishhouse theatre, and dived off into the bay. The wharf was high, and the fish house higher, and he reaped quite a reward of admiration for a casual and graceful dive." When Max attempted the same dive the next day, he failed "to notice that the tide was running out." He hit the bottom and for several days "could not move [his] head or any muscle in [his] back without excruciating pain."[71]

Jack also promoted Gene's career. He gave Max two of Gene's poems, "The Louse" and "Submarine." Presumably, Louise gave these to Jack after Floyd Dell had rejected Gene's love poems, "Tides" and "On the Dunes." "The Louse" condemns the idler who lives on the blood of workers and the workers who are stupefied by the braying of their leaders. "The Louse" was not accepted. "Submarine," however, appeared in the February 1917 *Masses*. It was not political, as "The Louse" was, but instead revealed a misanthropic poet:

> My soul is a submarine
> My aspirations are torpedoes
> I will hide unseen
> Beneath the surface of life
> Watching for ships . . .
> I will destroy them
> Because the sea is beautiful . . .

It is not entirely clear how much Jack knew about the extent of the Louise–Gene affair, how much he believed the rumors, or how much he cared. As Jack did with most controversy, he defiantly met it head-on. He wrote a farce, *The Eternal Quadrangle*, that was performed on August 8 as part of the third bill. Jack was not demure about his love affairs. Free love was fair game to the true bohemian, and Jack and Louise were archetypical bohemians. *The Eternal Quadrangle: A Farce Adapted from the Wiener-Schnitzler* poked fun at marriage, the double standard, and cuckoldry.

The main character, played by Jig Cook, is a stock market magnate, wedded to business and happy to share his wife with lovers. The wife was played by Louise Bryant. The dramatic crisis occurs when the maid informs the husband that his wife is tiring of her latest lover and another one must be found. Reed played Archibald, the butler, who is selected as the substitute lover, a perfect choice, according to the script, because: "He's shallow, clever with a sort of Broadway cleverness, rough with women, and has a kind of barbaric rhythm about him like ragtime." Reed as Archibald performed some "fancy roller skating" on Lewis Wharf. The wife, however, sees Archibald as a Nietzschian or Shavian who wants to mold women. The denouement gives women the edge: "It is for us Superwomen to make men what they will be." *Eternal Quadrangle* gave approval to free love. It was Reed's explicit statement to the gossipmongers that he was aware of Bryant's interest in O'Neill. And so the triangular love affair continued.

EUGENE O'NEILL JOINED IN on the summer's confessional hijinks. Uncharacteristically for a tragedian, he wrote a full-length comedy, *Now I Ask You, a Three Act Farce-Comedy*. (*Ah, Wilderness!* is O'Neill's only other comedy; for him it expressed "a nostalgia for a youth I never had.") In *Now I Ask You*, O'Neill satirized a quadrangular love relationship, much as Reed had in the *Eternal Quadrangle*. The four main characters in *Now I Ask You* are composites of himself, Louise, and Jack. Louise Bryant is depicted in his play as Lucy Ashleigh, "an intelligent healthy American girl suffering from an overdose of undigested reading and has mistaken herself for the heroine of a Russian novel," and Leonora Barnes, a bohemian artist who wears a painter's smock and sandals on her bare feet, rolls her own cigarettes, and asks to be called "Leo." Lucy resembles Louise in appearance, "a slender, beautiful girl with large eyes," but Leonora has Louise's flair and ultra-sophisticated manner and "no moral scruples." Gabriel, the impoverished poet with "long black hair and big soulful eyes," is O'Neill's depiction of himself.

Not until the end of the play is it revealed that the Village couple who have been living together for two years have also been married during all that time. They concealed their marriage (as Louise and Jack Reed would conceal theirs), partly because in Greenwich Village marriage was considered bourgeois. Marriage was for propagating and, in O'Neill's words, "artists shouldn't propagate." Lucy reluctantly married Tom Drayton (a close rendering of Jack Reed), a sensible, likeable businessman, "about thirty with large, handsome features." Lucy and Tom and Leo and Gabriel change partners and then revert to their original partners. Delusion sets in quickly when emotions are allowed to run free. O'Neill describes the dangers and ironies of unlicensed love. Free love "is less free than marriage," because one is open to the "malicious badgering and interference of all the moral busy-bodies."

O'Neill's comedy has a socially acceptable denouement. Both the bohemian and the suburban couples stay married to their original spouses. In his July 25, 1916, letter to Beatrice Ashe, O'Neill wrote, "[I will tell] you all about the place and the celebrities and their scandalous lives." There is no record of his having done so, but where he did deal with the bohemians was in his play.

For O'Neill, illicit affairs were difficult for him to handle; he was quick to marry his lovers, beginning with his clandestine first marriage. He married his second wife, Agnes Boulton, within weeks after they started living together in Provincetown; and in turn married Carlotta Monterey as soon as he was divorced from Agnes. Gene was physically attracted to Louise, to her Irishness and to her passion: "When Louise touches me with the tip of her little finger it's like a flame."[72] But he was put off by her unconventionality.

According to O'Neill's biographer, Louis Sheaffer, Louise most probably had an abortion while Reed was in the hospital and O'Neill most likely was the father. Louise was under a doctor's care, and, according to Sheaffer, "Various things suggest that her illness was an abortion."[73] O'Neill had agonized over the pregnancy of Kathleen Jenkins, whom he married despite his father's disapproval; likewise he was remorseful about abandoning Agnes Boulton and their children, Shane and Oona. Despite the intensity of his feelings, it is doubtful that he could have devoted himself wholeheartedly to Louise. Even at the beginning of the affair, O'Neill was ambivalent and acted out his emotions in contradictory ways. He was simultaneously writing love poems to Louise, composing a farce that mocked their love affair, and sending love letters to Beatrice Ashe.

Now I Ask You was never staged or published during O'Neill's lifetime. It is a departure from his usual dour outlook. George Jean Nathan said of O'Neill, "In all the many years of our friendship, I have heard Eugene O'Neill laugh aloud once and only once."[74] His days on the beach next to Snow's boathouse were exceptionally pleasant times. The future as a playwright had opened up to him, thanks to the enthusiastic support of the Players. In a rather expansive mood, the usually sullen O'Neill rather playfully delineated the antics of the bohemians. He catalogued their poses and fads, many of which were being dramatized on Mrs. O'Brien's wharf. In *Now I Ask You*, O'Neill talks of the "Futurist painter," "Greenwich eucalalie," "a tramp poet," "a long-haired sculptor smelling of absinthe," "Yogi mystic in a cerise turban," "Anarchist lecture," and "birth control," all elements of the ragtime generation.

O'NEILL WAS THE CONSUMMATE AUTOBIOGRAPHICAL WRITER. Writing was a release valve for his emotions and a substitute for personal contact. It was his anodyne for anxiety and in his words, his "vacation from living." His contemporaries said relatively little of a personal nature about him in their memoirs, for he gave them little to write about. The prevailing comments were that he worked hard and that he protected his solitude. Harry Kemp was most persistent in trying to break through O'Neill's silent barriers, to the point of even mimicking O'Neill's reclusiveness; he took over an abandoned hen house at the new Peaked Hill Station. On most occasions when Kemp approached O'Neill on the beach, O'Neill would get up and quietly leave.

In her unpublished notebook, Susan Glaspell placed O'Neill in her "misfits" category, one who complained that "no one in the world understands my slightest impulse."[75] Even in his everyday relations with his wives, O'Neill often wrote out rather than enunciated his feelings. He left intimate notes in small and measured handwriting around the house and when away, even for short periods of time, mailed ardent love letters to "my own little wife." Carlotta Monterey, his third wife, complained bitterly about his silences. O'Neill, a sullen, passive-aggressive type, squirreled away both emotions and grudges, caching them in his writings. Louis Sheaffer characterized him as an "emotional hemophiliac" who bled all his life over any slight or offense.

Not surprisingly, O'Neill spent the rest of his career exorcising Louise Bryant. The love poems he wrote about her in Provincetown and subsequently in the Village Hell Hole bar expressed the romantic and sentimental side of the affair. But the bitter side—rejection and guilt—he handled in his plays. With typical sang-froid, O'Neill wrote the farce, *Now I Ask You*, satirizing the affair. The moral and emotional dilemmas consequent to the affair erupted in various forms in his later plays. For instance, in *Strange Interlude*, he expounded the moral difficulties of a triangular relationship and an abortion. These paralleled the events in his affair with Louise Bryant.

O'Neill's outward behavior and his inner feelings were typically contradictory. He could not have missed the irony and the subterfuge surrounding the love poems he gave to Louise, for they in turn were given to Jack for publication. The explicit poems, "Your body is warm and undulating as the sand dunes" ("On the Dunes"), "Low tide—I burn, Where shallows are . . . " ("Tides") were sent to Floyd Dell at the *Masses*, with the endorsement of both Louise and Jack. In fact, the nomadic O'Neill wrote on the bottom of these poems that "after October 1" he could be reached at Jack Reed's apartment at "43 Washington Square South, New York City."[76]

During Reed's hospitalization in Baltimore in the fall of 1916, Bryant and O'Neill continued their affair. After Louise's abortion and Jack's return to New York, the affair cooled. Jig wrote to Sue on December 23, 1916:

O'Neil (*sic*) isn't seeing Louise now and is nearing the snapping point of suspense and tension. Jack Reed seems pretty well. Saw him four or five days ago at Harvard Club. O'Neil's nervous tension is a thing that I feel instantly when I see him. I mean that I instantly catch it from him feel it myself in myself. Sort of anxiety complex. He likes to be with me since he discovered that I feel what he feels. But it isn't good for me.[77]

When Jack returned from the hospital in early December, he and Louise left the Village and retired to their home in Croton, an hour away from the Village. Gene sequestered himself in the Hell Hole and wrote poems about love and rejection. His poem "Good Night" has the notation "Hell Hole—1916."

> Chatter, chatter, chatter
> Runs the little talk
> Of the little people
> As they lie
> To each other...

Another poem, untitled, reads in part:

> Ah, Love
> Indecent
> Beautiful,
> How I miss you . . .[78]

In May 1917, when *Now I Ask You* was copyrighted, O'Neill was back in Provincetown. Louise followed him there, and Jack rode in for the day trying to contact Louise. O'Neill had returned to Provincetown in March 1917, along with his drinking buddy Harold DePolo, and was staying at the Atlantic House. (Others have stated that he stayed at the

Central House, but it was closed for the season.) The Louise affair took Gene through the gamut of emotions—lust, jealousy, despair, guilt, and anger. While the relationship did not completely end even after O'Neill had married Agnes Boulton in April 1918, the affair was cooling down when Louise searched out O'Neill at the Atlantic House. Louise wrote an unpublished poem, "Spring in Provincetown," at the time, in which she foresees the end of the relationship:

> Stretches of wind swept water,
> Purple—blue-green
> Flashes of wings and of sails
>   A cold sun
>   That promises nothing.
> And over it all a white peace
> To heal old wounds.[79]

THREE MONTHS OF COMBUSTIBLE ACTIVITY on Mrs. O'Brien's wharf forged some successes. O'Neill's pivotal play, *Bound East*, withstood the test of the summer, beginning with its first review. Heywood Broun, in the *New York Tribune*, wrote that "[O'Neill] strikes a rich vein, the old Kipling vein," with his familiar talk and creation of mood. Glaspell's *Trifles* is to this day a staple of Little Theater groups and a model play for feminist studies. Other plays, like Jack Reed's *Eternal Quadrangle* did not survive, and *Freedom* only for a short time. As was the case with the other Players, Reed had not limited all of his creative talents to the little 25-by-35-foot theater on Mrs. O'Brien's wharf. Reed was readying himself for a larger stage, the world of international politics.

There would be no other summer like that of 1916 for the Provincetown Players. That flashpoint of high excitement and intense activity would never again be repeated. America went to war the next spring, and the original Players and their

215

careers turned away from Mrs. O'Brien's wharf. A nucleus of the newly organized Players went to New York and scarcely looked back. Eugene O'Neill moved from despair to confirmation following his baptism as a playwright; Susan Glaspell reluctantly committed herself for the next six seasons to the theater in New York and moved from fictive idealism to dramatic realism; and Jig Cook moved as close as he would get to his dream of an ideal Grecian community. Conversely, Mary O'Brien moved away from romantic settings and wharves to the harsh world of labor disputes and strikes, and Jack Reed moved farther away from poetry and theater to the world of revolution, and to his premature death.

Twelve days after the last performances on Lewis Wharf, Jig wrote to Sue on September 14, 1916: "Took down the theatre curtain a little while ago, and felt a little regret at that symbolic closing of the wharf."[80] It was a bitter-sweet moment. The curtain that he planned to take to New York that fall represented both the ending of a successful Provincetown season and an uncertain beginning in the Village. Jig, however, optimistically added in his letter to Sue: "The stamp on this envelope came from an autograph seeker in Boston! Such is the fame of the Provincetown Players."

September in Provincetown was warm and the Village crowd stayed on. Jig wrote to Sue: "a lot of kids left the wharf here awhile ago for a picnic on the point [Long Point]." Jig wrote to Sue daily while she recuperated from the strenuous summer at Gates Farm, North Hartland, Vermont. Jig was awaiting word from Floyd Dell in New York about renting a building for the Players. Under the guidance of their patron and realtor John Francis, Jack and Louise were making trips to Truro, looking for property to buy. O'Neill and Steele were meeting with "the Baltimore woman" from the Vagabond Theater, who offered to pay $30 for each play to be put on a "guarantors" list. There were parties and dinners at Jack's place, at Hutch's, and at Mary's. The weather was mellow and so were the lingering Villagers, as Jig wrote: "It is perfectly gorgeous weather here now cool—bracing—sunny. The town seems emptied of summer folk—though when you think who's gone away of our crowd—they are nearly all here yet. It is that unknown respectable crowd that has gone."[81]

All seemed reluctant to abandon the darkened theater on the wharf. The curtain was still up when the Players met there and drew up a manifesto on September 4 and 5. The first meeting held in the fishhouse theater was at 8:00 P.M. on a Monday night. There were twenty-nine active members listed. The presiding officers were Robert E. Rogers, Chairman; Louise Bryant, Secretary pro-tem; succeeded by elected officers: Cook, President; Margaret Nordfeldt, Secretary; Reed, Dell, and Bryant, executive committee. Jack Reed had drafted a constitution overnight, which the members accepted the next evening. The name, "Tryout Theatre," was voted down in favor of the name "Provincetown Players." O'Neill had wanted the troupe to be called "The Playwright's Theatre." As a compromise, it was agreed that the playhouse would be called that.[82]

What had begun in July as the Players Club geared toward summer fun ended in September on a formal, serious note. The change began after the reading of *Bound East for Cardiff* in the Cooks' living room. In midsummer, even before the production of *Bound East* on July 28, Jig had solicited money by subscription to support a New York theater. Jig requested that people who had seen the first bill contribute "one dollar for the three remaining bills . . . to give American playwrights of sincere purpose a chance to work out their ideas in freedom."[83]

Jig was in charge of both raising subscription monies

and arranging for newspaper coverage. The *Provincetown Advocate* of August 31, 1916, announced that the Provincetown Players would give a show on Friday and Saturday, September 1 and 2, at the Modern Art School wharf. Tickets were 50 cents and were available at Arequipa cottage next to the wharf, at Francis's store a few doors to the east of the wharf, and at Adams Pharmacy in the center of town. This final bill was staged specifically to raise money for the move to New York.

Financial help came from the "First Subscription List," which was started before the first bill (June 21 is next to Jig Cook's name); contributors were mainly the Players themselves, who each gave $5. The penniless O'Neill contributed nothing, but was given an honorary membership. For $2, others became associate members, many of whom were lady artists.

Among the artists were Maud Squire and Ethel Mars, Provincetown printmakers and friends of Gertrude Stein. They were the subject of an early Stein verbal portrait, namely, *Miss Furr and Miss Skeene*. Mars and Squire, who behaved like prim Midwesterners during their first year in Paris in 1906, quickly adapted to bohemian life. They colored their hair in flaming colors and wore heavy make-up that resembled the café habitués depicted in Toulouse-Lautrec posters.

Boston newspapers carried two stories on separate Sundays: on August 13 in the *Boston Globe* and on September 10 in the *Boston Post*. The first account, "Laboratory of the Drama on Cape Cod's Farthest Wharf," linked the Players Club with the Beachcombers. Most likely the art colony lured the reporters to Provincetown, for the most prestigious artists in the country were summering there. Ross Moffett in 1964 commented on the importance of the artists: "Several of the painters who appeared here at this time [1916], or slightly later—Max Bohm, George Elmer Browne, Richard Miller, Gifford Beal, and William Paxton—were what for that time may be called big-named artists. As members of the National Academy of Design, they enjoyed the aura that then emanated from that institution. Indeed, it may be said that the prestige held by these men, along with Charles Hawthorne, has perhaps no exact parallel at the present time."[84]

The August 13 *Boston Globe* article described the Players as "a pretty serious group" and theatrical "revolutionists." The reporter listed the following "notables" among the Players: writers Mary Heaton Vorse, John Reed, Hutchins Hapgood, Neith Boyce, Susan Glaspell, Louise Bryant, and George Cram Cook. Publicist Cook took pains to have himself listed last. Also cited in the article were Frederick Burt, "a popular actor"; [Teddy] Ballantine, the sculptor and member of the Washington Square Players; and other artists "Bros [*sic*] Nordfeldt and Mr. and Mrs. Zorach." Under the heading "Plays that Succeeded" is mentioned O'Neill's *Bound East for Cardiff*, Susan Glaspell's *Trifles*, and Louise Bryant's *The Game*. There are photographs of the three: Louise and O'Neill both in bathing suits, Glaspell under a wide-brimmed picture-hat. O'Neill, the article continued, "has written some little plays which have made a very deep impression on those who have seen them produced here." There is a synopsis of *Bound East* and reference to *Thirst* and *Fog*. (*Fog* was not produced but may have been considered.) Under the spell of Jig Cook, the reporter spouted hyperboles about the Players: "Idealists! Dreamers! Yes. They admit it, and are not the least ashamed of it . . . full house at every performance."

Jig finally persuaded Floyd Dell to travel down for the final bill—Dell, who earlier said he could not afford the railroad fare. He also convinced Edna Kenton, a newspaper woman and long-time friend, to make the trip. Kenton later wrote that she became a member of the Provincetown Players in mid-summer. Although she was not on the subscription list, she was a member "of its executive committee from its first New York season in 1916 to its last . . . in 1922." Cook ushered Kenton off the Boston boat and over to the "old remodeled fish house on the wharf" to "inspect 'the theatre'—circus-seated, sand strewn, and sea-weed hung." According to Kenton, Jig was prophetic about Gene's plays: "'You don't know Gene yet,' he told me. 'You don't know his plays. But you will. All the world will know Gene's plays some day.'"[85]

Jig Cook arranged for publicity in advance of the Players' move to New York. The *Boston Post*, September 10, 1916, article, "Many Literary Lights Among Provincetown Players," announced their plans. Jack Reed said they wanted to "get a little place around Washington Square in New York—perhaps an old stable remodeled to seat two or three hundred people." The first New York theater was not an old stable but a renovated brownstone, 139 MacDougal Street, next to the Liberal Club. "There's no stopping it," continued Jack Reed. Jig Cook, as the new president of the Players, claimed credit for the first time: "the manager of the Provincetown players . . . It was George Cram Cook's idea." Another significant aspect of this *Post* article was the Players' fictionalized retelling of their beginnings. It read like one of the one-acters produced on Lewis Wharf:

> "Why shouldn't we have a little theatre and try out our new plays?" said he (Cook) one day as they were all sunning on the beach after a swim. "Just the thing!" cried Jack Reed. "I've got two that I'd like to try next week." "Where shall we have the theatre?" said they. "Why not out there on the

wharf?" suggested someone. An old sea captain was looked up and told they wanted to rent his old shed on the pier for a theatre. "That ain't no theatre," said he. "You wait and see!" said Freddie Burt.

With this distorted account, particularly the looking up of "an old sea captain . . . to rent his old shed on the pier for a theatre," began the myths surrounding the Provincetown Players.

"139 MACDOUGAL STREET leased by Provincetown Players! Hurray! Paid $50 first month's rent from October 1st. So that much is settled," stated Jig's last letter from Provincetown, as he hurried to catch the boat to Boston, escorting his mother and his two children who had spent the summer in Provincetown.[86] He put them on the train to Chicago; he himself was scheduled to take the 11:40 P.M. train for New York. Jig barely made the connection in Boston because the Provincetown boat was late. "I have an upper berth. Jack Reed gave me a key to one of his rooms at 43 Washington Square South."

Mary O'Brien stayed on in September after the Provincetown Players left. Mary Pyne, the wife of Harry Kemp (and, like him, one of the Provincetown Players), wrote Mary O'Brien a significant letter about the bustling activities of the Players in mounting the first productions in New York:

[Sept 1916?]

Mary [O'Brien] darling—

. . . Between cleaning the house and attending rehearsals and try-outs, life here is certainly a mad rush . . . There were two parts for me to try—Paula the girl in John Mosher's "Sauce for the Emperor," and the women in Neith's "Enemies." . . . I am to read Neith's play tonight, she is to be there—Lucian Cary's wife (or sister-in-law) is to read it too

221

but I believe I can have it. Either Jean [Gene O'Neill] or Justus S. will do the man—I hope it's anybody but Justus, I have a kind of physical antipathy for him—he makes me think of a human herring which I think Terry says is the most cold blooded of the fishes.

Hutch was around the theatre last night in a very mellow mood—we all went over to Gonfarone's [a restaurant on 8th St. and MacDougal] and sat and talked a while there, Stuart, Mr. & Mrs. Ben—Hippolyte, . . . Bayard Boyesen—Harry [Kemp], Hutch & Jig and Susan and I—Hutch declared he already saw a decadent spirit in the P.P [Provincetown Players] in the form of a certain longing for efficiency—Jig—on the contrary maintained that he wasn't worried about anybody being too efficient and Hippolyte and Hutch finished the argument.

Jig and Nordfeldt are working like galley slaves—painting, hanging beams, sawing wood—Jig looks awfully tired, he says he hasn't had time to twist his forelocks—the theatre is lovely—the benches are lavender—the walls dark dull grey, with emerald green doors and panelling, the archway over the stage gold squares and a purple design at each side—and the curtain a wonderful royal purple affair with a cerise band across it—the curtain will part in the middle.

The Game has many more gestures in it, and two nice girls—Jack Reed rehearses his gestures between courses at meals. Freedom is going on the next bill instead of the Mosher play, Harry [Kemp] is going to take Jack's part—he's quite good in the Cardiff play—Jean's brother was around last night and gave them some valuable criticism, not knowing Teddy was an actor, he tells him to speak up etc.

I saw Jean at Christine's last night. I told him Terry was asking for him—he says Terry told him he could write—Before Breakfast is going on the third bill.

I think I've told you every littlest thing now—everybody asks for you and Terry too—and wants to know when you're coming back—I haven't seen Don [Corley] yet, he didn't show up at rehearsal last night.

Provincetown seems like a land of dreams—infinitely far off and unattainable—how is your work going—I'll write you about the opening. Dear Mary I hope you're serene and happy—

love Mary [Pyne][87]

Despite the war, despite financial difficulties and personal squabbles, the Players were successful in New York and never staged another play on Mrs. O'Brien's wharf. That was unfortunate, for Provincetown would have gladly welcomed them back. "Provincetown . . . had rather got used to the 'reds' who contributed to the *Masses*," the *Boston Herald* reported the next summer. "There is no Watch and Ward Society or mayoral arbiter of morality to stop the show." F.W. Coburn of the *Herald* further reports how quickly the town accepted the new avant-garde painters: "Go into the executive offices of the town hall and you find business transacted in a room whose walls are adorned with pictures . . . over the desks of assessors and registrars of deeds."

Those first years in New York were difficult. The Players had to find ways to avoid the law that objected to wholesale renovations on the brownstone and to placate the authorities who questioned the propriety of their productions. There were also problems with expanded productions and swollen egos. Jig was thinking back to simpler days on Lewis Wharf when, in 1918, he wistfully wrote to Sue: "I think probably I will come back to Mary O'Brien's Fish-House."

CHAPTER EIGHT

Traces of the Provincetown Players

*Do you realize we've made very little impression
on this town? It's a fishing town—tough. By
tough I mean impossible to destroy.*

—Susan Glaspell, *Judd Rankin's Daughter*

EDMUND WILSON WROTE, in his journal *The Thirties*, about "poor" Carl Van Vechten going to Provincetown in 1936 thinking he could photograph O'Neill's house and the Wharf Theatre. Van Vechten was unfortunately too late. The sea claimed Lewis Wharf in 1922, and then O'Neill's Peaked Hill house in 1931. In Provincetown, there are no shrines to the Provincetown Players nor, for that matter, to any writer or artist who ever lived there. There is, however, a roadway named after Provincetown Player Harry Kemp, the self-styled "Poet of the Dunes." And there are commemorative plaques on private homes once occupied by Players. Two houses are significant in terms of the Players' beginnings: the former Hapgood cottage, where *Constancy* and *Suppressed Desires* were first performed, and the Glaspell house, where *Bound East for Cardiff* was first read.

The essential Provincetown, the maritime town, has changed little since the time of the Players. Standing on an old wharf in Provincetown harbor as the tide washes in and a foghorn sounds, one can easily relive that July evening in 1916 when *Bound East for Cardiff* was staged for the first time on Lewis Wharf. Geographically Provincetown is the same: a natural harbor with the town hunching at its edge along a three-mile waterfront—a sand-locked, water-locked town at the far end of a sandy peninsula. As in 1916, one sees houses jumbled about the side streets. To walk down the narrow, twenty-two-foot-wide Commercial Street is an intimate social experience. Except for garish facades in the commercial center, most of the buildings—such as the white clapboard houses and architectural exteriors of the Town Hall and the Library and Pilgrim Monument—are the same. Above all it is a mariner's town, with a long wharf jutting out to meet incoming vessels.

Peaked Hill, on the oceanside, was for the Players as inspirational as Lewis Wharf. The muse of Peaked Hill is found on the ocean bluffs—where the wind howls, where the long stretch of the Atlantic curves beyond sight, where *Beyond the Horizon* was written. There, in the old Peaked Hill Life-Saving Station, Susan Glaspell found a setting for *The Outside*, a one-act play depicting life's struggle for survival, which she likened to the fight against the encroaching sea. Wilbur Daniel Steele, in the years before the station was abandoned in 1914, gathered story material from the station keeper, Captain William W. Cook, who told endless tales about his merchant service and his whaling years. Mary Heaton Vorse recounts, in *Time and the Town*, how she would take lobsters across to Peaked Hill: "The Captain loved to pick a lobster. We would sit around the campfire, with Mrs.

Cook, to hear him spill out tales of wrecks and rescues and of adventure on the sea."

What the Players left behind is what they first found: an intimate and imaginative retreat. They came during the ragtime era; some left during the frantic Twenties; others, such as Glaspell, Vorse, and the Hapgoods, came and went, but chose to spend their last years in Provincetown. Underneath Mary Heaton Vorse's "summer froth" is the intrinsic Provincetown, a vulnerable yet resilient outpost.

Provincetown is its geography. It is Thoreau's "filmy sliver of land" surrounded by a sweeping harbor and ocean beaches that offer a special chromatic palette. Provincetown's oceanside drew Thoreau to where "white breakers were rushing to shore." It kept O'Neill there where "breakers crashed below our feet." And again one is reminded of the agrarian Jig Cook, who dreamed by the edge of the sea of being "a Greek Thoreau, living with Homer . . . the sailors and the sea."

At first fishing, then sand dunes, then painters, later Pilgrim Monument, and finally writers brought outsiders to Provincetown. The original Provincetown Players were the town's first renown wave of writers, the "literary lights" of 1916. Writers followed on the heels of one another; for example, the Players' pioneer, Mary Heaton Vorse, in 1907 was led there by *McClure's* editor Viola Roseboro. In 1914 Margaret Sanger, the birth-control advocate, summered there because Provincetown was "a favorite inexpensive gathering place for artists and intellectuals." In keeping with the bohemian trend, Sanger "took a lover" for the summer. In 1917 Sanger bought one of Reed's two properties in Truro. Jig Cook's daughter Nilla, in her memoirs, fantasized about Provincetown "as a pagan kingdom, cut off from the rest of America."[1]

In 1920, outside media interest in the writers' colony

accelerated when O'Neill won the Pulitzer Prize for *Beyond the Horizon*. There was enough curiosity to warrant a journalist's grueling August trip over the dunes to O'Neill's home, the old Peaked Hill Life-Saving Station. Olin Downes of the *Boston Post* interviewed O'Neill and found him in a rare expansive mood. O'Neill reminisced about his seaman days, the poetry of sailing, and the despair of waterfront life in Buenos Aires and in New York. Following the publicity surrounding O'Neill's prize, Provincetown summers exploded with invading tourists and a new wave of Village bohemians. The new, fast roads brought in more tourists who preferred the automobile to the train, which shuffled "along so slowly that it might have been plodding through the sand," as Edmund Wilson complained.[2]

To escape the frenzy, Provincetown's first-wave writers relocated—to Truro, Nantucket, Maine, and New Hampshire. Even O'Neill's remote sanctuary, Peaked Hill, was jeopardized; he left in 1924 for sojourns in Bermuda and Connecticut. "Provincetown was no longer the quiet fishing village," lamented Glaspell. "In summer motors jam the narrow winding street which faithfully followed the line of the sea, and never meant to be a highway. Having been much tormented the summer before, we bought an abandoned farmhouse . . . near Truro."[3]

The Roaring Twenties in Provincetown were followed by quieter, economically and emotionally depressed periods: the Depression and World War II. Not until the late Fifties and Sixties did Provincetown echo the literary, artistic, and tourist heyday of the Twenties. In the decades after World War I and then again after World War II, if you wrote or painted in Greenwich Village during the winter, you most likely summered in Provincetown. It was Floyd Dell who first dubbed Provincetown the suburb of Greewich Village.

* * *

PROVINCETOWN'S GRANDE DAME, octogenarian Hazel Haw-thorne, lived through most of Provincetown's literary history.[4] In 1918, as a bright, beautiful, sixteen-year-old aspiring au-thor, she first came to Provincetown to be near the famous writers who summered there. As a minister's daughter living in a restrictive Massachusetts small town, Hazel found escape in the poetry and fiction of *Scribners*, *McClure's*, and *Harpers* magazines. After analyzing Edward J. O'Brien's annual *The Best Short Stories*, she discovered that the most popular writ-ers of the day were in Provincetown. Hazel thereupon con-trived to spend the summer as an *au pair* for family friends.

She fell irreversibly in love with the town and began her long association with Provincetown's literati: Eugene O'Neill, Edmund Wilson, John Dos Passos, and Norman Mailer. In the early Fifties, her local reputation was so firmly established that Mailer asked her to arrange a dinner party so that he might meet Wilson. What Hazel Hawthorne regretted about that evening is that Wilson, shunning other topics, gave endless accounts of Harry Kemp's Rabelaisian antics. For Hawthorne it was an unfortunate choice because Kemp was not one of her favorite writers. She found Kemp boorish, but did admit that he had some charm, for "Harry did leave one with a laugh."

In 1918 the East End of Provincetown was a literary paradise, in Hazel Hawthorne's eyes. She often happened upon her idols walking along Commercial Street, sitting on the beach, or chatting in John Francis's grocery store. O'Neill and his new bride, Agnes Boulton, were living close by in Francis's Flats over the grocery store; the Cooks were across the street; and Mary Heaton Vorse was a little way "up along" Commercial Street. The Steeles, although "way up along" in the West End, often made their way to the East End.

Hazel recalls vividly the excitement of a chance meeting with Mary Heaton Vorse: "She was wearing a large picture hat and underneath gave me a warm smile as she said hello. I was still something of a child and Mary liked children." That summer Hazel had a poem published in the July issue of the *Liberator*. Like any neophyte author she wanted immediate approval, so she went about asking for opinions. The criticisms were mixed. She especially remembers showing her poem to O'Neill as he lounged on the beach. He graciously and professionally offered his critique: he liked all but the last four lines, which he thought were insincere. Hazel of course agreed.

After her first summer, Hazel was not able to return to Provincetown until the mid-Twenties. By then the original "literary lights" had scattered. Harry Kemp disliked the fact and said to Edmund Wilson: "dozens of dumb artists—literary people gone." Jig Cook, with Greek honors, lay buried in Delphi; John Reed, a Communist hero, was interred in the Kremlin wall; Mary Heaton Vorse, disillusioned with the new liberals, was traveling abroad; the Steeles had relocated to Nantucket; and the Hapgoods had moved to a farm in New Hampshire. Renting out her Provincetown house, Susan Glaspell summered in her Truro home, located near the estate of Shebnah Rich, the 19th-century local historian.

A satellite summer colony developed in Truro. One summer resident was Edna St. Vincent Millay, who wrote for and acted in the New York Provincetown Playhouse. Hawthorne, desperately wanting to meet Millay, set out from Peaked Hill one hot summer day and walked barefoot across the scorching dunes, then along the railroad tracks to Truro. Hawthorne's feet were so severely blistered that she was in bed for several days. Unfortunately, on arriving in Truro, she found that Millay had gone to Provincetown for the day.

Edmund Wilson, in his *Twenties* journal, describes

Hazel as "very young and very pretty" with "quite a remark-able literary gift, as yet in rather an immature state." Hazel Hawthorne's long association with Edmund Wilson began in 1927, when he rented O'Neill's Peaked Hill home. Wilson knew O'Neill through Wilson's first wife, Mary Blair, who acted in several of O'Neill's plays, notably *The Hairy Ape.* In 1924, Wilson's play, *The Crime in the Whistler Room,* was staged in the Provincetown Playhouse.

In the summer of 1927, Hazel Hawthorne was again in town, this time with her minister husband and their four children. They had rented a shack near the O'Neill's, one built by a Coast Guardsman out of lumber from shipwrecked schooners. (Most Guardsmen were carpenters, an avocation that filled the long, uneventful hours on duty.) When O'Neill moved into Peaked Hill in the spring of 1919, he was well enough known by the Guardsmen that they welcomed him with a surprise wedding gift, a driftwood desk. Agnes O'Neill especially remembered the bouquet of wildflowers and the considerate way they readied the kerosene lamps and stove.

O'Neill, one of the hardest-working writers, was also the most inaccessible. On the rare occasions when Hawthorne saw O'Neill at Peaked Hill, he was swimming far off-shore. Occasionally he waved and smiled as she walked along the beach. The sea safely cocooned O'Neill, a marathon swim-mer, as did his hard-to-get-to seaside home. O'Neill was in-trigued by the cavernous old Life-Saving Station, with its history of grisly rescues. O'Neill's study was once the area where bloated cadavers dragged from the sea were laid out. While the sea was his inspiration, he turned his back to it when he wrote; his flotsam desk faced a windowless south wall. In this second-story room, even the small casement win-dows hid the sea because they had been made opaque by the blasting sand.

At the time of Hazel Hawthorne's return to Provincetown, O'Neill was readying to leave. In 1922 he had bought a winter home—one he never grew to like—in Ridgefield, Connecticut, close to New York City. In 1924, following Wilbur Daniel Steele's lead, he went to Nantucket for the summer; then he wintered in Bermuda. There followed other residences—in France, Georgia, California, and again Massachusetts. After leaving Peaked Hill, O'Neill embarked on a life-long, fruitless odyssey in search of the perfect sea home.

"ALL I KNOW IS THAT IT WAS ONE HELL OF A FIGHT," recalled Alice Joseph, a former Provincetown librarian. Her comment sums up the town's memories about the fierce argument between Eugene O'Neill and Abbie Putnam, town librarian. Exploiting his skill as a writer, O'Neill routinely got even with anyone who offended him. And so he did with Abbie.

O'Neill, an avid reader, was a frequent visitor to Putnam's tightly run domain. Abbie Putnam, a petite spinster who ran the library for a generation (1901–1935), was nearly deaf. O'Neill spoke in a muted baritone and was frequently inaudible. It's a wonder they ever communicated. Their contretemps may have occurred for a number of reasons. Other than the communication problem, Abbie mistrusted strangers and O'Neill, as an unknown visitor, was—in town parlance—a stranger. "Stranger" was the actual term Abbie used in the annual Town Report to describe unknown visitors to the library. O'Neill may well have broken some cardinal rule of Abbie's library—perhaps he did not return books on time, or he read them on the beach, where they were soiled, or, worst yet, he lost them.

Abbie Putnam and her family were playfully eccentric. Her father, A.L. Putnam, was a library trustee. They lived in the

Figurehead House, so-called because Putnam had boldly placed a figurehead over the front door that was noticeable to anyone coming down Commercial Street. It was a half-figure of a bare-breasted woman; the more suggestive lower half had been sawed off. On Sundays, after dressing for church, Putnam exited the house by gleefully sliding down the bannister, followed close on by his son. Abbie's sister was a talented artist who painted the floors to look like carpets, an innovation much talked about in town. Later in her life and despite growing deafness, Abbie learned to play the trumpet and on occasion blasted out a cacophonous tune on her front lawn. An occasion for rendering her favorite piece, the *Battle Hymn of the Republic*, might be either a spectacular sunset or the election of a Republican president. Theodore Roosevelt was her hero. She said that meeting Teddy Roosevelt, during the dedication of the Pilgrim Monument in 1907, was more memorable for her than having been blessed by the Pope at the Vatican.

Stories about Abbie's deafness are legendary. Heaton Vorse often retold an off-color anecdote. It concerns a visiting French sailor who approached Abbie and asked to use the men's room. Abbie, not understanding the Frenchman, asked him to repeat the question. He did so three times: "Is there a men's room?" Each time his voice and Abbie's voice grew louder. Finally an exasperated Abbie shouted out, "No there isn't, and you can't take it out unless you have a library card."

In the library logbook, in Abbie's large Pitman-style handwriting, O'Neill's name was first entered under March 1917. As a visitor—that is, one who did not qualify for a resident library card—O'Neill was not allowed to write his own name in the logbook. Instead, he had to say his name aloud to Abbie. She misspelled it "O'Neil." Like all other patrons entering the library, O'Neill was immediately confronted by Abbie. She vigilantly stationed herself at the far end of the first floor behind a long wooden railing that shielded her and the shelves of fiction books behind her. (This railing, along with library shelving, is now on display in Provincetown's Heritage Museum.) As a self-appointed guardian of literature, Abbie favored only a few card holders; these few she allowed to browse in the fiction section. Hazel Hawthorne remembers that she was not among the chosen and soon despaired of using the library. She says, "I read Andersen's *Fairy Tales* and Jane Austen's novels and stopped at the B's."

Abbie also dictated how many fiction books could be checked out at any one time. Children were closely monitored. Town resident Mary Lewis recalls that as a child she routinely presented Abbie with a request list, from which Abbie selected books. Abbie frowned on those who returned books the very next day. She suspected they had not read the books. Grace Collinson, a long-time resident, recalled that Abbie never allowed her to take out what were then considered risqué books. In that category was Harry Kemp's *Love Among the Cape Enders*, a *roman à clef* account of the Greenwich Villagers' escapades in Provincetown. Abbie carefully restricted the circulation of novels written by Provincetown's East-Enders, ones like Glaspell's *Fidelity*, which dealt with divorce. Abbie Putnam nevertheless viewed herself as quite liberal. In the 1919 Town Report, in response to the item "Describe any changes in the direction of more liberal library rules," she penned in large script: "No changes. Same rules. We always try to be as liberal as possible."

In 1917, at the time of O'Neill's first recorded visit to the library, it is doubtful that he had the $1.25 deposit required to check out books. As an adult visitor, however, he was allowed to use the second-floor reading room freely. Children were not permitted above the first floor. Therefore it became a favorite game of the town boys to pique Abbie by playing tag on the staircase leading to the second floor. In 1917, the Library's reading room was a welcome retreat for O'Neill, because he was staying in a room over the noisy Atlantic House bar. The reading room housed quite a large assortment of newspapers, magazines, general reference works, and non-fiction books. O'Neill read his favorite periodicals, *The New York Times* and *The Saturday Evening Post*, in the quiet, well-lighted reading room that was heated in the winter with coal and shaded in the summer by a large chestnut tree. It had elegant appointments: red-flocked wallpaper, large wooden tables, and a rare modern convenience—a newly installed water closet. Here O'Neill perhaps worked on the sea plays he was composing that winter (*In the Zone*, *The Long Voyage Home*, and *The Moon of the Caribbees*), the series that was set aboard the S.S. *Glencairn*, which is also the setting for *Bound East for Cardiff*.

At the time, O'Neill was interested in Eastern mysticism. Terry Carlin wrote to him about Mabel Collins' *Light on the Path*, a popular book, but a rather sentimental rendering of cult philosophy. This book was among the library's acquisitions and was shelved in the non-fiction section of the second floor. O'Neill copied out several phrases that appealed to him, made some minor revisions, and added exclamation points. It has been speculated that it may have been Charles Demuth who painted the precept on the rafters of O'Neill's apartment in Francis's Flats. The inscription, which is still intact, reads:

> Before the eyes can see, they must be
> incapable of tears!
> Before the ear can hear, it must have
> lost its sensitiveness!
> Before the voice can speak, it must have
> lost the power to wound!
> Before the soul can fly, its wings must
> be washed in the blood of the heart!

During the winter months strangers rarely visited Provincetown, much less the library. The records from January to March 1917 show that O'Neill was only the fifth visitor that year. The gruff and grim O'Neill, dressed in seaman garb, aroused Abbie's worst suspicions. If Abbie had had any inkling that O'Neill was staying at the Atlantic House, she would have been doubly distressed, for it catered to visiting seamen and allowed drinking, gambling, and prostitution. She closely watched O'Neill as he walked up the wooden steps to the reading room and more carefully scrutinized him for evidence of purloined newspapers, magazines, or books as he came down the stairs. With America about to enter the war, all strangers were doubly suspect. That same month, in overreaction to the impending war, local authorities arrested O'Neill and his buddy, the pulp writer Harold dePolo, on charges of spying. They had wandered too close to the United States radio station in Truro.

When O'Neill stayed in the East End, he routinely passed by Abbie's house on his way to the center of town. He did not see the whimsical Abbie but an inverted, shy person, much like himself. While in Provincetown in 1917, O'Neill outlined a scenario called *The Trumpet*.[5] This play, never completed, is a farce about a deaf librarian, a dumb town crier, and a blind beach-cleaner. The setting is "in the public library of a small town on the N.E. sea-coast." He describes a librarian much like Abbie, "a slight little woman about 38 with a small, homely face; dark brown hair faintly tinged with grey; a hesitating, wistful smile; eager hazel eyes, anxious to please but continually clouded with a dreaded perplexity, due to her self-consciousness about her affliction. Her voice is soft and gentle. She wears a simple, dark dress." To Abbie's credit, Abbie was forty-eight-years-old, ten years older than O'Neill's estimate. In 1917, O'Neill portrays Abbie sympathetically. Five years later his portrayal is venomous.

In January 1918, the library was one of the first places O'Neill took Agnes Boulton to see on her first visit to Provincetown. At the top of the visitors' log for 1918, next to numbers one and two, Abbie Putnam registered O'Neill and Boulton. Again boldly and carefully she misspelled his name "O'Neil"; she also misheard Agnes' last name as "Burton" rather than "Boulton." Neither mistake was corrected because Gene and Agnes did not want to call undue attention to their being together. John Francis had reluctantly set them up in an apartment off Conwell Street and was not happy about their unmarried co-habitation. O'Neill did not tell Francis ahead of time that he would not be alone. In April 1918, Gene and Agnes did marry, in Provincetown.

In December 1920, Gene and Agnes applied for library cards. They were now Mr. and Mrs. E.G. O'Neill and owned property. "O'Neill" was spelled correctly this time, for card holders were permitted to sign the register. They gave their address as 199 Bradford. The O'Neills had left Peaked Hill for the winter and rented this house in town. That year O'Neill had gained major recognition. On February 2, 1920, *Beyond the Horizon*, his first full-length play to be staged, was a Broadway success. This triumph was followed in June by the awarding of his first Pulitzer Prize.

It was about that time, according to Grace Collinson Goveia, that O'Neill and Putnam had their fierce quarrel. Quite drunk, O'Neill staggered into the library and belligerently pointed his finger at Abbie Putnam, yelling "Now, do you know who I am?" The imperious Abbie, whose only hero was Teddy Roosevelt and who passionately protected the sanctity of the library, shouted back, "No, I don't young man.

But I do want you to leave this library, now!" O'Neill's revenge came sometime in 1923, when he was writing *Desire Under the Elms* at Peaked Hill. In that play, Abbie Putnam, the mild-mannered, eccentric spinster of *The Trumpet*, became—as a product of O'Neill's revenge mill—a character actually named "Abbie Putnam," a woman who committed adultery and murdered her own child.

EUGENE O'NEILL FELL IN LOVE with the Peaked Hill Bars Life-Saving Station the first time he saw it in the summer of 1916. From then on he was a frequent visitor to the vicinity of the unoccupied cottage. Agnes remembered O'Neill taking her there in 1918 and saying, "This is the house you and I should have. We would live here like sea gulls." The following year, as newlyweds, they moved in. This, his first home, sitting a few feet from the ocean surf and about two miles from Lewis Wharf on the bayside, was important to his development as a playwright. In 1921 he wrote to Pierre Loving: "The place has come to mean a tremendous lot to me. I feel a true kinship and harmony with life out there. Sand and sun and sea and wind . . . There is always the monotone of surf on the bar . . . You can walk or swim along the beach for miles, and meet only the dunes—Sphinxes muffled in their yellow robes with paws deep in the sea."[6]

To reach Peaked Hills is a grinding mile-long walk leading easterly to the Atlantic Ocean. One leaves the highway on the outskirts of Provincetown and takes a sandy path that is faintly described on clear days by footprints. The path snakes through the remnants of a forest ravaged by early settlers into a sandbowl and then crosses two ridges of sand dunes. From atop the first towering dune—a barricade of sliding sand—there spreads out a surrealistic vista. Eastward is the Atlantic Ocean—an uncluttered watery horizon that bends toward Spain; around the base of the dune is wave after wave of sand anchored by scrub pine, green velour bayberry bushes, red rosehips, silvery dusty miller, and verdigris beach grass. A half-turn to the west and one sees Provincetown's granite, gargoyled Pilgrim Monument jutting skyward over the sand and water, an Italianate tower marking a moment in recorded time, the first landing of the Pilgrims in 1620.

On this part of the peninsula, a stretch of sand anchored between the sea and the rest of America, can be found the history of Provincetown and the history of America. The Nauset Indians of Cape Cod foraged here. Bartholomew Gosnold surveyed the waters around the sandy peninsula, found codfish rife in the waters, and named it Cape Cod. Miles Standish and the Pilgrims scouted here for a settlement site and for lurking Indians in the winter of 1620 while the *Mayflower* was anchored in Provincetown harbor. Renegade fishermen, pirates and privateers in their unmarked vessels, and sailors in armed frigates—with English, French, and Spanish ensigns mounted aggressively on high—plowed the nearby churning waters.

In the sea at the foot of Peaked Hill are underwater sand bars that erratically and dangerously shift. Beneath the sand bars are buried wrecks of frigates, schooners, and fishing smacks. Here the sand and sea also pulverized the remains of a Life-Saving Station that sat too close to the sea, the Station that served as Eugene O'Neill's first home. When Shane O'Neill, Eugene O'Neill's son, remembered the storms at Peaked Hill, he referred to it as "the place where the wind blows." Shane spent his first four summers in the old Peaked Hill Bars Life-Saving Station while his father successfully worked through his apprentice years as a playwright.

Peaked Hills is a living laboratory of geological change. Wind and sand eat away the barrier beaches and bluffs; prevailing winter winds move the surface sand to the south, while currents under the sea plow the sand northward. The first settlers laid waste the vegetation by releasing cows, horses, and oxen to graze on the thinly pastured dunes. They felled pine, oak, and birch to build ships and houses, and scrub pine for tar and pitch. Without the stability provided by anchoring vegetation, the dunes accelerated their primitive sculpting. Cranberry bogs were covered, freshwater ponds were blotted dry, and stunted trees and bushes were calcified by windblown salt.

"Coming from the country as I did . . . this was perhaps the most novel and remarkable sight that I saw on the Cape." This was Thoreau's comment as he first came upon Peaked Hills in 1849. To him the sparse vegetation weaving through the carpet of dunes "was like the richest rug imaginable spread over an uneven surface; no damask nor velvet . . . nor the work of any loom, could ever match it."[7]

Peaked Hills was popular with early travelers, who wanted to see this region of towering sand dunes that they called a Sahara. Thoreau's descriptions lured other writers to retrace his steps. In 1918 Helen Henderson, a Philadelphia art critic and friend of the artist Charles Demuth, walked over to see Thoreau's tapestry. She found her "dream of dunes, ponds, and cranberry bogs" was "infested with a belligerent horde of mosquitoes." Today mosquitoes are more controlled; the dunes are not walking about as much; there are vestiges of cranberry bogs; and, after a heavy rain, freshwater ponds miraculously appear.

PEAKED HILL BARS was one of the two original Life-Saving Stations erected in 1872 in the vicinity of Provincetown. The other was Race Point Station. Each was strategically located along the Atlantic Coast, where the most shipwrecks occurred as vessels headed around the outer reaches of Cape Cod. Peaked Hill Bars Station witnessed more wrecks than the Race Point Station because of the ever-shifting sand bars in its vicinity. In 1872, the new U.S. Life-Saving Service erected and manned nine stations along the coast of Cape Cod. These stations were identical in construction. None survive. The original wooden structures were 18 feet wide by 42 feet long, two stories high, with two rooms on each floor. On the bottom floor was the larger boat room and the smaller messroom; one of the upper rooms was a sleeping barracks, the other a storeroom. In 1889, the stations were remodeled and enlarged. A storage lean-to was added to either side of the original structure and the main roof was extended over each addition. The building was shingled from roof to foundation. The overall intended effect was that of a then-fashionable summer resort cottage.

The Life-Saving Service was issued uniforms in 1889. The public was invited to watch the surfmen practice their life-saving drills, held each day except Sunday. On Mondays and Thursdays, the crew practiced with the beach apparatus, such as the Lyle gun—a type of cannon that was fired at a practice "wreck" pole shaped like a ship's mast seventy-five yards away. The projectile was a line on which was rigged a breeches buoy, a life preserver with leggings that was designed for transporting shipwrecked persons from ship to shore. On Tuesdays, the surfmen launched their boats through the surf. The keeper, who was in charge of the station, stood erect in the stern of the lifeboat with his sweep (steering) oar. Boats were deliberately capsized, then righted. This activity was an unfailing crowd pleaser.

Surfmen were paid a meager $65 per month and had no retirement benefits; with the inauguration of the U.S. Coast Guard in 1915, guardsmen were given retirement benefits, but their salary was still marginal. There were advantages to being stationed near home; most of the Peaked Hill crew were native Provincetowners who shunned the greater uncertainties and hazards of fishing. During its first decade (1871–80), the Life-Saving Service experienced its greatest growth and greatest number of rescues. The effectiveness of the service declined as ships became steam-powered and carried improved navigational equipment. In 1914, the opening of the Cape Cod Canal reduced passage through the treacherous waters of the Outer Cape and drastically cut the need for rescue services.

PHYLLIS HIGGINS, A PROVINCETOWN NATIVE, was a daughter of Surfman Charles Higgins, who served both at the old Peaked Hill Station and at the new Coast Guard Station.[8] One of Phyllis's delights as a child was to visit, or—on rare occasions—to spend the night with her father at the Station. She remembered walking across the dunes with a playmate, stopping to collect drinking water from the freshwater ponds. They would name the ponds after themselves and stand spellbound when the ponds magically disappeared. She recalled the smell of freshly baked bread that greeted her on arrival at the Station. In the upstairs room of the old Station, which O'Neill eventually used as a study, were lockers filled with clothes that had been reclaimed from shipwrecks. One time, when Phyllis and a friend had been caught in a hailstorm, they were allowed to change into oversized, heavy serge dresses with long skirts and high lace collars. The north upstairs storage room was usually occupied by a surfman who snored loudly. He was ousted when Phyllis slept there. Her father would cautiously place a chair at the head of the doorless companionway so that she would not tumble down it in the dark.

Surfmen supplemented their meager stipends by working off-season as painters, carpenters, or cooks. When on duty, the Surfmen paid for and pooled their rations; sharing their food with visitors was a hardship for the Surfmen, so visitors usually brought food with them. Youngsters sometimes brought cake or candy in exchange for the privilege of riding on the breeches buoy, "the only amusement ride in town."[9] Each Surfman had one of the many wild cranberry bogs for his own use. As a special treat, Charles Higgins would bake cranberry bread, to the delight of his two daughters. To the west of Snail Road, near Cape Cod Bay, was a cranberry bog frequently pirated by local youngsters. The owner was a scold who routinely searched the children for stolen cranberries. One of the local boys, knowing she would thrust her hand into his pockets, removed his undergarments and the stitching from his pockets. What the bog owner found that day, as she jammed her fingers into his pockets searching for cranberries, kept her from ever again reaching into the pockets of little boys.

IN 1915, THE OLD PEAKED HILL LIFE-SAVING STATION was converted into a shining palace built upon the sand. In 1914, John Francis had arranged for the original sale of the Station to Sam Lewisohn of New York City; he arranged for its sale again in 1919 to James O'Neill, Eugene's father, who gave it to Gene as a wedding present. Lewisohn spent a few weeks there in 1914; Mabel Dodge spent the summer of 1915. Although he had never been a guest of Dodge or of Lewisohn, O'Neill knew the particulars of the furnishings before he took occupancy, for he often had prowled around the empty station. His new bride, Agnes Boulton, however, was surprised to see a well-appointed interior. Other than his clothes, a trunk of books, and his manuscripts, Gene took little else to his first home.

Once again John Francis had cleaned and readied the

place. In 1930, less than a year before the old station surrendered to the elements, O'Neill inquired through his lawyer about selling it. Edmund Wilson had expressed interest. John Francis replied that "$1000 would be the best one could get." This was the original selling price in 1914. Mabel Dodge had spent another $1,000 of Lewisohn's funds in decorating it. Francis recommended to O'Neill's lawyer in 1930 that "it would be wise for him to let go if he has no further use of the place otherwise if he intends to keep it he will have to lay out a lot of money to preserve it as it is very expensive to get supplies and people to work out there." John Francis was protecting himself from another renovation.

The dogged and patient John Francis had more than earned his reputation as the saint of the Greenwich Village crowd during the winter of 1914–15, when, under the long-distance supervision of Mabel Dodge, he carried out the renovation of Peaked Hill. In addition to the difficult logistics of hauling materials and workmen across the dunes to install a modern bathroom and kitchen, and a two-story fireplace, there was the task of decorating to meet Dodge's sophisticated tastes. For example, Francis carried out the meticulous job of seeing that the walls were precisely covered with layer after layer of white glistening paint, and the oak floors painted to a translucent blue.

Among the furnishings Dodge sent to him from New York were two stuffed couches that had belonged to Isadora Duncan, and new white wicker chairs and a wicker chaise lounge. (Edmund Wilson, in his journal *The Thirties*, recalled that he and his wife Margaret enjoyed gymnastic love-making on the wicker lounge.) Against the radiant white walls were arranged heavy blue linen couches and chairs accented with pillows striped in yellow and blue. Sand-colored rush mats were centered on the blue floors. Carton after carton of color-coordinated Italian pottery was unpacked and scattered throughout the living- and dining-room areas: flower jars, lamps and inkpots. At either end of a long high shelf in the dining room was set a highly glazed white pottery fruit bowl. White pottery against white walls was strangely, aesthetically right. The living room became a chambered nautilus of golden diffused light that emanated from the two south windows flanking the fireplace. A room that had housed lifeboats, breeches buoys, sweep oars and—on one grisly day—twenty-seven drowned corpses became a decorator's showcase. Peaked Hill Bars Life-Saving Station was thus transformed into a summer camp, suitable for the New York wealthy.

John Francis employed the Carr brothers for the cartage service. Peter and Dick Carr were taciturn, tobacco-chewing bachelors. Every time the freight train came in or was ready to leave, one could hear throughout town the rumble of their wagons running up and down the ramp connected to the freight cars. Their dray fees were exhorbitant, but they provided the only way—except for the services offered through the good graces of the Coast Guard—to transport baggage or passengers across to Peaked Hill. Usually one walked the distance of just over a mile from the Bay to the Ocean. On cool summer days the walk was a routine half-hour hike to the John Francis store in the East End. On hot days, or when burdened with a heavy load, a walker found the trek over the sand ridges arduous and exhausting.

John Francis, a guileless man, was an extraordinary facilitator of goods and services. For example, in arranging for O'Neill's visit in January 1918, he attended to the smallest detail: "I will give you a two burner oil stove and I will let or lend you the coal heating stove that I have in my back shop ... you can have the studio for $75 to Dec 31 this year and I will pay the water bill only be careful and report any leak as I have a meter there and no old maid underneath of you to keep me in hot water like the one did last summer. The electric lights if you want to use them and bulbs are extra." His procurement skills were rather cruelly tested by the Players. They once asked him to acquire a camel for their productions, a practical joke initiated most likely by Hutch Hapgood. Not until Francis was totally exasperated did they discharge him from the fake task.

"Many a wise thing I have heard him say and many a kind act I have seen him perform," wrote Hutchins Hapgood upon Francis's death in 1937.[10] When John Francis died, Susan Glaspell sent condolences from Chicago: "[he] was always a good friend. He, more than anyone else there, seemed a part of our lives. The town will not be the same without him." John Francis's mother was Irish, his father Portuguese. The senior Francis turned from the hardships of fishing to the uncertainties of farming. Eventually he branched out into the grocery business. His son helped with the farm and the store; then, as tourism grew, he turned to real estate. John Francis negotiated house rentals and sales for the Village crowd. He was eventually successful enough to send his son and daughter to Boston colleges. Celia Francis, his daughter, bequeathed the family inheritance to the town for college scholarships.

At Peaked Hill, O'Neill was insulated from the crowds of Provincetown, but he was not as isolated as has usually been reported. The new Coast Guard Station was only a quarter of a mile away and visible across the dunes. The Guardsmen performed many services for him. Frequently they took his telephone messages, picked up his mail from town, and transported his groceries and other necessities. O'Neill was comfortable with male companions. As a merchant sailor he thrived on the camaraderie of shipboard life, and he was intrigued by the renegade street gang, the Hudson Dusters, who

frequented the Village Hell Hole, and by the Coast Guardsmen at Peaked Hill. The Station was manned ten months of
the year and was visited frequently by families and friends
and tourists. Hazel Hawthorne claimed that tourists with
cameras frequently walked right into the old station without
knocking. When O'Neill became financially secure, he hired a
live-in nursemaid and a cook, and entertained frequently.

WHEN HE WAS RENTING THE O'NEILL HOME, the impractical
Edmund Wilson one summer's day scurried to town for ice, in
a last-minute preparation for a cocktail party he was giving.
Hazel Hawthorne watched Wilson's progress over the dunes,
his robust form struggling in the sliding sand, buttons loos-
ened at the knees of his flapping golf pants, and the ice dripping from a gunny sack he was carrying at the end of this
outstretched arm. Looking at his bouncing, rolling form she
observed: "I knew then why they called him Bunny." What
little was left of the ice was placed in a galvanized box. But
Wilson forgot to close the lid. By the time the guests arrived,
the ice had melted and Wilson had locked himself in the
former mess room and fallen asleep. The early guests helped
themselves to Wilson's Prohibition-era bathtub gin. When
they left to telephone the other guests and to ask them to bring
ice, Wilson locked them out.

Hazel recalled that Wilson shaved with ginger ale
when the gasoline-driven water pump failed. He was nevertheless fastidious about the condition of the cottage; he insisted that all the walls be freshly whitewashed before he
moved in. Wilson spent two summers at Peaked Hill (1927
and 1930). In 1927 Hazel Hawthorne had rented a nearby
shack. She recalled that the jovial Wilson, in his "high-pitched
voice, would lectured her on their beach walks, slapping the
side of his leg when amused." For the summers of 1928 and

1929, Hawthorne rented the O'Neill cottage and wrote *Salt House*, a novel thinly disguising her amorous escapades at Peaked Hill and in Provincetown itself. *Salt House* describes some of the luminescent interior of Peaked Hill cottage: "These high windows, table, shelf, make three long lines in the narrow room. White walls and ceiling."

O'Neill deeded the property to his older son and namesake Eugene. Several times O'Neill contemplated returning but never did. O'Neill was living in LePlessis, a French Chateau outside Paris, with his third wife, Carlotta Monterey, when his Peaked Hill house collapsed into the ocean on January 10, 1931. Seventeen years after it had been declared uninhabitable by the U.S. Life-Saving Service, the old station finally crumbled and surrendered to a winter storm.

The Station tottered for three months and then finally slid into the sea. John Dos Passos and Edmund Wilson were among the crowds that flocked to watch as the sea eroded the sandy base. Dos Passos and Wilson climbed up an iron ladder in the bedroom to the lookout tower on the roof as the station canted at a 45-degree angle on its slow descent. The collapse of Peaked Hill, as well as that of Lewis Wharf, marked the end of a literary moment in Provincetown's history. When O'Neill staged his debut on Lewis Wharf the sea had given him a gift—fog, waves, and a high tide. Fifteen years later the sea took away his shining palace built on sand.

LIVING AT PEAKED HILL BARS LIFE-SAVING STATION WAS, for O'Neill, an extension of his shipboard life and his seaside New London childhood home. It was a profound inspiration. "At least twenty of his plays, and the majority of the early one-acters . . . take place on or near the sea. Moreover, many plays that take place on land have as an integral part of their symbolism . . . sea life."[11] O'Neill's description, in *A Long*

Day's Journey into Night, is like a description of the other-worldliness of Peaked Hill:

> Out beyond the harbor, where the road runs along the beach, I even lost the feeling of being on land. The fog and the sea seemed part of each other.

THOREAU AND O'NEILL were both attracted to the ocean. Thoreau, the naturalist, ventured to Cape Cod because, as he said, he "came to see the ocean." O'Neill's attachment was intensely metaphysical: his dream was to be "dissolved in the sea." Thoreau, on the other hand, expressed his reluctance to enter the sea in his verse, "My years are like a stroll upon the beach, / As near the ocean's edge as I can go." Both spent time on the same Atlantic cliffs overlooking the sea: Thoreau in North Truro at Highland Light and O'Neill at Peaked Hill, about six miles to the north. Both took long walks along the same ocean bluffs and beaches. Each had a history of tuberculosis and walked for his health as well as for inspiration. Thoreau, the Poet-Naturalist, collected information and marine specimens for his essays and lectures, while O'Neill, the Poet-Dramatist, wrestled with the interior voices of his characters and with himself.

For O'Neill, the Peaked Hill house was a legendary Walden; this was where he sequestered himself and wrote intensely for over five years, completing his journeyman period. Here he got news of his first Pulitzer Prize for *Beyond the Horizon*. Even at Peaked Hill, however, there was not all the solitude O'Neill wanted. Between Peaked Hill and the center of Provincetown, a distance of nearly three miles, there was a well-beaten path, just as there had been a well-traveled path between Walden Pond and Concord, a mile and a half apart. Hardly a day went by that Thoreau did not visit the village or was not visited at the pond. It was nearly the same for O'Neill at Peaked Hill. One or more of the Provincetown Players were there often, sometimes spending the night, for the accommodations there were commodious by Provincetown standards. Compared to Thoreau's cabin at Walden Pond, it was palatial.

Thoreau characteristically did not probe into other people's lives: "As for the interior of the inhabitants I am still in the dark about it." In Provincetown, Thoreau made a faint attempt to call upon a resident who kept open house on the Sabbath. Upon approaching the house, Thoreau found "stretched across . . . (the) gateway a circular cobweb of the largest kind and quite entire. This looked so ominous that I actually turned aside and went in the back way."

Thoreau's longest stay by the ocean was two weeks. He was a landsman more at home on inland rivers than at the sea; he preferred to stay within the confines of Concord. One is again reminded of his propensity for home, so evident in his statement: "I have travelled a good deal in Concord." His view of the ocean and the people was that of a detached outsider. He was most himself overlooking the ocean from the bluffs or atop a sand dune, surveying the harbor of Provincetown. From that elevation he could overlook the operations of the inhabitants almost as completely as if the roofs had been taken off.

O'Neill was the antithesis of Thoreau in his obsession with the sea and the people of the sea. He probed deeply into both. O'Neill was a marathon swimmer, at one time an able-bodied seaman, and one who for most of his life lived next to the sea. The sea was redemption and ecstasy and a persistent theme in his plays. In *A Long Day's Journey into Night*, Act IV, Edmund speaks about the "high spots" in his "memories."

They're all connected with the sea. [While on a] square rigger bound for Buenos Aires. Full moon in the Trades ... I lay on the bowsprit, facing stern, with water foaming into spume under me, the masts with every sail white in the moonlight, towering high above me. I became drunk with the beauty and singing rhythm of it, and for a moment I lost myself—actually lost my life. I was set free: I dissolved in the sea, became white sails and flying spray ... the moment of ecstatic freedom ... when I was swimming far out, or lying alone on a beach, I have had the same experience ...

It was a great mistake, my being born a man, I would have been much more successful as a sea gull or a fish. As it is, I will always be a stranger who never feels at home.

PAINTERS HAVE BRUITED WORLDWIDE the narrow streets and arcing skies of Provincetown. Jumbled houses, narrow lanes, and curving shoreline have been sketched and re-sketched, thus rendering what is distinctively Provincetown. Writers generally do not publicize the town as its painters do. Harry Kemp, the self-styled "Poet of the Dunes," was the exception. Harry Kemp publicized Provincetown as much as he did himself. He roamed the streets and bars of Provincetown, and was as highly visible as any outdoor artist. Part of his advertising campaign was to costume himself as a Pilgrim and to re-enact the 1620 winter landing. He was personally offended that Provincetown did not have proper status in history books. He first came to town late in the summer of 1916 to be part of the Provincetown Players. The record is not clear as to the extent of his participation, for his name is not on the first subscription list.

Harry Kemp Way is a roadway, a by-pass that runs parallel to Bradford Street, eastward to Snail Road and then northward to Peaked Hill. It was Kemp's beach route as he walked "bent-kneed, like a man going through snow drifts" to his dune shack. The *Provincetown Advocate* describes him making his annual spring trek to "his lonely shack out on the Great Shore near Peaked Hill and Eugene O'Neill's early isolation. In one hand he carried a battered portable typewriter. In the other an even more battered oil stove. Around his neck he had slung a sack of provisions."

On the last day of spring, Harry Kemp emerged briefly from his dune shack to read his spring verse on the steps of the Town Hall. On one occasion he tied a passerby to a chain of flowers, named her "Gloria of Greenwich Village," and led her onto the steps where he read his verse. Antics such as this, and particularly the yearly re-enactment of the Pilgrim's Landing, endeared him to the town.

Toward the end of his life, Kemp relinquished Greenwich Village and stayed year-round in Provincetown, where he found generous landlords, particularly John Francis and his son, John Francis, Jr. When the latter died, Sonny Tasha became Kemp's benefactor. She built him the shack where he died on August 8, 1960, at the age of seventy-six. Despite much resistance by the local undertaker, his body was sent out to be cremated. As Kemp requested, his ashes were scattered at Peaked Hill and on the streets of Greenwich Village, two important places in his life. According to local legend, a few Provincetowners went to the Village and scraped up Kemp's ashes as Sonny Tasha strewed them upon the sidewalk.

Harry Kemp prided himself on being a "tramp poet" or "box-car bard," in the tradition of Vachel Lindsay, the vagabond poet—a type of anti-hero who lived not for the robber barons and industrial America but for poetic beauty. Kemp was about six feet tall and had craggy features, pale-blue eyes, and spindly arms and legs. He dressed for attention. He never wore a hat, tousled his matted hair, and wore sandals, corduroy pants, and vivid cotton shirts, partially unbuttoned to reveal his hairy chest. Kemp staged events to advertise himself and called his stunts "spectacularism." He illegally rode a box car to the University of Kansas, heralding his arrival as a student—a stunt covered by the newspapers. In 1913 he became the "stowaway poet" when he blatantly boarded, without passage, the liner *Oceanic*, bound for England. Before boarding, he alerted the press. The stunt backfired. The Captain assigned him to kitchen duty and, upon the ship's arrival in Southampton, had him thrown into jail. He was finally released when some of his friends interceded for him. Kemp chronicled this event as a *Poet's Pilgrimage*.[12]

Although he was but briefly a part of the Provincetown Players, Harry Kemp wanted to be remembered as a Player. Only one of his plays, *The Prodigal Son*, was staged. This took place in 1916–17, during the Players' first winter in New York. Kemp acted in three plays that first New York season, including the role of Davis in *Bound East for Cardiff*. The Players, though experimental and sometimes capricious, found Kemp too undisciplined. He skipped over lines and according to Alfred Kreymborg "ranted like Bottom . . . and tramped about as if life indeed lay underfoot."[13] Kemp left the Players after the first season and set up his own little theater, the Harry Kemp Playhouse, but it was not successful. When the writer Maxwell Bodenheim went to the Village in the 1920s, he supplanted Harry Kemp as the Village's poet. Kemp then retired to his dune shack at Peaked Hill.

Right after her marriage to Kemp in 1915, the lovely young redhead Mary Pyne underwent a serious operation, most probably a hysterectomy. She was ill throughout their short marriage and died in 1919 from tuberculosis. Marriage itself was troublesome to Kemp, for it limited his freedom: "when one marries, everything becomes much more complicated."[14] Pyne was an actress with the Provincetown Players in New York. Theodore Dreiser was enamored of her and portrayed her as Esther Norn in *A Gallery of Women*; in the novel, Dreiser depicted Hutch Hapgood as an ardent suitor of Pyne. Hapgood angrily insisted that the relationship was platonic. Djuna Barnes was also infatuated with Mary Pyne. Both she and Hutch befriended Mary when Harry neglected her during her last illness.

Kemp later claimed more of a role with the Players than facts substantiate. He was never part of the inner circle. Jack Reed referred to him as "unkempt Harry Kemp"; Jig Cook found him a good drinking partner but exasperating. On one occasion Kemp swam the shoreline of Provincetown harbor with a poem in his teeth that he delivered to a bemused Neith Boyce. Hazel Hawthorne, in her *Salt House*, portrays Kemp as "Johnny Otto, an old friend of everybody, a poet . . . vastly out of place . . . He kept carrying the sonnet he was writing into the bathroom with him, stuffed into his pocket like a piece of cloth." The hardest workers in the group—O'Neill, Vorse, and Glaspell—found him disruptive. Kemp needed continual reassurance. Day or night he banged on doors bellowing for attention and for someone to listen to a newly written poem. As he grew older and his alcoholism worsened, these intrusions occurred more frequently and at more ungodly hours. Once he pounded unrelentingly on Mary Heaton Vorse's front door at 3:00 A.M., waving a poem he had dedicated to her. She sent him off. O'Neill refused to unlock his door, yelling to Harry whenever he knocked to "Get the Hell out."

In his later years, Kemp was a rollicking, ribald, and—at times—cavalier drunk who cadged drinks by composing on-the-spot verse tailored to his benefactor. They were acrostic verses that spelled out the donor's name with the beginning letter of each line. He is affectionately remembered for his clever and humorous versification of Provincetown nicknames, mostly Portuguese, which he set to verse in "Rhyme of Provincetown Nicknames." "Next I weave on my versicles' difficult loom, Swede, Swifty, Rocky, and Titti-boom." Harry Kemp spent half of his adult life on the dunes of Peaked Hill. One of his best verses is "The Dunes." Perhaps this is the way to remember him:

> Back from the wave-carved ramparts of the beach
> Skyward the gray, enormous sand-dunes reach
> Stippled with far-seen trails of wandering feet
> That walk up distant summits, cross, and meet
> And merge into the road where lies the Town . . .

FOLLOWING THEIR SUCCESSFUL 1916–17 SEASON on Mac-Dougal Street in New York, the Provincetown Players as a troupe did not return to Provincetown. Artists Margaret Steele and Lucy L'Engle set up easels on Lewis Wharf, and a group of art students who called themselves the "Sixes and Sevens," for two summers operated a coffee shop and a "dry" night club in the old theater building. Costumed in sailor attire, the artists served tea and sandwiches, played musical instruments, and sang. At night there was a cover charge of eleven cents because the club was open until 11 o'clock or "until the last bus of the day would honk outside on Commercial St."[15] By 1922, Lewis Wharf was gone. "Fire and ice and the sea destroyed the Lewis wharf," recounted Mary Heaton Vorse in her memoirs of the town. Courtney Allen, one of the Sixes-and-Sevens artists, constructed a scale model of the wharf and its buildings, which is now displayed in Provincetown's Pilgrim Monument Museum.

Susan Glaspell vehemently objected to a theater group that came to Provincetown in the summer of 1946 and called themselves the Provincetown Players. "The name Provincetown Players still stands for an amazing burst of creative energy. Now comes a group of people from New York and without so much as by-your-leave to us, these Broadway actors fill the town with posters declaring they are the Provincetown Players. If the haddock began calling themselves mackerel, would the fish-minded be fooled."[16]

There have been other groups through the years that have tried to exploit the name and reputation of the Players. Some groups, however, have tried to revive the spirit of the Players. None succeeded. The Wharf Theater, organized in 1924, is often confused with the original Provincetown Players. Mary Heaton Vorse commented: "They had nothing in common except the fact that they both gave plays in the same town."[17] In 1940, when that wharf was destroyed, Susan Glaspell commented: "Provincetown has had a storm tossed winter. The wharf theater put out to sea."[18] The writer Norman Matson, like his common-law wife Glaspell, was happy when it collapsed in a gale: "like a righteous critic" the gale "pulled it apart; it exposed it."

In 1924, Frank Shay, editor and bookseller, transformed his barn on Bradford Street into the Barnstormer's Theater. This theater, more than any other local theater, followed the experimental approach of the Provincetown Players; in fact, O'Neill and Vorse were part of this organization. O'Neill was present at the first bill of the Barnstormers, when it staged his *Before Breakfast* and revived four of his sea plays, which were produced for the first time as a group, with the title *S.S. Glencairn*. Mary Heaton Vorse told of Gene's quiet coaching of the lead actress in *Before Breakfast* and described his appearance: "He is well, but has lost the look of security and sweetness which made him so lovable last summer. His face shows the pain he went through at his brother's death. He is remote and absorbed within."[19]

Immediately after the first bill of the Barnstormers, a rump group that became the Wharf Theatre moved their property out of the Barn. According to Mary Heaton Vorse, a Mrs. Aldis early one morning "got a truck which she had backed up to the theater. From it she removed all the benches, all the props, even the light bulbs, and carried them off to her studio . . . The rest of the season Mrs. Aldis had plays in her studio by the water with the furniture from the Theatre." The Wharf Theatre staged conservative fare, while Frank Shay's Barnstormers produced more robust and shocking plays. Vorse continues: "[Provincetown was amused when] Rita Byrd and a friend went to the costume ball as sandwich boards, advertising the two theaters. One advertised the 'Lewd and Stewed' and the other the 'Rude and Prude.'" One of the Barnstormers, Ray Moore, moved forty miles away from Provincetown to Dennis, Massachusetts, where he established the still-operating Cape Playhouse.

THE PROVINCETOWN PLAYERS' FICTION reveals little about their personal lives in Provincetown. One needs to consult their autobiographies, letters, and diaries that have been preserved in university and private archives. Their first years in Provincetown were creative, youthful, and optimistic; there followed subdued times, years of shared memories, melancholy, and nostalgia. Susan Glaspell's letter written near the end of her life reflects on this: "Funny how this place became home to some of us who came from places so different . . . but how nice that we feel we belong together, and that this is our home."[20]

Susan Glaspell devoted only a small part of her fiction to Provincetown. Of her nine novels, only *Judd Rankin's Daughter* has a setting—and that only partially—in Provincetown. In it she characterizes the durability of Provincetown as a tough fishing town. Of her fourteen plays, two have Provincetown settings, *The Outside* and *Tickless Time*, the latter co-authored with Jig. The locale of *The Outside* is Peaked Hill, and it was written three years before O'Neill moved there. She portrayed this stretch of dunes as a place where one could escape from life and engage in a symbolic fight with the encroaching sea. Her description foreshadows what O'Neill eventually did when he moved to Peaked Hill. One of Glaspell's major short stories, *Government Goat*, deals in mock-epic form with the struggle for survival in Provincetown, an impoverished environment.

Hutchins Hapgood was the only Player to publish a full-length autobiography. Hapgood's *A Victorian in the Modern World* is not a happy memoir despite his claim: "I have sinned, I have suffered, I have wasted, but how I have enjoyed." In retrospect, he blamed world events, particularly the feminism movement, for his and other men's failures. Formerly close women friends—Mabel Dodge, Susan Glaspell, and Mary Vorse—were blamed. He relates his quarrel with Glaspell when he challenged her true intentions in writing her posthumous tribute to Jig Cook, *Road to the Temple*. He accused her of missing the true spirit of Jig: "You perhaps, like most women, wanted him to be practical." Mary Vorse received the harshest treatment; he objected to her wit and claimed that she "had a very amusing tongue which she did not hold in check." Mabel Dodge escaped his harshest criticism because she spoke of Hutch with admiration and respect in her memoirs, which predated Hapgood's. Nevertheless, he analyzed in detail Dodge's failures at love, concluding that she was "a cripple" who tried "all her life to become well, whole."

Mary Heaton Vorse's scattered reminiscences are found in *Time and the Town* and *Footnote to Folly*. The latter is primarily about her struggles in labor activities. Vorse regaled her friends with stories about Provincetown, but her fiction dealt only marginally with the town. She donated story ideas about Provincetown to others such as Steele and O'Neill. One such tale became O'Neill's one-act play *Ile*, which was about John A. Cook, Provincetown's abusive whaling captain.

PROVINCETOWN, FOR O'NEILL, was "hard to get to and get out of but a grand place to be alone and undisturbed when you want to work." For Gene, it was his home for nearly nine years, another sea-home for this "Sea-Mother's Son" who had lived most of his life along a seacoast or aboard ship. Born in New York City, O'Neill spent his summers in New London, Connecticut, in the family's modest but elegantly furnished cottage along the Thames River near where it widens into Long Island Sound. For O'Neill, the sea was his escape and his metaphorical salvation. Childhood summers near the sea were O'Neill's happiest times, for Fall meant either boarding school and being away from his parents, or endless train rides and lodgings in hotels or rented houses with his touring parents.

O'Neill adapted rapidly to Provincetown, like a hermit crab backing into a new shell. At this period in his life, he intensely needed the sea around him; he thrived on scruffy waterfronts, sailors and fishermen, fish lumpers and wharf rats, shacks to flop in, and time to write about sea-related things. He relished the oceanside: "Beautiful surf rolling in with slumberous roar." Provincetown had this and more— people who finally understood and appreciated his plays. Jig and Susan Cook immediately recognized his talent, as did Louise Bryant and Jack Reed; many others said they did in retrospective writings.

Moving to Provincetown was psychologically and practically easier for Gene than for the rest, for example, the

Cooks, who were from Midwest farmland, or Mary O'Brien, who each season moved a full household of children and servants. Gene was unencumbered and his family home was only a couple of hours away by rail in New London, midway between Provincetown and New York City. On trips to New York, Gene frequently stopped over in New London to visit his parents. His family had begun to summer there before Gene's birth and in 1883 renovated a cottage with the finest materials, such as walnut woodwork and tile fireplaces. James O'Neill, Sr., named it "Monte Cristo" after his successful role in the play, *Count of Monte Cristo*. It gradually became their permanent home as James O'Neill's touring activities diminished.

As O'Neill recorded in his notebooks, he deliberately left New London and Greenwich Village in 1916 and made Provincetown his home. In these notebooks, he divided his life into seven-year cycles that were centered around significant events in his creative and personal life. Provincetown was one of these cycles, as cited in his notebooks for 1916–17: "PT [Provincetown]-G.V. [Greenwich Village] last of N.L. [New London] home." Within these nine years, he married for the second time, acquired a house, had a second son, ended his period as a journeyman playwright, and won a Pulitzer Prize. When he left Provincetown in 1924, he was the only remaining member of the O'Neill family; both parents and Jamie were dead. He came as an apprentice and left as a master craftsman, confident and rich.

A critical turning-point in O'Neill's life occurred July 28, 1916, on Mrs. O'Brien's wharf, when *Bound East for Cardiff* was staged. O'Neill's instincts were theoretically sound when he chose *Bound East for Cardiff* for his premiere. It was his best play to date, despite the criticism of Professor Baker at Harvard, who said that it was not a play at all. It did not have the conventional structure and plot of contemporary plays, but was instead a prolonged dialogue and mood piece about a sailor facing his death on a fogbound ship. O'Neill had taken *Bound East for Cardiff* to Harvard, as well as his volume of five one-act plays, *Thirst*. The plays were not well received there. To conform to course expectations, O'Neill wrote rather conventional plays for Baker, nothing that he valued. Though O'Neill stated later, in 1935, that he learned a great deal from Baker on a personal level, he concluded that "the plays I wrote for him were rotten."[21]

O'Neill had a strong sense of place. As a dramatic realist and the observant son of a seasoned actor and theatrical producer, he correctly assessed the potential of the seaport atmosphere of Provincetown and the rustic setting of Mrs. O'Brien's wharf, and then selected his best sea play as a fitting first production. When, in 1935, O'Neill looked back on the importance of *Bound East for Cardiff*, he wrote: "Very important from my point of view. In it can be seen, or felt, the germ of the spirit, life-attitude, etc., of all my more important future work. It was written before my work under Professor Baker at Harvard."[22]

O'Neill, the outsider, was embraced by the Players. How far and how fast he would have gone without them will forever be conjecture. Susan Glaspell noted, in 1927, that the Provincetown Players under Jig Cook's direction allowed audiences to see "those dramas of the sea written by Eugene O'Neill. No one else was producing him then."[23] Mary Heaton Vorse echoed this: "We know, had Mr. O'Neill not had the Provincetown Players as a medium of expression, he might yet be waiting for the recognition that is his just due."[24] O'Neill himself wrote to Barrett H. Clark, his first biographer, that "I owe a tremendous lot to the Players—they encouraged me to write, and produced all my early and many of my later plays. But I can't honestly say I would not have gone on writing plays if it hadn't been for them. I had already gone too far ever to quit."[25]

The Players were not landscape writers; seldom did they look directly at the sea and the dunes and describe what lay around them. Searching for Provincetown in the writings of the Players who called Provincetown home, one finds melancholy. There is Glaspell's recurrent plaintive motif, her nostalgia for her Midwestern roots: "home to some of us who came from places so different." There is Mary Heaton Vorse's loss of the romantic, sea-faring past of Lewis Wharf: "the old fish wharf could not go on living." There is O'Neill's constant search for the cleansing redemption of the sea, "A melancholy . . . chant, faint and faroff, drifts, crooning, over the water."[26] Steele's sinewy descriptions and masculine bravado mask a deeper, recurring theme, a nostalgic search for lost spirituality: "He doesn't even know it, that the immortal soul of him has gone out."[27] Hutchins Hapgood expressed melancholy in his memoirs, bemoaning the loss of the romance of living. Most of the writers were introspective; their own interior landscapes were more important to them than the external scenery.

The most telling melancholy image of Provincetown is O'Neill's, of ships lying at anchor in Provincetown Harbor during a fog: "It is ten o'clock at night. Dense fog shrouds the barge on all sides, and she floats motionless in a calm . . . The doleful tolling of bells, on Long Point, on ships at anchor breaks the silence at regular intervals."[28]

For O'Neill, the Sea-Mother's Son, Provincetown was a sea home. O'Neill turned again and again to the sea for metaphor and sustenance. The sea give him his first stage and his first home, and then took them both away. He died in a Boston hospital only fifty miles across Cape Cod Bay from Provincetown. He had come full circle from where his sea journey had begun.

Plays Staged in Provincetown by the Provincetown Players*

Play	Playwright	Stage
SUMMER 1915		
Constancy	Neith Boyce	Hapgood Cottage
Suppressed Desires	Susan Glaspell	Hapgood Cottage
	George Cram Cook	
Change Your Style	George Cram Cook	Lewis Wharf
Contemporaries	Wilbur Daniel Steele	Lewis Wharf
SUMMER 1916**		
Winter's Night	Neith Boyce	Lewis Wharf
Enemies	Neith Boyce	Lewis Wharf
	Hutchins Hapgood	
Trifles	Susan Glaspell	Lewis Wharf
Not Smart	Wilbur Daniel Steele	Lewis Wharf
The Game	Louise Bryant	Lewis Wharf
Freedom	John S. Reed	Lewis Wharf and Town Hall
Eternal Quadrangle	John S. Reed	Lewis Wharf
Bound East for Cardiff	Eugene O'Neill	Lewis Wharf
Thirst	Eugene O'Neill	Lewis Wharf

*See Robert Karoly Sarlos, *Jig Cook and the Provincetown Players,* for further discussion of chronology and cast; also for the children's play, *Mother Carey's Chickens.*

**Reprise of 1915 plays is not repeated here.

Notes

Abbreviations of frequently cited collections:

HUH   Harvard University, Houghton Library
HUT   Harvard University, Theatre Collection
IUL   Indiana University, Lilly Library
LC   Library of Congress
NYPL   New York Public Library, Berg Collection
SUA   Syracuse University, George Arents Library
SUL   Stanford University Libraries, Special Collections
UVA   University of Virginia, Alderman Library
WSU   Wayne State University, Archives of Labor & Urban Affairs
YCAL   Yale Collection of American Literature, The Beinecke Rare Book and Manuscript Library

Note: See Bibliography for complete citations for books and periodicals.

INTRODUCTION

1. "Many Literary Lights Among Provincetown Players," *Boston (Sunday) Post,* September 10, 1916, p. 44.

CHAPTER 1

1. WSU, Mary Heaton Vorse papers, Mary Vorse to John Francis, March 3, 1916.
2. Susan Glaspell, *Road to the Temple,* p. 252.
3. William Zorach, *Art is My Life,* p. 45.
4. Glaspell, *Road,* p. 253.
5. *Ibid.,* p. 254.
6. O'Neill letter, June 13, 1922, in Bogard and Bryer, *Selected Letters of Eugene O'Neill,* p. 170.

CHAPTER 2

1. Mary Heaton Vorse, *Time and the Town*, p. 118.
2. *Ibid.*, p. 9.
3. *Provincetown Advocate*, October 19, 1916.
4. *Ibid.*, November 25, 1915.
5. Edmund Wilson, *The Thirties*, pp. 26–28.
6. Vorse, *Time*, p. 118.
7. *Ibid.*, pp. 118–119.
8. WSU, Vorse papers, Mary to Joe [n.d. Sept. 1915?].
9. Robert K. Sarlos, *Jig Cook and the Provincetown Players*, p. 210.
10. *Provincetown Advocate*, June 18, 1916. [Carpenters were Jig Cook, Bror Nordfeldt, Teddy Ballantine, and Joe O'Brien, cf. Susan Glaspell, *Road to the Temple*.]
11. WSU, Vorse papers, Don to Mary [1916].
12. *Provincetown Advocate*, July 13, 1916.
13. WSU, Vorse papers, Don to Mary [1916].
14. *Ibid.*
15. Hutchins Hapgood, *A Victorian in the Modern World*, p. 557.
16. Helen Deutsch and Stella Hanau, *The Provincetown: A Story of the Theater*, p. 19.
17. *Provincetown Advocate*, October 13, 1916.
18. Dee Garrison, *Rebel Pen*, p. 26.
19. Phyllis C. Robinson, *Willa: The Life of Willa Cather*, p. 130.
20. IUL, Viola Roseboro papers, Viola to Sam McClure [1907].
21. Heaton Vorse, "The Province of Bohemia," 1985 *Arts Directory*, p. 15.
22. Jane K. Graham, *Viola, the Duchess of New Dorp*, pp. 110–115 *passim*.
23. Garrison, *Rebel Pen*, pp. 38–39. [Garrison's interviewee mistakenly identified Viola as Mary Vorse's secretary.]
24. Martin Bucco, *Wilbur Daniel Steele*, pp. 24–25 *passim*.
25. WSU, Vorse papers, Wilbur to Mary [n.d. 1909?].
26. *Ibid.* [n.d. 1911?].
27. Max Eastman, *Enjoyment of Living*, p. 399.
28. Lawrence Langner, *The Magic Curtain*, p. 70.
29. Hapgood, *Victorian*, p. 372.
30. YCAL, Hapgood papers, Neith to Hutch [n.d. July 1911?].

31. NYPL, Cook papers, Jig to Sue, March 17, 1913.
32. *Ibid.*, March 23, 1913.
33. *Provincetown Advocate,* May 29, 1913.
34. WSU, Vorse papers, Susan to Mary and Joe, May 8, 1913.
35. Hapgood, *Victorian,* p. 373.
36. WSU, Vorse papers, Susan to Mary and Joe [October 1914?].
37. Dorothy G. Seckler, "History of the Provincetown Art Colony," p. 23.
38. *Provincetown Advocate,* April 15, 1915.
39. Michael Jacobs, *The Good and Simple Life,* pp. 7 and 17.
40. Mary Heaton Vorse, "The Portuguese of Provincetown," *Outlook,* p. 410.
41. Vorse, *Time,* p. 359.
42. *Ibid.,* p. 115.

CHAPTER 3

1. Henry David Thoreau, *Cape Cod,* p. 316.
2. John Brereton, *Brief and True Relation, 1602,* in Shay and Shay, *Sand in Their Shoes,* p. 6.
3. William Bradford, *Mourt's Relations, 1622,* in Shay and Shay, pp. 19–36.
4. Henry Howe, *Prologue to New England,* pp. 183–187.
5. Shebnah Rich, *Truro-Cape Cod,* pp. 84–85.
6. George F. Dow, *Everyday Life in the Massachusetts Bay Colony,* p. 110.
7. Frederick Freeman, *History of Cape Cod: Annals of the Thirteen Towns of Barnstable County,* p. 629.
8. Dow, *Everyday Life,* pp. 207–225.
9. William Bradford, *History of Plimoth Plantation,* pp. 474–476.
10. Rich, *Truro,* p. 282.
11. David Freeman Hawke, *Everyday Life in Early America,* p. 152.
12. Freeman, *History of Cape Cod,* p. 628.
13. *Ibid.,* p. 629.
14. Simeon L. Deyo, *History of Barnstable County, Massachusetts,* p. 965.

15. Henry C. Kittredge, *Cape Cod, Its People and Their History,* p. 160.
16. S.P. Leatherman, *Environmental Geologic Guide to Cape Cod National Seashore,* p. 211.
17. Edward Augustus Kendall, *Travels Through the Northern Part of the U.S., 1807–8,* p. 152.
18. Timothy Dwight, *Travels; in New England and New York,* p. 91.
19. James Warner Barber, *Massachusetts Historical Collections,* pp. 50–51.
20. James D. Graham, *A Report upon the Military and Hydrographical Chart of the Extremity of Cape Cod,* p. 8.
21. Rich, *Truro,* p. 218.
22. Thoreau, *Cape Cod,* p. 114.
23. *Ibid.,* pp. 265–266.
24. Freeman, *History of Cape Cod,* p. 646.
25. Thoreau, *Cape Cod,* p. 307.
26. *Ibid.,* p. 269.
27. Elias Nason, *A Gazetteer of the State of Massachusetts,* p. 422.
28. Mary Heaton Vorse, *Time and the Town,* p. 87.
29. Kittredge, *History of Cape Cod,* p. 182.
30. Deyo, *History,* p. 976.
31. *Ibid.,* p. 969.
32. Thoreau, *Cape Cod,* p. 256.
33. *Ibid.,* p. 44.
34. Freeman, *History of Cape Cod,* p. 624.
35. *Ibid.,* p. 647.
36. Alexander Starbuck, *History of the American Whale Fishery,* p. 490 *fn.*
37. Charles Nordhoff, *Whaling and Fishing,* pp. 362–363. (See also: W.D. Steele, "The 'Killers' of Provincetown.")
38. Samuel E. Morison, *The Maritime History of Massachusetts,* pp. 305–312 *passim.*
39. Thoreau, *Cape Cod,* p. 326.
40. Rich, *Truro,* pp. 444–445.
41. Thoreau, *Cape Cod,* p. 326.
42. Walter Harding, *The Days of Henry Thoreau,* p. 273.
43. Henry S. Canby, *Thoreau,* p. 373.

44. *Dictionary of American Biography,* 1936 ed., p. 306.
45. Cortland Auser, *Nathaniel P. Willis,* p. 56.
46. Henry Beers, *Nathaniel Willis,* p. 323.
47. N. Parker Willis, *Hurry-Graphs,* pp. 32–71 *passim.*
48. Thoreau, *Cape Cod,* p. 262.
49. Samuel Nash and Lorenzo Warriner, unpublished letters, 1831.
50. *Provincetown 1874 Town Report,* p. 43.
51. *Ibid.,* p. 42.
52. *Ibid.,* p. 44.
53. Robert Carter, *Summer Cruise on the Coast of New England,* pp. 45–57 *passim.*
54. Morison, *Maritime History,* p. 314.
55. HUT, Agnes Boulton to Eugene O'Neill, January 22, 1920.

CHAPTER 4

1. *Salem Gazette,* January 1, 1839 (cited in Alvin F. Harlow, *Steelways of New England,* p. 153).
2. *Provincetown Advocate,* July 23, 1873.
3. Charles Nordhoff, "Cape Cod, Nantucket, and the Vineyard," *Harper's Monthly,* 1875, p. 55.
4. Samuel Drake, *Nooks and Corners of the New England Coast,* p. 319.
5. William W. Nolen, "Provincetown," *Our Country East—In New England,* p. 204.
6. Katharine Lee Bates, "Cape Cod Towns" in Lyman P. Powell, *Historic Towns of New England,* pp. 358–359.
7. Charles Dickens, *American Notes,* p. 62
8. Alvin Harlow, *Steelways of New England,* p. 402.
9. Dickens, *Notes,* p. 61.
10. Hildegarde Hawthorne, *Old Seaport Towns of New England,* p. 217.
11. John Sloan, *New York Scene,* p. 145.
12. Helen Henderson, *Loiterer in New England,* p. 45.
13. *Ibid.,* pp. 46–48.
14. Roger W. McAdam, *The Old Fall River Line,* p. 55.
15. Roger Williams McAdam, *Priscilla of Fall River,* p. 128.
16. Mary Heaton Vorse, *The Passing of the Fall River Line,* p. 3.

17. Drake, *Nooks and Corners,* p. 312.
18. Howe, *New England,* p. 27.
19. Leo Pap, *The Portuguese-Americans,* pp. 35–36.

CHAPTER 5

1. Henry F. May, *The End of American Innocence,* p. 283.
2. IUL, Neith Boyce to ? [n.d. 1913?].
3. Otis Pease, ed., *The Progressive Years,* p. 3.
4. Alfred Kazin, *On Native Grounds,* pp. 165–173 *passim.*
5. Ralph Pendleton, ed., *The Theatre of Robert Edmond Jones,* p. 15.
6. Dee Garrison, *Rebel Pen,* pp. 36–61 *passim.*
7. WSU, Vorse papers, Mary to Wilbur, March 15, 1915.
8. Mary Heaton Vorse, *Footnote to Folly,* p. 73.
9. Mabel Dodge Luhan, *Movers and Shakers,* p. 23.
10. James R. Mellow, *Charmed Circle,* p. 169.
11. Max Eastman, *Enjoyment of Living,* p. 523.
12. Hutchins Hapgood, *A Victorian in the Modern World,* p. 353.
13. *Ibid.,* p. 351.
14. Lincoln Steffens, *Autobiography,* p. 653.
15. Hapgood, *Victorian,* p. 353.
16. HUT, Jones papers, Westcott letter [n.d. June ? 1913].
17. Luhan, *Movers,* pp. 212–216 *passim.*
18. HUH, John S. Reed papers, Jack to Eddy Hunt, July 20, 1913.
19. YCAL, Hapgood papers, Mabel to Neith, September 29, 1913.
20. Mabel Dodge Luhan, *European Experiences,* p. 159.
21. HUH, Reed papers, Jack to Eddy Hunt, December 16, 1913.
22. Luhan, *Movers,* p. 282.
23. *Ibid.,* pp. 284–285.
24. Robert A. Rosenstone, *Romantic Revolutionary,* p. 191.
25. June Sochen, *Movers and Shakers,* p. 27.
26. For further discussion, see Adam Weisman, "Susan Glaspell: A Woman's Modernism."
27. June Sochen, *The New Woman in Greenwich Village 1910–20,* p. 37.
28. Eastman, *Enjoyment,* p. 425.

29. Hapgood, *Victorian,* p. 360.
30. *Ibid.,* p. 134.
31. *Ibid.,* pp. 150–154.
32. NYPL, Cook papers, Jig to Sue, December 10, 1907.
33. Allen Churchill, *The Improper Bohemians,* pp. 177–178.
34. Robert Karoly Sarlos, *Jig Cook and the Provincetown Players,* p. 10.
35. Constance D'Arcy Mackay, *The Little Theatre in the United States,* p. 16.
36. Susan Glaspell, *Road to the Temple,* p. 250.
37. Floyd Dell, *Homecoming,* pp. 202–203.
38. NYPL, Theatre Collection, Susan Glaspell to Eleanor Fitzgerald, May 7, 1929.
39. WSU, Vorse papers, Mary to Neith, March 10, 1915.
40. *Ibid.,* Neith to Mary, January 20, 1915.

CHAPTER 6

1. Hutchins Hapgood, *A Victorian in the Modern World,* pp. 385–390 *passim.*
2. John S. Reed, *The War in Eastern Europe,* p. 98.
3. *Ibid.,* p. 311.
4. Mary Heaton Vorse, *Footnote to Folly,* p. 128.
5. *Ibid.,* p. 127.
6. NYPL, Cook papers, Cook's unpublished autobiography, holograph, 1914.
7. Lawrence Langner, *The Magic Curtain,* p. 71.
8. *Provincetown Advocate,* September 17, 1914.
9. *Ibid.,* August 25, 1915.
10. Van Deren Coke, *Nordfeldt the Painter,* pp. 35–48.
11. Robert Karoly Sarlos, *Jig Cook and the Provincetown Players,* p. 18.
12. Susan Glaspell, *Road to the Temple,* p. 245.
13. Helen Deutsch and Stella Hanau, *The Provincetown,* p. 8.
14. WSU, Vorse papers, Mary to Wilbur, March 15, 1915.
15. Martin Bucco, *Wilbur Daniel Steele,* pp. 17–39 *passim.*
16. WSU, Vorse papers, Sue to Mary [n.d. 1915].

17. Bucco, *Steele*, p. 17.
18. Mabel Dodge Luhan, *Movers and Shakers*, p. 403.
19. *Ibid.*, p. 405.

CHAPTER 7

1. *Provincetown Advocate*, July 20, 1916.
2. *Ibid.*, July 27, 1916.
3. *Ibid.*, August 17, 1916.
4. HUT, Jones papers, Bobby to Florence Westcott [n.d. June 1916].
5. Van Deren Coke, *Nordfeldt the Painter*, p. 46.
6. William Zorach, *Art is My Life*, p. 44.
7. Alfred Kreymborg, *Troubadour*, p. 139.
8. SUA, Louise Bryant papers, unpublished TS autobiographical sketch.
9. HUT, Jones, Westcott letter.
10. *Ibid.*, Westcott letter.
11. SUA, Bryant autobiographical sketch.
12. O'Neill letter in Bogard and Bryer, *Selected Letters of Eugene O'Neill*, p. 73.
13. SUA, Bryant autobiographical sketch.
14. HUH, Reed papers, Jack to Louise, June 18, 1916.
15. Hutchins Hapgood, *A Victorian in the Modern World*, pp. 394–395.
16. Mabel Dodge Luhan, *Movers and Shakers*, p. 482.
17. HUH, Reed papers, Marsden Hartley to Louise and Jack [n.d. June 1916].
18. Kreymborg, *Troubadour*, p. 113.
19. YCAL, Marsden Hartley papers, TS "The Great Provincetown Summer."
20. William Carlos Williams, *Autobiography*, p. 52
21. Marsden Hartley, "Farewell, Charles," *passim*, in *The New Caravan*.
22. Louis Sheaffer, *O'Neill: Son and Playwright*, p. 353.
23. HUT, Jones papers, Westcott letter.
24. Lincoln Steffens, *Autobiography*, p. 654.
25. Mary Heaton Vorse, *A Footnote to Folly*, p. 128.

26. WSU, Vorse papers, Griffin Barry to Mary O'Brien [n.d. 1916].
27. Dora Russell, *The Tamarisk Tree*, pp. 205–262 *passim*.
28. Edmund Wilson, *The Thirties*, p. 354.
29. Townsend Ludington, *John Dos Passos*, pp. 82–83.
30. WSU, Vorse papers, Joe to Mary [? 1914].
31. SUL, Steele papers, Wilbur to parents, June 28, 1916.
32. Robert Karoly Sarlos, *Jig Cook and the Provincetown Players*, p. 210 *fn*.
33. YCAL, Hapgood papers, Neith Boyce to father-in-law, July 16, 1916.
34. Sarlos, *Jig Cook*, p. 21.
35. YCAL, Hapgood papers, Neith Boyce to Carl Van Vechten, December (?), 1915.
36. *Ibid.*, Hutch to Mabel, December 15, 1915.
37. UVA, Glaspell papers, holograph notebook, n.d.
38. Helen Deutsch and Stella Hanau, *The Provincetown*, p. 26.
39. Hapgood, *Victorian*, p. 392.
40. *Ibid.*, p. 395.
41. UVA, Glaspell papers, Jig to Sue [n.d. 1916?].
42. Susan Glaspell, *Road to the Temple*, pp. 255–256.
43. Lawrence Langner, *The Magic Curtain*, p. 70.
44. WSU, Vorse papers, Sue to Joe and Mary, May 8, 1913.
45. Glaspell, *Road*, p. 278.
46. Marcia Noe, *Susan Glaspell*, p. 44.
47. William Zorach, *Art is My Life*, p. 47.
48. NYPL, Cook papers, Glaspell to Fitzgerald, May 7, 1929.
49. Alice Rohe, "The Story of Susan Glaspell," *New York Morning Telegraph*, December 18, 1921.
50. Reginald Cabral Collection, Provincetown.
51. SUL, Steele papers, Wilbur to parents, July 28, 1916.
52. Sarlos, *Jig Cook*, p. 111.
53. SUL, Steele papers, Jig to Wilbur [n.d. 1913?].
54. Sarlos, *Jig Cook*, p. 21.
55. *Provincetown Advocate*, August 17, 1916.
56. Ted Robinson, *The Beachcombers*, pp. 8–9
57. *Provincetown Advocate*, August 31, 1916.
58. John Reed, "Fog," *Scribners*, LXVI, August 1919.
59. Art Young, *On My Way*, p. 110.

60. Hapgood, *Victorian,* p. 352.
61. HUL, Reed papers, Jack to Louise, April 10, 1917.
62. Glaspell, *Road,* p. 302.
63. SUA, Bryant autobiographical sketch.
64. HUL, Reed papers, Reed to Sally Robinson, December 4, 1915.
65. SUA, Bryant autobiographical sketch.
66. Williams, *Autobiography,* p. 142.
67. Zorach, *Life,* p. 46.
68. SUA, Bryant autobiographical sketch.
69. Louise Bryant, "Six Poems," *The Masses,* October 1916.
70. HUL, Reed papers, "On the Dunes," Eugene G. O'Neill.

Note: A typed manuscript of O'Neill's poem "On the Dunes" is in the Reed papers, with the handwritten subscript: "until Oct. 1st {Provincetown Mass.} after that {c/o Jack Reed 43 Wash. Sq. So. New York City.}" A variation of the poem appears as "Fragments" in *Eugene O'Neill Poems, 1912–1944,* ed. Donald Gallup, pp. 71–72.

O'Neill cancelled in pencil the following lines:

Your body is warm and undulating
As the sand dunes.
Eager with tremulous heat waves
Beneath my kisses
Your passions stretch upward
Their frantic, quivering hands.

I shall come to you
In the delirium of noon.

71. Max Eastman, *Enjoyment of Life,* p. 564.
72. Arthur and Barbara Gelb, *O'Neill,* p. 324.
73. Sheaffer, *O'Neill: Son and Playwright,* p. 365.
74. George Jean Nathan, "Portrait of O'Neill" in Cargill, et al., *O'Neill and His Plays: Four Decades of Criticism,* p. 50.
75. UVA, Glaspell papers, holograph notebook.
76. HUL, Reed papers, TS, O'Neill poems [1916].
77. NYPL, Cook papers, Jig to Sue, December 23, 1916.
78. Donald Gallup, *Eugene O'Neill Poems, 1912–1944,* pp. 56 and 83.

79. HUL, Reed papers, TS, Bryant [1917].
80. NYPL, Cook papers, Jig to Sue, September 14, 1916.
81. *Ibid.,* September 13, 1916.
82. New York Public Library Theater Collection. Minute Book of the Provincetown Players, Inc., dated September 4, 1916 to November 11, 1923.
83. Glaspell, *Road,* p. 255.
84. Ross Moffett, *Art in Narrow Streets,* p. 13.
85. George Cram Cook, *Greek Coins,* p. 18.
86. NYPL, Cook papers, Jig to Sue, September 15, 1916.
87. WSU, Vorse papers, Mary [Pyne] to Mary [O'Brien] [n.d. September 1916?].

CHAPTER 8

1. Nilla Cram Cook, *My Road to India,* p. 458.
2. Edmund Wilson, *The Shores of Light,* p. 759.
3. Susan Glaspell, *Road to the Temple,* pp. 291–292.
4. Interviews with Hazel Hawthorne, Provincetown, 1984–1985.
5. Virginia Floyd, *Eugene O'Neill at Work,* pp. 5–6.
6. Pierre Loving, "Eugene O'Neill," *Bookman,* p. 516.
7. Henry David Thoreau, *Cape Cod,* pp. 232–234.
8. Interviews with Phyllis Higgins, Provincetown, 1984–1985.
9. Interview with Jean Hanson Johnson, Bethesda, Md., 1991.
10. Reginald Cabral Collection, Hutch Hapgood to Cecilia Francis, August 1937.
11. John Henry Raleigh, *The Plays of Eugene O'Neill,* p. 20.
12. William Brevda, *Harry Kemp,* pp. 195–198 *passim.*
13. Alfred Kreymborg, *Troubadour,* p. 307.
14. IUL, Kemp to Dave [Carb], October 8, 1915.
15. Ross Moffett, *Art in Narrow Streets,* p. 39.
16. *Provincetown Advocate,* July 11, 1946.
17. Mary Heaton Vorse, *Time and the Town,* p. 197.
18. Reginald Cabral Collection, Susan Glaspell to Martha Robinson, February 27, 1940.
19. Vorse, *Time,* p. 200.
20. Reginald Cabral Collection, Glaspell to Robinson, November 12, 1946.

Notes

21. Barrett H. Clark, *Eugene O'Neill: The Man and His Plays,* p. 36.
22. Richard Dana Skinner, *Eugene O'Neill: A Poet's Quest,* p. viii.
23. Glaspell, *Road,* p. 264.
24. WSU, Vorse papers, Vorse to Mary Bicknell, October 24, 1923.
25. Clark, *O'Neill,* p. 20.
26. Eugene O'Neill, *Moon of the Caribbees.*
27. Wilbur Daniel Steele, "The Dark Hour."
28. Eugene O'Neill, *Anna Christie,* Scene. Act II.

Bibliography

Alexander, Doris. *The Tempering of Eugene O'Neill*. New York: Harcourt, 1962.

Allen, Gay Wilson. *Melville and His World*. New York: Viking, 1971.

Angoff, Charles. *The World of George Jean Nathan*. New York: Knopf, 1952.

Atkinson, Jennifer McCabe, ed. *Children of the Sea*. Washington, D.C.: NCR/Microcard, 1972.

Auser, Cortland P. *Nathaniel P. Willis*. New York: Twayne, 1969.

Barber, John Warner. *Massachusetts Historical Collections*. Worcester: Dorr, Howland, 1839.

Beer, Thomas. *The Mauve Decade*. Garden City, N.Y.: Garden, 1926.

Beers, Henry A. *Nathaniel Parker Willis*. New York: AMS, 1969.

Bogard, Travis. *Contour in Time: The Plays of Eugene O'Neill*. New York: Oxford UP, 1972.

———— and Jackson R. Bryer, eds. *Selected Letters of Eugene O'Neill*. New Haven: Yale UP, 1988.

Boston Chamber of Commerce. *Concerning the Port of Boston*. Boston, 1919.

Boulton, Agnes. *Part of a Long Story*. Garden City, N.Y.: Doubleday, 1958.

Bradford, William. *Bradford's History of Plimoth Plantation*. Boston: Wright & Potter, 1899.

Breese, Jesse Martin. "A Home in the Dunes," *Country Life in America* 45 (1923): pp. 72–76.

Brevda, William. *Harry Kemp*. Lewisburg, Pa.: Bucknell UP, 1986.

Bryant, George. "The Port of Provincetown 1776–1900," *29th Annual Blessing of the Fleet*. Provincetown: Shank Painter, 1976.

Bryant, Louise. "Six Poems," *The Masses,* October 1916.

Bucco, Martin. *Wilbur Daniel Steele*. New York: Twayne, 1972.

Burgess, Dorothy. *Dream and Deed: The Story of Katharine Lee Bates*. Norman, Okla.: Oklahoma UP, 1952.

Bynner, Witter. *Journey with Genius.* New York: John Day, 1951.

Canby, Henry Seidel. *Thoreau.* Boston: Houghton, 1939.

Cargill, Oscar, N. Bryllion Fagin, and William J. Fisher, eds. *O'Neill and His Plays: Four Decades of Criticism.* New York: New York UP, 1961.

Carpenter, Frederic I. *Eugene O'Neill.* New York: Twayne, 1964.

Carter, Robert. *Summer Cruise on the Coast of New England.* Boston: Nichols & Hall, 1870.

Chadwick, Henry. "The Wind-Built Hills," *Education Magazine* 28 (1908).

Chamberlain, Barbara Blau. *These Fragile Outposts.* Garden City: Natural History, 1964.

Churchill, Allen. *The Improper Bohemians.* New York: Dutton, 1959.

———. *The Literary Decade.* Englewood Cliffs, N.J.: Prentice-Hall, 1971.

Clark, Barrett H. *Eugene O'Neill: The Man and His Plays.* New York: McBride, 1929.

Coke, Van Deren. *Nordfeldt the Painter.* Albuquerque, N.M.: New Mexico UP, 1972.

———. *Andrew Dasburg.* Albuquerque, N.M.: New Mexico UP, 1979.

Commins, Dorothy, ed. *Love and Admiration and Respect: The O'Neill–Commins Correspondence.* Durham, N.C.: Duke UP, 1986.

Committee of the City Council. *An Account of the Celebration Commemorative of the Opening of Railroad Communication between Boston and Canada.* Boston: 1852. (287 pp.)

Cook, George Cram. *Greek Coins.* New York: Doran, 1925.

——— and Frank Shay, eds. *The Provincetown Plays.* Cincinnati: Kidd, 1921.

Cook, Nilla Cram. *My Road to India.* New York: Furman, 1939.

Cram, W. Bartlett. *Picture History of New England Passenger Vessels.* Hampden Highlands, Maine: Burntcoat, 1980.

Cuningham, Charles E. *Timothy Dwight.* New York: Macmillan, 1942.

Dell, Floyd. *Love in Greenwich Village.* New York: Doran, 1926.

———. *Homecoming.* Port Washington, N.Y.: Kennikat, 1961.

Deutsch, Helen, and Stella Hanau. *The Provincetown: A Story of the Theater.* New York: Farrar, 1931.

Deyo, Simeon L. *History of Barnstable County, Massachusetts.* New York: Blake, 1890.

Dickens, Charles. *American Notes.* New York: St. Martin's, 1985.

Dow, George Francis. *Everyday Life in the Massachusetts Bay Colony.* New York: Benjamin Blom, 1967.

Drake, Samuel Adams. *Nooks and Corners of the New England Coast.* New York: Harper, 1875.

Dwight, Timothy. *Travels: in New England and New York.* New Haven: Timothy Dwight, 1822.

Eastman, Max. *Enjoyment of Living.* New York: Harper, 1948.

Edel, Leon. *Henry James, A Life.* New York: Harper, 1985.

Everett, Patricia R. *Mabel Dodge: The Salon Years 1912–1917.* New York: Barbara Mathes Gallery, 1985.

Farnham, Emily. *Charles Demuth: Behind a Laughing Mask.* Norman, Okla.: Oklahoma UP, 1971.

Ferguson, Edith. *The 1850 Federal Census.* Bowie, Md.: Heritage, 1983.

Finn, William J. *Tourists Guide to Boston Harbor.* Boston: Finn, 1914.

Flint, Janet Altic. *Provincetown Printers: A Woodcut Tradition.* Washington, D.C.: Smithsonian, 1983.

Floyd, Virginia, ed. *Eugene O'Neill at Work.* New York: Ungar, 1981.

———. *The Plays of Eugene O'Neill: A New Assessment.* New York: Ungar, 1985.

Freeman, Frederick. *History of Cape Cod: Annals of the Thirteen Towns of Barnstable County.* Boston: Piper, 1869.

Gallup, Donald, ed. *Eugene O'Neill Poems, 1912–1944.* New Haven: Ticknor, 1980.

Gardner, Virginia. *Friend and Lover: The Life of Louise Bryant.* New York: Horizon, 1982.

Garrison, Dee. *Rebel Pen.* New York: Monthly Review, 1985.

———. *Mary Heaton Vorse: The Life of an American Insurgent.* Philadelphia: Temple UP, 1989.

Gassner, John, ed. *O'Neill: A Collection of Critical Essays.* Englewood Cliffs, N.J.: Prentice-Hall, 1964.

Gelb, Arthur and Barbara. *O'Neill*. New York: Harper, 1962.

Gelb, Barbara. *So Short A Time*. New York: Norton, 1973.

Gilmer, Walker. *Horace Liveright*. New York: David Lewis, 1970.

Glaspell, Susan. *The Road to the Temple*. New York: Stokes, 1927.

———. *Judd Rankin's Daughter*. New York: Lippincott, 1945.

Goldman, Arnold. "The Culture of the Provincetown Players," *Journal of American Studies,* December 1978, pp. 291–310.

Graham, James D. *A Report upon the Military and Hydrographical Chart of the Extremity of Cape Cod*. Washington: Corps of Topographical Engineers, 1836.

Graham, Jane Kirkland. *Viola, the Duchess of New Dorp*. Columbia, S.C., 1955.

Green, Martin. *New York 1913: The Armory Show and the Paterson Strike Pageant*. New York: Scribner's, 1988.

Hahn, Emily. *Romantic Rebels, An Informal History of Bohemianism in America*. Boston: Houghton, 1967.

———. *Mabel*. Boston: Houghton, 1977.

Hapgood, Hutchins. *A Victorian in the Modern World*. New York: Harcourt, 1939.

Harding. Walter. *The Days of Henry Thoreau*. New York: Knopf, 1965.

Harlow, Alvin F. *Steelways of New England*. New York: Creative Age, 1955.

Hartley, M. "Farewell, Charles." *The New Caravan*. New York: Norton, 1936.

Hawke, David Freeman. *Everyday Life in Early America*. New York: Harper, 1987.

Hawthorne, Hazel. *Salt House*. New York: Stokes, 1934.

Hawthorne, Hildegarde. *Old Seaport Towns of New England*. New York: Dodd, 1916.

Henderson, Helen W. *Loiterer in New England*. New York: Doran, 1919.

Hicks, Granville. *John Reed: The Making of a Revolutionary*. New York: Macmillan, 1936.

Howe, Henry F. *Prologue to New England*. New York: Farrar, 1943.

Jacobs, Michael. *The Good and Simple Life: Artist Colonies in Europe and America*. Oxford: Phaidon, 1985.

Bibliography

Jennings, Herman A. *Provincetown*. Reprint. Provincetown: Peaked Hill, 1975.

Kaplan, Justin. *Lincoln Steffens*. New York: Simon, 1974.

Kazin, Alfred. *On Native Grounds: An Interpretation of Modern American Prose Literature*. New York: Reynal, 1942.

Kellner, Bruce. *Carl Van Vechten and the Irreverent Decade*. Norman, Okla.: Oklahoma UP, 1968.

Kendall, Edward Augustus. *Travels Through the Northern Part of the U.S., 1807–8*. LC microfilm 01291, reel 129, No. 3 E.

Kenrick, John, et al. *Report of the Committee on Cape Cod Harbor*. Boston: Massachusetts Public Document #36, 1857.

Kinne, Wisner Payne. *George Pierce Baker and the American Theater*. Cambridge: Harvard UP, 1954.

Kittridge, Henry C. *Cape Cod, Its People and Their History*. Boston: Houghton, 1930.

Kreymborg, Alfred. *Troubadour*. New York: Boni, 1925.

Kuchta, Ronald A. *Provincetown Painters*. New York: Visual Arts, 1977.

Langner, Lawrence. *The Magic Curtain*. New York: Dutton, 1951.

Leatherman, S.P. *Environmental Geologic Guide to Cape Cod National Seashore*. Amherst: Massachusetts UP, 1979.

LeBlond, Richard. "Keeping Pace with the Dunes," *OCEA NEWS* 3 (1981): 2–3.

Loving, Pierre. "Eugene O'Neill," *Bookman*, August 1921, pp. 511–520.

Ludington, Townsend. *John Dos Passos*. New York: Dutton, 1980.

Luhan, Mabel Dodge. *European Experiences*. New York: Harcourt, 1935.

———. *Movers and Shakers*. New York: Harcourt, 1936.

Mackay, Constance D'Arcy. *The Little Theatre in the United States*. New York: Holt, 1917.

May, Henry F. *The End of American Innocence*. New York: Oxford UP, 1959.

Mayerson, Charlotte Leon, ed. *Shadow and Light*. New York: Harcourt, 1952.

McAdam, Roger Williams. *The Old Fall River Line*. New York: Stephen Daye, 1955.

————. *Priscilla of Fall River.* New York: Stephen Daye, 1956.

McCausland, Elizabeth. *Marsden Hartley.* Minneapolis: Minnesota UP, 1952.

Mellow, James R. *Charmed Circle.* New York: Praeger, 1974.

Middleton, George. *These Things Are Mine.* New York: Macmillan, 1947.

Miller, Perry, ed. *The American Puritans.* New York: Doubleday, 1956.

Moffett, Ross. *Art in Narrow Streets.* Falmouth, Mass.: Kendall, 1964.

Morison, Samuel Eliot. *The Maritime History of Massachusetts.* London: Heinemann, 1923.

————. *The European Discovery of America.* New York: Oxford UP, 1971.

Nash, Samuel, and Lorenzo Warriner. Unpublished letters, c. 1830. Courtesy of Alice N. Nash, New York City.

Nason, Elias. *A Gazetteer of the State of Massachusetts.* Boston: B.B. Russell, 1874.

National Collection of Fine Arts. *Marguerite Zorach: The Early Years, 1908–1920.* Washington, D.C.: Smithsonian, 1974.

National Park Service. *Archeology of Cape Cod.* Washington, D.C., 1984.

Noe, Marcia. *Susan Glaspell.* Macomb, Ill.: Western Illinois Monograph Series, 1983.

Nolen, William W. "Provincetown," *Our Country East—In New England.* Boston: Perry Mason, 1911.

Nordhoff, Charles. "Cape Cod, Nantucket, and the Vineyard," *Harper's Monthly,* LI, Nov.–June 1875: 52–66.

————. *Man-of-War Life.* Cincinnati: Moore, Wilstach, Keys, 1856.

————. *Whaling and Fishing.* New York: Dodd, 1895.

O'Neill, William L., ed. *Echoes of Revolt: THE MASSES 1911–1917.* Chicago: Quadrangle, 1966.

Pap, Leo. *The Portuguese-Americans.* Boston: Twayne, 1981.

Pease, Otis, ed. *The Progressive Years.* New York: Braziller, 1962.

Pendleton, Ralph, ed. *The Theater of Robert Edmond Jones.* Middletown, Conn.: Wesleyan UP, 1958.

Pool, Maria Louise. *Sand 'n' Bushes.* Chicago: Herbert S. Stone, 1899.

Powell, Lyman P., ed. *Historic Towns of New England.* New York: Knickerbocker, 1898.

Provincetown Art Association & Museum. *Days Lumberyard Studios.* Provincetown, Mass.: Shank Painter, 1978.

Raleigh, John Henry. *The Plays of Eugene O'Neill.* Carbondale, Ill.: Southern Illinois UP, 1965.

Reed, John S. *The War in Eastern Europe.* New York: Scribner's, 1916.

———. "Fog," in *Scribners,* LXVI, August 1919.

Reynolds, J. *Peter Gott: The Cape Ann Fisherman.* Boston: John P. Jewitt, 1856.

Rich, Shebnah. *Truro-Cape Cod.* 2nd ed. Boston: D. Lothrop, 1884.

Robinson, Phyllis C. *Willa, The Life of Willa Cather.* Garden City, N.Y.: Doubleday, 1983.

Robinson, Ted. *The Beachcombers.* Provincetown, Mass.: Advocate, 1947.

Rohe, Alice. "The Story of Susan Glaspell," *New York Morning Telegraph,* December 18, 1921, Glaspell Papers, Barrett Library, University of Virginia.

Rosenstone, Robert A. *Romantic Revolutionary: A Biography of John Reed.* New York: Vintage, 1975.

Rudnick, Lois Palken. *Mabel Dodge Luhan, New Woman, New Worlds.* Albuquerque, N.M.: New Mexico UP, 1984.

Russell, Dora. *The Tamarisk Tree: My Quest for Liberty and Love.* New York: Putnam, 1975.

St. John, Bruce, ed. *John Sloan, New York Scene.* New York: Harper, 1965.

Sargent, Porter E. *A Handbook of New England.* Boston, 1917.

Sarlos, Robert Karoly. *Jig Cook and the Provincetown Players.* Amherst, Mass.: Massachusetts UP, 1982.

Seckler, Dorothy Gees. "History of the Provincetown Art Colony," in *Provincetown Painters,* Visual Arts, 1977.

Shay, Edith, and Frank Shay. *Sand in Their Shoes.* Boston: Houghton, 1951.

Sheaffer, Louis. *O'Neill: Son and Playwright.* Boston: Brown, 1968.

———. *O'Neill: Son and Artist.* Boston: Brown, 1973.

Skinner, Richard Dana. *Eugene O'Neill: A Poet's Quest.* New York: Longmans, Green, 1935.

Sloan, John. *New York Scene.* New York: Harper, 1965.

Sochen, June. *Movers and Shakers.* New York: Quadrangle, 1973.
———. *The New Woman in Greenwich Village 1910–20.* New York: Quadrangle, 1972.
Spears, John R. *The Story of the New England Whalers.* New York: Macmillan, 1910.
Starbuck, Alexander. *History of the American Whale Fishery.* Waltham, Mass.: Author, 1878.
Steele, Wilbur D. "The Dark Hour," in *The Best Stories of Wilbur Daniel Steele.* New York: Doubleday, 1946.
———. "The 'Killers' of Provincetown," *Harper's Magazine,* March 1917, 457–466.
Steffens, Lincoln. *Autobiography.* New York: Literary Guild, 1931.
Sterne, Maurice. *Shadow and Light.* New York: Harcourt, 1965.
Thoreau, Henry David. *Cape Cod.* Boston: Houghton, 1914.
———. *The Journal of Henry D. Thoreau* (in 2 vols.). New York: Dover, 1963.
Tyler, David Budlong. *Steam Conquers the Atlantic.* New York: Appleton, 1939.
Vorse, Mary Heaton. *A Footnote to Folly.* New York: Farrar, 1935.
———. *Time and the Town.* New York: Dial, 1942.
———. "The Portuguese of Provincetown," *Outlook* (1911): 409–416.
———. *The Passing of the Fall River Line.* Unpublished mss., n.d.
Waterman, Arthur E. *Susan Glaspell.* New York: Twayne, 1966.
Watson, Steven. *Strange Bedfellows: The First American Avant-Garde.* New York: Abbeville, 1991.
Weisman, Adam Paul. "Susan Glaspell: A Woman's Modernism." Master's thesis, Oxford University, 1989.
Whicher, George G. *Walden Revisited.* Chicago: Packard, 1945.
Whittemore, Reed. *William Carlos Williams.* Boston: Houghton, 1975.
Williams, William Carlos. *Autobiography.* New York: Random, 1951.
Willis, N. Parker. *Hurry-Graphs.* Auburn: Alden, Beardsley, 1854.
Wilson, Edmund. *The Shores of Light.* New York: Farrar, 1952.
———. *The Twenties.* New York: Farrar, 1975.
———. *The Thirties.* New York: Farrar, 1980.
Young, Art. *On My Way.* New York: Liveright, 1928.
Zorach, William. *Art is My Life.* Cleveland: World, 1967.

Index

Index

Index

Index

Index

291

Index

Index

Index

Index